I0540401

GUNBOAT JUSTICE

British and American Courts in China and Japan
(1842 to 1943)

Volume II
Destruction, Disorder and Defiance (1900-1927)

Douglas Clark

Gunboat Justice

By Douglas Clark

Volume 1 - ISBN-13: 978-988-82730-8-9
Volume 2 - ISBN-13: 978-988-82730-9-6
Volume 3 - ISBN-13: 978-988-82731-9-5

This book has been reset in 10pt Book Antiqua. Spellings and punctuations are left as in the original edition.

HISTORY / Asia / General

EB055

Published by Earnshaw Books Ltd (Hong Kong)

In memory of my maternal grandfather

The Honourable Mr Justice Russell Skerman

Supreme Court of Queensland

Foreign Office Map Of The Main

MAP N⁰ 8.

PARTS OF

SIA & THE PACIFIC

Scale of English Miles.

Treaty Ports In East Asia, 1925

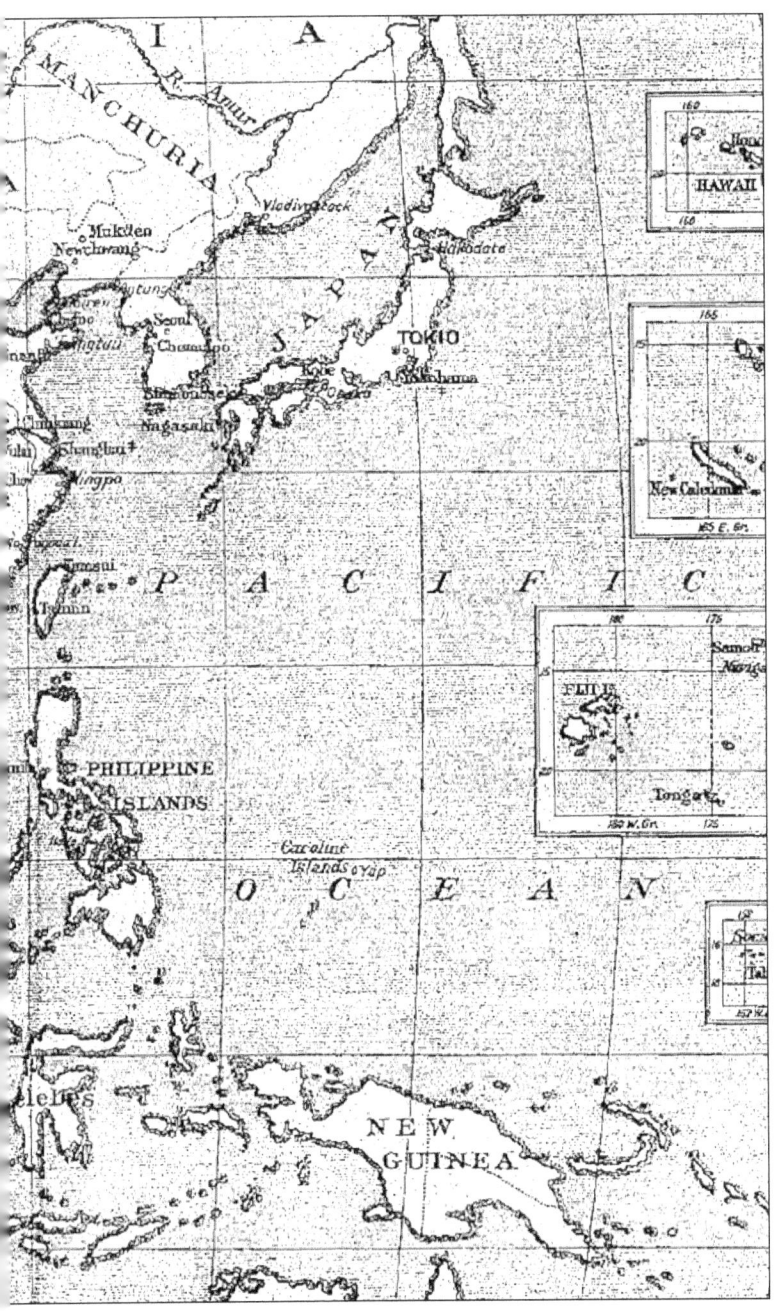

Contents

Volume II Destruction, Disorder and Defiance (1900-1927)

Volume III Revolution, Resistance and Resurrection (1927-1943)

Romanisation and place names

I have used transliterations of Chinese personal and place names in accordance with the transliterations used during the period covered by this book. Where someone is now much better known by a different transliteration, I have used this.

For place names in China, for any reference prior to the Communist Revolution in 1949, I have generally used the contemporaneous English names, such as Canton and Amoy. Beijing is referred to as Peking for the most part but also as Peiping for the period that was its official name. This is the way the names appear in the documents of the time and would have been spoken in English.

For street names in Shanghai, I have used the pre-World War II street names. Where appropriate I give the current street name in parentheses.

For references to places and personal names in China after the Communist Revolution, I have used Hanyu Pinyin, except where a person is much better known by a different transliteration.

For Japanese names, I have used modern romanisations. For Korean names I have used contemporaneous transliterations.

For all quotations or names of publications I have kept the original spelling.

Currencies in Shanghai

There were four major currencies in use in Shanghai during the period covered by this book. For almost the entire period, the Pound Sterling to United States Dollar exchange rate was £1 = US$5. For a time, the US dollar was also referred to as the Gold Dollar (G$). The other two currencies in use were Mexican silver dollars and the Chinese Tael (based on the price of silver). The value of these currencies fluctuated wildly. In 1930, US$1 was equal to about 3 taels and $3.5 Mex. However, at other times the Mexican dollar was equivalent to or worth more than the US$.

I have not attempted to give any conversions of currency in the book.

File References
Unless indicated otherwise, all files references are to the UK National Archive file reference for a document. PRONI files refers to the Wilkinson Papers kept at the Public Records Office of Northern Ireland. Where possible full file references have been given for the PRONI papers. However, these were not always available.

Cartoons and Illustrations
All cartoons and illustrations accompanying the text, with two exceptions, are contemporaneous drawings published at the time. The exceptions are the sketches of the Supreme Court and George French's grave which have been made from photographs.

INTRODUCTION TO VOL II

Destruction, Disorder and Defiance

BELOW IS A SHORT INTRODUCTION for Volume II of this book. For readers who do not have or have not read Volume I, the Introduction to Volume I is reproduced as an appendix. This should be read first before reading the following.

Volume I of the book described the development and practice of extraterritoriality in Japan and China in the 19th century. We have seen how consular jurisdiction developed, followed by the opening of the British Supreme Court for China and Japan. Over the years, through case law, new Orders in Council and new treaties, a workable system of jurisprudence was built up in the British Courts in both China and Japan, and later, Korea. America did not establish any formal court systems in China, Japan or Korea, relying instead on consular courts. In the Ross case, the US Supreme Court confirmed the constitutionality of the consular court system and that there was no right to trial by jury.

Japan responded to its forced opening and the imposition of extraterritoriality by engaging in a massive program of political, economic and legal reform. Through this it was able to bring an end to extraterritoriality and become a power in its own right, including defeating China in a war in 1895. China, on the other hand, failed to respond to the challenge posed by foreign countries and continued a long decline as the Manchus hold on power became weaker and weaker. By the end of the 19th century, the Manchus appreciated the need for reform but were not yet willing to implement it. That would take another major defeat, which was to come very soon, in

1900, with the failed Boxer Rebellion and the almost complete destruction of Peking by the foreign powers.

The end of extraterritoriality in Japan also did not mean the end of Japan as a player in our story. The Japan that had just joined the "family of nations" wanted to become a great power and was increasingly asserting itself. First, it took control of Korea without, at first, annexing it, bringing extraterritoriality back to a Japanese-controlled territory. This led to the British authorities being forced to bring cases against one of their own nationals to defend Japanese interests.

The beginning of the 20th century marked a new era in the British courts. All but one of the judges and lawyers who had played important roles in China and Japan in the 19th century had retired or died. The one remaining judge, H.S. Wilkinson, was about to achieve his long-held ambition to be Chief Justice of the Supreme Court. Once H.S. Wilkinson retired, the British court also saw major changes in the way it was staffed. Instead of local appointments, judges were for many years brought in from outside China.

America also set out about reforming its practice of extraterritoriality in China and Korea, finally establishing a United States Court for China. This court went through a number of teething pains with poorly drafted legislation and an unsatisfactory appointment for the first judge. Eventually a judge, Charles Lobingier, was appointed who, very much in the mold of Edmund Hornby, the first British Chief Judge, set the court on a solid foundation for the rest of its life.

The arrival of a "sister" court (as they referred to each other) and the increase in international trade and business brought new challenges to the British Court. New jurisdictional and legal issues arose including how to deal with witnesses who perjured themselves in each other's courts. In one major case, the British brought a criminal prosecution against an Irish newspaper editor for defaming the new judge of the United States Court.

The new century was not all bad news for China. The Republican Revolution in 1911 brought hope for change with the introduction of democracy and serious legal reform. But this hope was soon snuffed out by a failed attempt to restore the monarchy which caused the country to collapse into a civil war and almost total disorder that continued for more than a decade.

War was, throughout the 20th Century, a constant theme for both British and American courts. World War I brought a variety of cases before the courts. Japan also increased its demands on China, taking over German concessions and territory during World War I. The civil war in China from 1916 up to the Nationalist Party's victory in 1927 generated numerous cases involving smuggling, sedition and gun-running to name just a few.

The Chinese people did however start to defy foreign power, launching national protest movements in 1919 - against the terms of the Treaty of Versailles at the end of WWI - and in 1925 - against the killing by Shanghai police of protestors.   In one case, the Ningpo Guild brought a prosecution in the British Supreme Court against British policemen for torture. Indians in China also started to agitate for freedom resulting in a number of prosecutions for sedition. Still in 1926, the foreign powers still felt comfortable enough to issue a report by the long-awaited Extraterritoriality Commission putting off the end of extraterritoriality way into the future.

China had not been able to properly assert itself because it had been weakened by constant domestic and foreign wars and the need to pay indemnities to foreign powers.

The biggest and most crippling indemnity was that owed as a result of the destruction wrought by the Boxer Rebellion in 1900, to which we now turn.

PART SIX

CHINA BOXED IN
(1900 TO 1905)

CHAPTER 28

The Boxer Rebellion

THE 20TH CENTURY STARTED very badly for China and the Qing Dynasty. Things got so bad that British Judge Frederick Bourne thought that there may be full out war in China between the foreign powers which if won by one of Britian's rivals could result in the "Chinese being exported as industrial slaves."[1]

While there was no full out war, the disturbances did lead to three major cases - all involving journalists - coming before Bourne in the British Supreme Court for China and Corea. In the first, a newspaper editor was sued for defamation by another editor for alleging reports of a massacre of foreigners in Peking were faked. In the second, the plaintiff in the first case was prosecuted for criminal defamation of the Judge of the newly-established United States Court for China. In the third, Bourne travelled to Korea to try a British journalist for sedition against the Japanese-controlled government of Korea.

Starting in the late 1890s, a rebellion begun by the Boxers, a religious group that claimed to be immune to foreign bullets and weapons, swept Northern China. The Boxers were particularly ferocious in Shantung and Manchuria, driving most foreigners out from remote areas or killing them. The Chinese government supported attacks on foreigners. In June 1900, the Boxers descended on Peking with the slogan "Support the

---

1 Royal Botanic Gardens, Directors Correspondence, Directors' Correspondence 150/40-41, Letter from Bourne to Sir William Thiselton-Dyer, 10 Septemeber, 1900

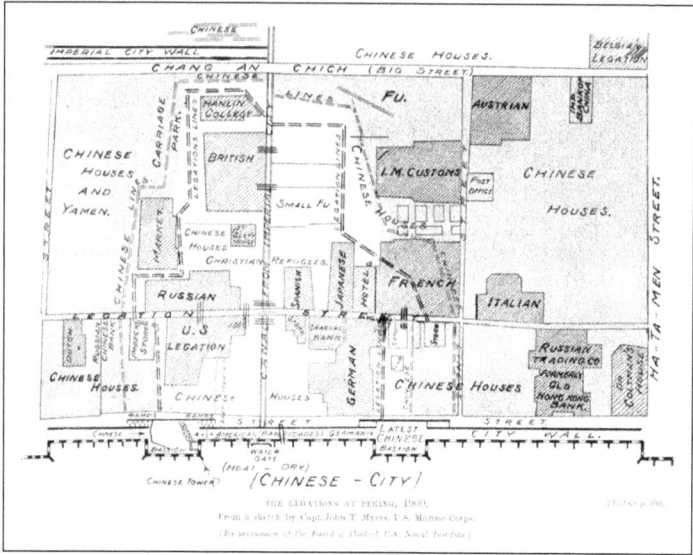

A contemporaneous map shows the small legation area surrounded
by Chinese troops

Qing, exterminate the foreigners." The battles resulted in June 1900 in the killing of senior German and Japanese officials.[2]

China declared war on all eight major foreign powers: Great Britain, France, Germany, the United States, Russia, Austria-Hungary, Italy and Japan. From June 1900, Chinese troops laid siege to the foreign legations in Peking where most foreigners had retreated. Given that five years before China had not been able to defend themselves against the Japanese alone, this was foolishness of the greatest degree. The dowager Empress, Cixi, in one of the war councils justified the support of the Boxers on the need to retain the support of the people. She said:

> "China has been extremely weak; the only thing we can rely upon is the hearts of the people. If we lose them,

2   For an account of the Boxer Rebellion, see, I Hsu, The Rise of Modern China (4th ed.), p390 to 406; For an account of the Boxer Rebellion in Manchuria, see M. O'Neill, *Frederick: The Life of My Missionary Grandfather in Manchuria*, pp61-67.

how can we maintain our country?"

Kang-I, another high-ranking official, emphasized the anti-foreign feeling by saying:

"When the legations are taken, the barbarians will have no more roots. The country will then have peace."

Needless to say, many other high Chinese officials did not support attacks on foreigners. Provincial governors, including Li Hongzhang in Canton and Yuan Shikai in Shandong as well as the governors in Nanking and Wuhan, all refused to recognise the declaration of war. They reached agreements with the foreign powers that there would be no fighting between their troops and foreigners in areas they controlled. More importantly, Rong Lu the commander in chief of the Beiyang forces in Peking and in charge of the siege of the legations, only attacked half-heartedly. He ordered that blanks be fired and refused to bring up larger caliber cannon.

During the siege, London newspapers, particularly the *Daily Mail* and *Daily Express* published lurid accounts of a massacre of the foreigners in the legations. The *Daily Mail* published a "Massacre Telegram" from its Shanghai correspondents recounting a heroic last stand:

"Towards the end of the third watch, about 5 a.m.,
the allies had practically defeated the besiegers, who
were wavering and were gradually withdrawing when
General Tung-fua-siang arrived from the vicinity of
Tdien with a large force of Kansu braves. By this time
the walls of the Legation had been battered down, and
most of the buildings were in ruins from the Chinese
artillery fire. Many of the allies had fallen at their posts,
and the remaining small band who were still alive took

refuge in the wrecked buildings, which they endeavoured to hastily fortify. Upon them the fire of the Chinese artillery was now directed. Towards sunrise it was evident that the ammunition of the allies was running out, and at 7 o'clock, as the advances of the Chinese in force failed to draw a response, it was at once clear that it was at length completely exhausted. A rush was determined upon. Thus standing together, as the Sun rose fully, the little remaining band, all Europeans, met death stubbornly. There was a desperate hand-to-hand encounter. The Chinese lost heavily, but as one man fell others advanced, and finally, overcome by overwhelming odds, every one of the Europeans remaining was put to the sword in a most atrocious manner." [3]

The *Daily Express* followed with an even more lurid account of a massacre sourced from its correspondent, Henry O'Shea, who was also publisher and editor of the *China Gazette* in Shanghai.

"The end has come, and the worst horrors have been but too terribly accomplished. Every European in Peking has been massacred by the savage, bloodthirsty miscreants who now represent the supreme authority in China.

"...... The central figure and ringleader in the atrocity was Prince Tuan, who overruled the more moderate party and declared for extermination. It was by his order that the Legations were surrounded and supplies cut off, that they were decimated by incessant fire, bombarded and eventually massacred on the night of June 30 and morning of July 1, the dates originally given by our respondent.

3 Reproduced in the *Times*, July 16, 1900.

"A last desperate sortie was made by the doomed victims. It is a picture that will live for all time. The horror square led by soldiers and civilians, the hapless women and children in the centre, the last murderous attack by the infuriated Boxers. 'Then the foreigners went mad,' said the courier who brought the story to Sheng. 'They killed the women and children, shooting them with their revolvers instead of using them on the Boxers.' Upon this awful climax, the true inwardness of which we realise with a shudder of fiercest indignation, the curtain went down on a worse tragedy than Cawnpore."[4]

In Cawnpore, India in 1857, the British had been under siege and brutally massacred by Indian troops. As it would

The Daily Express reports on the "Peking Massacre"
Robert Hart, Inspector-General of Chinese Customs was one of those reported killed.

4   Extracted from the case report for *O'Shea v Cowen*, *North China Herald*, June 25, 1902, p1255 et seq.

turn out, this was no Cawnpore and no tragedy, at least, not for the foreigners. Both stories were complete tissues of lies. Thanks mainly to Rong Lu's lackluster attacks, the legations were able to hold out until they were relieved.

While not a tragedy for foreigners, it was a tragedy for the people of Peking and the people of China.

Peking's position inland meant that gunboats could not come to the rescue of the legations. But on August 4, 1900, a foreign army of over 18,000 men, made up of 8,000 Japanese, 4,800 Russian, 3,000 British, 2,100 American, 800 French, 58 Austrian, and 53 Italian troops set out from Tientsin and made their way very quickly to Peking in 10 days. They arrived on August 14, 1900 to relieve the legations. German troops were also sent to join the attack but did not arrive in time.

After taking Peking, the troops looted the city and massacred the Chinese population. The looting went on for many months, leaving behind a devastated city. Ernest Satow, previously British Minister in Japan who had just been appointed British Minister in China, described his arrival in Peking in October 1900:

"So through the Hatamen and along legation street, which showed terrible marks of devastation. A feeling of profound melancholy took possession of me, such as I have never experienced. It was like entering a city of the dead where the tombs had been thrown down and enveloped in dust." [5]

During the war, the Emperor, Emperess Dowager and all other officials fled Peking. Li Hongzhang was called upon to negotiate with the foreigners. While the capture of Peking could have led to the end of the Qing Dynasty, this did not suit the foreign powers who were more content to continue to

5   I. Ruxton (ed), *Sir Ernest Satow's Peking Diary (Vol 1, 1900-1903)*, p34.

carve up China while leaving a weak government in power.

The negotiations for a peace settlement resulted in yet more onerous terms being imposed on China. This included a massive indemnity of 450 million taels (£67.5 million pounds at the time) to be paid over 39 years. The "Boxer Indemnity" was divided up between the foreign powers with Russia and Germany receiving 49% between them. Japan, despite having contributed the largest number of troops and also having seen one of its officials killed, only received 7.7%.[6] Russia, which had occupied Manchuria during the fighting, stayed there despite promises to leave. The result of these negotiations were seen as a great failure in Japan and were one of the principal drivers of Japan's attack on Russia three years later. Payment of the Boxer Indemnity crippled China economically for years to come.

Liar, Liar, the legations were not on fire!

On January 18, 1902, the *Shanghai Times* published an article reporting on an expose by the *Chinese Times* in Tientsin of how the famous "Massacre Telegram" came about. The report said that the two temporary correspondents for the *Daily Mail*, W. Sutterle alias Sylvester, in conjunction with Chesney Duncan had made the story up and sent it to the *Daily Mail*. "The *Daily Express* determined to do as well as the *Mail* or better wired to its Shanghai Correspondent H. D. O'Shea to get a move on or words to that effect."

Then, coming to the crux, the *Shanghai Times* said:

"So O'Shea then wired as much blood and thunder as his conscience permitted and the Express came out next day with a bigger pack of lies than the *Mail*."

The *Shanghai Times* added the caveat that the *Daily Mail*

6 I .Hsu, , *The Rise of Modern China* 4th Ed, p401-2.

had published the original telegram it received to show it had
been misled. The *Express* did not do so, so therefore "part or
all of lies therefore may be not O'Shea's." The next paragraph
all but destroyed this caveat by adding:

> "But he is a man who can lie when he tries and he
> certainly had in this case a chance to 'tell the truth and
> shame the devil' by wiring a flat contradiction of the
> massacre or some reassuring message discounting the
> story instead of which he or his London accomplices
> told a lie big enough to put the devil in the amateur
> class."

This was clearly intended to attract a defamation suit. The
article ended:

> "Now watch for the Shanghai libel case."

O'Shea and Duncan took the bait. Each sued the editor
of the *Shanghai Times*, Mr T.C. Cowen, for defamation. Duncan soon dropped his claim but O'Shea proceeded claiming
15,000 taels in damages.

The trial was heard by Frederick Bourne as Acting Chief
Justice and a jury of five. It commenced on June 19, 1902 and
lasted four days.[7] Duncan McNeill and F. Ellis appeared for
O'Shea and Vernon Drummond and A.M. Latter for Cowen.
Cowen's defence was that what had been said about O'Shea
was true. There was no doubt that the massacre stories were
false. The foreigners had not been massacred. The question
to be answered was: had O'Shea sent telegrams to the *Daily
Express* knowing them to be false?

In court, O'Shea said that the *Daily Express* had used his
and other correspondents' materials to prepare their reports

----

7   *O'Shea v Cowen, North China Herald,* June 25, 1902, p1255. The jury members were F.
Large, J.E. Judah, R. Viccajee, J. Valentine and T. Cock.

and what he had sent, he believed to be true based on information that he had received. He added that "he considered it was the duty of a correspondent to send home what rumours he heard; but at the same time it was his duty to warn his papers at home that these rumours were not to be accepted as news." He suggested that the defendant had published the article about him out of spite because, at the time Cowen had also been a correspondent for the *Daily Express* and O'Shea had rejected some of his articles.

O'Shea recovered from the archives of the Chinese Telegraph Office 86 telegrams that he had sent. A key problem for the defence was that none of these were a telegram detailing the massacre as reported in the *Daily Express* on July 16. O'Shea swore that these were all of the telegrams he sent. He added, in cross-examination, that on July 16, he had been informed that the Japanese Consulate in Tientsin had received a telegraph from Baron Onishi that the legation was safe. He had sent a telegram to London to that effect.

In order to deal with the lack of a "smoking gun," the defence called James Ballard, a director and editor of the *Shanghai Mercury*. Ballard said that he had seen O'Shea at the telegraph office on July 15 writing a long telegram at a desk reserved for correspondents. Ballard said that O'Shea had told him that the report confirmed the massacre in Peking and that Ballard was free to use it. Ballard told O'Shea that he did not believe the report was accurate and did not use it. Not bad evidence, but Ballard had a problem with credibility himself: he was not a member of the Shanghai Club. That may not have been so telling to the jury, but, worse, he had once been a member of the club but had been expelled some years before due to a defamatory article he had written.

In another report, O'Shea reported that the British Consul-General, Sir Pelham Warren, had officially told him he believed that all in the Peking legations had been killed. Given his position, Warren was not expected to give evidence at the trial. Instead, Sir Pelham gave a deposition at a separate hearing. Sir Pelham denied he had ever made such a statement officially, although there had been times when he felt the legations had fallen. He added, interestingly, that he had been in direct telegraphic contact with Yuan Shikai who had been providing him and other Consuls with information about the siege. Yuan had never told him the legation had fallen.

Cowen gave evidence and denied that he had written the article out of ill will to the defendant, but rather that "because I thought it a matter of duty for anyone able to go into it, that this massacre telegram should be sifted and exposed if possible. I thought it would be for the public good." He conceded that at the time, there had been many rumours as to what was occurring in Peking. He said, however, that as a journalist it was necessary to be as accurate as possible.

Bourne summed up for the jury. He told them they needed to be satisfied that what Cowen had written was not true. If so, they could consider how much Cowen should pay in damages. The jury went out "for some considerable time." Upon their return they said they considered the words were untrue, but that the damages should only be a very small amount of 100 taels or, less than 6% of the 15,000 taels O'Shea had claimed. O'Shea was thus partially vindicated by the verdict, but the small award of damages suggests strongly that the jury were not impressed by him. Despite the small award of damages, Bourne ordered Cowen to pay the costs O'Shea had incurred in bringing the action. These costs were later assessed at $1,080.

Bourne thanked the jury for "the careful attention they had given to this long and tiresome case. They had done their duty most thoroughly, and he should be happy to exempt them from serving on a jury for the next three years."

It appears the costs and damages were never paid because one year later O'Shea and Cowen were back before Bourne with O'Shea seeking his money. Cowen was cross-examined as to income and assets. He said that the *China Times* had been transferred to his brother before the libel case and that he had no property and a small income of only $200 per month. O'Shea then asked for payment by installments. Bourne cannot have been too impressed with O'Shea because he did not order Cowen to pay anything. Instead he ruled that "he did not see how the defendant could pay installments, if his salary was $200 a month. There was nothing for the plaintiff to do but wait for the money until the defendant could pay it."[8]

Mr Cawnpore O'Shady defends

It appears that many others were not impressed by O'Shea and the result of the case. A couple of years later, the *North China Herald* published a spoof article parodying the trial.[9] The article reported on a case in the "International Court of Journalists" of *The Public vs Le Maire Emile* before Mr Robert Doyen (President) with Mr Orlando Ryte prosecuting and Mr Cawnpore O'Shady defending. The allegation was that the Defendant had failed to report the fall of Port Arthur, during the Russo-Japanese war. As we shall see later, the Japanese army had captured Port Arthur before Russia's Baltic fleet could arrive, sailing via the Cape of Good Hope to relieve the Pacific Fleet, which was blockaded in the harbour.

The prosecution alleged, "the first essential in an editor was a knowledge of a proper use of the word 'alleged,' in conjunction with a vivid imagination," and further:

"By the Statute of Mania (2nd Rsvlt. cap. 1, s.c. 01) it was definitely laid down that 'in any war between the Imperial Government of the Bear and the Imperial Government of the Rising Sun, it shall be lawful to surmise not more than three victories per diem, to suit the susceptibility of readers, and any paper neglecting

8   *North China Herald*, January 27, 1903, p188.
9   *North China Herald*, March 25, 1904, p621.

to record the sinking of a battleship at least once a week shall be subject to summary extinction.'"

A Baron Munchausen was called for the prosecution who said "he had searched through the file of defendant's paper since the beginning of the century and found no mention of the annihilation of St. Petersburg." In cross-examination he said, "he had just arrived from ten years holiday at the North Pole and met a Baltic squadron under full steam in the Arctic Ocean." The report concluded with the following unmistakable dig at the Shanghai Liar case:

> "Mr. O'Shady said that after the unanswerable evidence put in by the prosecution, he had advised his client to plead guilty and to throw himself on the clemency of the Court. There were extenuating circumstances, which the jury could not fail to discover.
> "The jury, without leaving the box, returned a unanimous verdict, honourably acquitting the accused.
> "The President thanked the jury for the close attention they had given to a particularly simple case and excused them from reading defendant's paper for a month of Sundays."

Beginning of Legal Reform in China
The Boxer Rebellion and its aftermath acted as a catalyst for reform in China. The Chinese now appreciated that Japan had been able to abolish extraterritoriality because it had made significant improvements in its legal system.

In a Commercial Treaty made between China and Britain in September 1902, the abolition of extraterritoriality was explicitly tied to improvements in the Chinese legal system. Article XII of the Treaty provided:

"China having expressed a strong desire to reform her judicial system and to bring it into accord with that of Western nations Great Britain agrees to give every assistance to such reform and she will also be prepared to relinquish her extraterritorial rights when she is satisfied that the state of the Chinese laws, the arrangement of their administration and other considerations warrant her so doing."[10]

The United States and Japan made similar promises in treaties signed at the same time.

A commission was formed to draft civil, criminal, commercial and procedural codes. The commission, logically given Japan had just completed the process of adapting European laws to Asian circumstances, appointed a number of Japanese experts and borrowed from the Japanese codes. The Chairman of the Chinese Civil Codification Commission, Foo Ping-Sheung, writing much later, explained the reason for relying on the Japanese experience:

"Since the new code was to be a complete departure from the general structure and principles of traditional Chinese law, it could not follow the distribution and phraseology of the Ta-Tsing Lu-li. Much therefore had to be imported from foreign jurisprudence, and the country from which the Codification Commission made their main borrowing was from Japan. Their reasons for this were obvious. Japan had just emerged from her old feudalism into a modern state. Her signal success in the process of modernization China was anxious to follow. It was quite natural for China to try to profit by her neighbour's experience. Besides, since the reform movement had been on foot in China,

10 G. Keeton, *The Development of Extraterritoriality in China*, Vol II. Keeton describes this process in detail at pp2-11.

hundreds of Chinese in search of modern knowledge
had gone to Japanese universities, principally to the
Japanese law schools, where their studies facilitated
by the great similarity of the two languages. Japan
at the time had completed her civil and commercial
codification, which she had modeled after the German
Codes. She had created a technical legal Japanese vo-
cabulary, translated a number of the leading juridical
textbooks of Europe, and produced a large Japanese
legal literature. The Chinese could then find in Japan
an adaptation to the Far Eastern mind, in a language
closely relate to their own, of what represented at the
time the most advanced stage of western scientific
juridical science."[11]

By 1907, regulations providing for modern courts and a
modern Criminal Code were promulgated. Sweeping reforms
were introduced, including the abolition of torture and the
use of the cangue. The overthrow of the Qing dynasty in 1911
and World War I intervened, thereby putting legal reform and
the abolition of extraterritoriality on the backburner. It was
not until the 1920s that serious discussions on the end of extraterritoriality resumed.

In fact, in the 1900s one more British court was established
in China, although it was not an extraterritorial court.

---

11 Introduction to Chinese Laws: Civil Code of the Republic of China, China-America
Council of Commerce and Industry, Legal Series 4, pp xi-xii.

CHAPTER 29

The High Court of Weihaiwei

As one British Court in the Far East, the Court for Japan, was wound down at the end of the 19th century, a new one was established at the beginning of the 20th century, the High Court of Weihaiwei. This court, however, was not subordinate to the Supreme Court for China and Corea. Instead it exercised full jurisdiction in Weihaiwei in Shandong Province.[1]

As part of the late 19th Century scramble by foreign powers for concessions in China, on July 1, 1898, British had signed a convention with China to take a lease of the city of Weihaiwei (now called Weihai) at the northeastern tip of the Shangtung Peninsula. Weihaiwei is about 130 kilometres directly south across the entrance to Bohai Bay from Port Arthur in Manchuria. In 1898 the Russians had occupied Port Arthur and the 1898 British-China convention explicitly stated in its preamble that the lease was to last "for so long a period as Port Arthur shall remain in the occupation of Russia."[2]

The Convention came into force on October 5, 1898 and Weihaiwei was established as a territory of the United Kingdom. As a territory, it was administered by the Colonial Office. In 1901, an Order in Council for Weihaiwei was issued to establish the government of Weihaiwei under a Commis-

---

1 For full details of British Justice in Weihaiwei, see C. Tan, *British Rule in China: Law and Justice in Weihaiwei 1898 to 1930*.

2 See Chapter 23 in 1898, The Germans had also obtained a 99-year lease for the Port of Kiaochow in Shangtung Province and the French a similar lease for the Port of Kwangchow. A number of railway concessions were also granted to foreign powers. See R. Akagi, *Japanese Foreign Relations, 1542-1936: A Short History*, pp181 to 183 for further details.

The Eastern Sketch features Weihaiwei on its front cover

sioner who was responsible for administrative and legislative matters as well as a High Court of Weihaiwei to handle judicial matters. English law was to be applied in Weihaiwei, however, the Commissioner could also directly enact ordinances in Weihaiwei as well as to extend Hong Kong ordinances to apply there.[3]

Before issuing the Order in Council, the Colonial Office had asked Sir Frank Sweetenham, then Resident General of the Federated States of Malaysia, to visit Weihaiwei and make recommendations on how the territory should be governed. Sweetenham made wide-ranging recommendations. With regards to law and order, he recommended the China and Japan Order in Council be extended to Weihaiwei and that a Supreme Court be established in Weihaiwei that had similar powers to a British Provincial Court in China. To limit the number of cases that would be sent to Shanghai he recommended the court's jurisdiction be increased to allow for more cases to be heard in Weihaiwei.[4]

This recommendation was not followed by the Colonial Office, most likely because it was considered there would be difficulties in applying an Order in Council designed for an extraterritorial court to a court with full jurisdiction.

Instead the 1901 Order in Council provided for the establishment of the High Court of Weihaiwei with full jurisdiction over all persons in Weihaiwei (that is, Chinese, British and all other foreigners). The only exception was for residents of the Weihaiwei walled city, who remained under Chinese jurisdiction except as necessary for "naval and military requirements of His Majesty or with the peace, order and good government of the said territories." This was the same exception that had been agreed in the lease of the New Territories in Hong Kong in relation to the Kowloon Walled City near the old Kai Tak Airport. After World War II when China was strong enough to assert its rights the Kowloon Walled City became an almost lawless enclave.

The Order in Council specifically ousted the jurisdiction of

....

3   The Administrative and Legislative Powers were granted to the Commissioner in S. 3 and Judicial Powers to the High Court in S. 12 of the Order in Council. The Power to proclaim Ordinances was granted by S.9.

4   C. Tan, *British Rule in China: Law and Justice in Weihaiwei 1898-1930*, p61-2.

the British Supreme Court for China and Corea in Weihaiwei by providing that the Orders in Council "relating to the exercise of Her Majesty's jurisdiction in China shall cease to have effect in the territories within the limits of this order."[5]

The High Court was to have one judge who was required to be a barrister of the High Court of England, Scotland or Ireland. The Commissioner was also granted judicial powers and he could sit alone or with the Judge. Appeals from the Court of Weihaiwei lay to the Supreme Court of Hong Kong (and not the Supreme Court for China and Corea) and then on to the Privy Council. It appears that no appeal was ever actually brought to Hong Kong. One writer at the time gave three reasons for this:

> "[F]irstly, there are in Weihaiwei neither barristers nor solicitors by whom litigants might be advised to appeal. Every party to a Suit appears in court in his own person, and states his case either orally or by means of written pleadings called Petitions. If he loses his case the matter is at an end unless he can show just cause why a re-hearing should be granted. Secondly, the legal costs of an appeal to a Hongkong court would be prohibitive for all but a minute fraction of the people of Weihaiwei. It is questionable whether, outside Liu-kungtao and Port Edward, there are more than a dozen families that would not be totally ruined if called upon to pay the costs of such an appeal. Thirdly, there are probably not twenty Chinese in the Territory who are aware that an appeal is possible."[6]

It was not completely true that parties were not repre-

---

5   Jurisdiction of the Court: Section 16; Judge's qualifications: Section 13; Judicial Power of Commissioner: Section 12 para 2; Exemption of Weihaiwei Walled City, S.11; Civil Appeals S.68 to 80; Criminal Appeals, S.35; Ouster of SCCC jurisdiction: S.85 of the Weihaiwei Order in Council.

6   R.F. Johnston, *Lion and Dragon in North China*, pp 100-101.

The Weihaiwei Walled City.

sented by lawyers. For the vast majority of cases which were heard by magistrates this was true, however, for important cases lawyers (and judges) would come from Shanghai to represent clients.

Due to the limited number of court cases, there was no need for a full-time judge in Weihaiwei. A judge could have been sent from Hong Kong, which was also administered by the Colonial Office, but this was a long trip of at least five days sailing, most likely stopping in Shanghai anyway. An agreement was therefore reached between the Colonial Office and Foreign Office for the Judge of the Supreme Court in Shanghai, Frederick Bourne, to be appointed the first judge of the Weihaiwei High Court in October 1904. Harrie Wilkinson, the Crown Advocate for China, was also appointed Crown Advocate for Weihaiwei. This was convenient for everyone. The Judge or Crown Advocate of the Supreme Court for China and Corea were able to visit Weihaiwei when they were on circuit in other treaty ports in North China.

Bourne was on leave when the first major case came before the High Court for Weihaiwei in June 1905. John Douglas, the

Registrar of the Supreme Court was appointed Acting Judge
to try the case. Harrie Wilkinson prosecuted and Francis Ellis,
also from Shanghai defended.[7] For the first time ever in Weihaiwei a jury, made up of five Englishmen, Mr T.C. Ramsey,
E.C. Ockenden, W.A. Lewis, Ernest Clark, and A. Merrilees
was empanelled.

The Defendants, Wang Cheng and Chi Chiu, were charged
with manslaughter. They must have been completely bewil-
dered to find themselves on trial before an English judge and
two lawyers all wearing white wigs and speaking English.
The case was certainly a change for the judge and lawyers.
This would have been the first time any of them had tried a
case against native Chinese. Wang and Chi were accused of
killing Hou Hsiping. Wang, Chi and Hou all lived together.
Wang was married to Hou's sister, Hou Wang Shih, and Chi
was married to a daughter in the family. Hou had been killed
after a fight involving the death of one of Hou's sons who
Hou had considered to be a waster. There were also family
disputes over the sale of a junk. Hou Hsiping had been beaten
by Wang and Chi and died of his injuries. The wife/sister,
Hou Wang-Shih gave evidence as did a number other family
members and the village headman. At the end of the trial the
jury convicted both Wang and Cheng of manslaughter. Douglas sentenced them both to seven years imprisonment each to
be served at Hong Kong.

Bourne heard his first two cases in Weihaiwei later that
year in October. They were prosecutions for manslaughter
and false imprisonment. Only very short case reports were
published for each case. In the manslaughter case the defendant was convicted and sentenced to imprisonment for one
year with hard labour and in the assault case three defendants were convicted and one acquitted.[8]

....

7   *R v Wang Cheng and Chi Chiu* , North China Herald, June 13, 1905, p655.

8   *R v Ma Shuang-His and R v Chia Yu-Wang and Others*, North China Herald, October 20,
1905, p 155.

A case of major interest came before Bourne the next year when he was called upon to decide which land law was to be applied in Weihaiwei: English land law or Chinese land law.[9] The question had arisen because the government wished to acquire certain lands. Bourne held that Chinese land law applied on the basis that English land law could only be applied if there was a specific provision in the Order in Council providing that English law applied (there was not) or if China was to be classed among "uninhabited and barbarous countries," so that when Britain had taken over Weihaiwei, English law had automatically applied. With regard to this latter point he held:

> "She is certainly not uninhabited; nor, from a legal point of view, as it seems to me, barbarous; she has had for centuries a system of land tenure and title and customary law."

He noted that in this particular case, one of the defendants had produced a title deed dated 1744. He then applied Chinese land law to determine if the land in question was private or government land and awarded compensation based on an "equitable rate" of the market value of the land plus 15% "for disturbance."

Bourne's decision of as judge of the High Court of Weihaiwei was effectively final. Bourne had no superior judge above him in Weihaiwei other than the judges of the Hong Kong Supreme Court. However, as we have seen, the cost of appealing was prohibitive.

Bourne did have a superior in Shanghai. That man had for many years desired a high judicial appointment. The early 1900s were to be his time.

---

9 *R v Chi Hsing –Nan and Others., North China Herald,* April 6, 1906, p39.

Chapter 30

Ambition Achieved: Wilkinson CJ

Wilkinson CJ

HIRAM SHAW WILKINSON achieved his greatest ambition, being formally appointed as Chief Justice of the Supreme Court for China and Corea in May 1900 following Nicholas Hannen's death. At the time, Wilkinson had not yet returned to Shanghai. He had left Japan in February, travelling Home via America. The end of extraterritoriality was a big story in the United States and "he was pounced upon by reporters" in Chicago. His view of the new system was mixed. He told the reporters:

"It is an open question whether or not the new Court system in Japan was not inaugurated too soon. The law of Japan is derived largely from the French and German codes, which are not as adaptable to the Japanese uses, and especially with reference to English and American subjects, as would have been English common law."[1]

He had originally intended to return to Yokohama in May to meet Hannen on his homeward voyage – this, of course,

1   *North China Herald*, April 25, 1900, p717, carrying a report from the *Japan Mail*.

could not happen. He did, however, go back to Yokohama where he took final steps to close the Court for Japan transferring remaining moneys either to the Treasury or Consulate and passing the archives of the court to the Yokohama Consulate. On 1 June 1900 he issued a final Circular to all Consuls informing them of the formal closure of the British Court for Japan.[2]

H.S. Wilkinson first sat as Chief Justice in Shanghai on June 26, 1900. There were no special formalities or speeches. Loftus Jones appearing for the Plaintiff, merely noted Wilkinson's appointment to the court to which "he had been so honourably associated for many years."[3] Presumably, Wilkinson had not thought it appropriate so soon after Hannen's death for there to be any celebration of his appointment. Hannen had appointed him executor of his will, leaving Wilkinson the sad duty of winding up his good friend's affairs in Shanghai.[4]

As Chief Justice, H.S. Wilkinson continued his practice of writing long, carefully considered, detailed and extremely soporific judgments. These included decisions on whether British subjects could run lotteries in China (they could not); whether British copyright was protected in China (it was); and whether British Courts should accept findings of fact made by consular courts of other nations between the same parties (they should).[5]

The fact that Wilkinson's son, Harrie, was the Crown Advocate was a matter of serious concern to the Foreign Office due to possible conflicts of interests, or at least, a perception of bias. Ernest Satow, now British Minister in Peking, noted in his diary that the Foreign Office wanted "to get rid of his son

2   PRO/30/6/6 p188 Note from Wilkinson to Satow dated December 28, 1900,(re meeting Hannen); C. Roberts, *The British Courts and Extraterritoriality in Japan*, 1859 to 1899, p337 (re formal closure of court)

3   *Yu Chun Shing v Cairney, North China Herald*, June 27, 1900, p1881

4   FO917/881. Wilkinson applied for probate on May 17, 1900 and it was granted on June 30, 1900.

5   *N. Moalle & Co v Khoo, North China Herald*, March 20, 1901, 551 (lotteries); *Pickwoad & Co v Shanghai Mercury, NCH*, March 27, 1901, p609 (copyright); *Norddeutscher Steamship Company v Ocean Steamship Co, NCH*, April 2, 1902, p635 (consular courts).

as Crown Advocate," and that H.S. Wilkinson had promised to arrange this.[6] In the first instance, the arrangement that was made was that Harrie would take leave. Satow then appointed him to serve as Commissioner for the Boxer Claims in 1901. In 1900, W.C. Platt took over as Acting Crown Advocate. Later, between 1901 and 1903 when Platt went on leave, Duncan McNeill, whose son, John, later served as the last Crown Advocate, served as Acting Crown Advocate. Platt took back over from McNeill when he returned from leave.[7]

As Commissioner for the Boxer Claims, Harrie Wilkinson worked as a single commissioner to assess the losses of British who had suffered at the hands of the Boxers.[8] He recalled later that it was "arduous work." He, however, considered himself very fortunate to be a single commissioner and not troubled by needing to reach agreement with other commissioners as to the compensation to be paid. Wilkinson arrived in Peking in June 1901 where, as he described, "the city had been parceled into zones ruled by various sections of the Allied Forces. The looting of curios had ceased, but they could be bought for ridiculously small prices." Wilkinson was required, as far as possible, to interview the claimants directly to assess their claims.

Recounting his claims work, Wilkinson said he could remember only one injustice – "one I have often wished I could remedy."

"A modest claim had been put in by a lady missionary whose mission was far in the interior. Her wardrobe was not such as one would expect in such circumstances, and I therefore cut one item of what would now be described as lingerie. I hope the claimant will read this and know that I admit that I was wrong."

6   I. Ruxton (ed), Sir Ernest Satow's Peking Diary (Volume I, 1900-1903), p3.

7   FO 656/101 Letter from *Duncan McNeill* to FSA Bourne Acting Chief Justice dated January 14, 1903 and letters dated February 25,1903 and February 27, 1903 resigning that position so that Mr Platt could resume acting after returning from long leave.

8   H.P. Wilkinson Reminiscences, *North China Herald*, October 31, 1925, p200-1.

WC Platt, Acting Crown Advocate in Harrie Wilkinson's absence

Wilkinson also said that he must have made mistakes, but the worst one was in setting the compensation for British houses in Peitaiho (Beidaihe). The Boxers had destroyed the houses and Wilkinson allowed the claims for new houses in full. It was pointed out to him later that: "You overlooked the fact that they may have knocked the houses down, but the Boxers did not take away the bricks, and the houses are being rebuilt with them."

After Harrie completed his claims work, from 1902 to 1903, father and son both took leave together.[9]

During their absence, Frederick Bourne acted as Chief Justice and Harold Frederick King, a consular officer, acted as Judge. King's younger brother, Gilbert Walter King, a solicitor in London, presumably on the recommendation of his elder brother, was appointed Assistant Clerk of the court during this time. He started work on April's Fool's day, April 1, 1903. Gilbert King was, however, no fool. Within fives years of joining he was appointed Registrar and after serving with distinction in that position for many years became a judge of the court. Both Bourne and Harold King received high praise from the *North China Herald* for their time in the acting positions.[10]

Satow continued to be a strong supporter of H.S. Wilkinson. In August 1902, Satow wrote to Barrington at the

A sketch by Harrie Wilkinson of the Clerk of the Court, most likely Gilbert King

9   *North China Herald*, October 2, 1903, p 728 reporting he had been on leave since April 1902;

10 *North China Herald*, April 9, 1902, p676. *North China Herald*, October 2, 1903, p728. Special thanks to Andrew Mussell of Gray's Inn for confirming the familial relationship of the Kings.

Foreign Office expressing his disappointment that Wilkinson had not been knighted. He said: "I was rather disappointed not to find the name of the C.J. at Shanghai in the list of Coronation honours, but perhaps it is being reserved to come out by itself, which always makes an honour seem so much bigger." He then pushed for perhaps a higher award:

> "To tell you the truth I am inclined to think that something more than a plain Knighthood would not be excessive in his case, for outside his judicial work he has been a most valuable counselor on intricate legal questions to successive ministers in both China and Japan for something like 30 years, and his memos of advice on matters of private international law seem to my humble appreciation, as good as anything of the kind that has ever been done."[11]

H.S. Wilkinson was knighted at Buckingham Palace, the following year, on June 26, 1903, while he was at Home on long leave. He left for Japan soon after the ceremony. In October 1903, he was due to return to Shanghai on board the HMS *Australien* from Kobe. Not far out of Kobe, the ship ran aground. Wilkinson took charge. After gently helping a little girl in a life jacket, he went off with the boat's crew to find help. To much praise from his fellow passengers, using his "knowledge of the language, tact and energy" he was able to arrange with local Japanese officials for all the passengers to get safely back to Kobe by either train or boat.[12]

H.S. Wilkinson was not always tactful. Later that year, he annoyed his strongest supporter, Ernest Satow. Satow wrote to Davidson of the Foreign Office about a difference of opin-

----

11 I. Ruxton (ed) *The Semi-official Letters of British Envoy Sir Ernest Satow from Japan and China (1895-1906)*, 1997, p315.

12 "To Kobe and Back: Some contrasts and a stranding" *North China Herald*, October 9, 1903, p751.

Ernest Satow, now British Minister in China. He remained a firm supporter of H.S. Wilkinson

ion that had occurred between Wilkinson and Bourne:

"You will have seen from Wilkinson's official letter to me that he is touched in his personal dignity by the words 'ignorance & inadvertence', & has no doubt sat on Bourne for treating the famous judgment he delivered when V-C at Kobe as pronounced by one who was not in fact endowed with judicial power. So I have it well to encourage Bourne with the idea which is held by those who sit in the seat of authority."[13]

Satow then expressed his concern about what to do with Harrie Wilkinson who was due to return as Crown Advocate from long leave:

"How we are to get over the difficulty about the C.J. & Crown Advocate being father & son I do not know? They doubtless feel that they have a hold over the Foreign Office of which they will make the best use."

A simple solution was found. Harrie Wilkinson was appointed as Acting Assistant Judge to the British Court of Si-

---

13 PRO 30/33 14/13 China (1-71) (May 8, 1902 – December 31, 1903). I have not been able to find what Bourne's said that so upset Wilkinson, nor Wilkinson's judgment delivered in Kobe. I suspect that the reference to the Kobe case is a reference to the *Hartley* case, which was in fact delivered in Yokohama. As we have seen, the Law Officers also considered Wilkinson did not have judicial power. (See Chapter 13)

am.[14] Harrie returned to Shanghai in June 1903 from leave a few months ahead of his father. He appeared in a number of cases in various courts, including the British Supreme Court, that month and then headed for Bangkok.[15] He had a rather ominous welcome:

"Going to Bangkok as British Acting Judge in 1903, the captain of the steamer said to me while steaming up the Menam River: 'Do you see that place on the right: that is the cemetery. You will be damned lucky if you ever see it on your left.'

"That was his opinion of the climate. I then and there made up my mind, hastily perhaps, that I would rather be a living Crown Advocate, than a dead Judge and therefore, though asked to remain, I came back to Shanghai in 1905 when my father's resignation as Chief Justice of the Court here left the way open for me to resume my work as Crown Advocate, and whatever was left of my private practice."[16]

Back in Shanghai, Harrie's father, H.S. Wilkinson, showed that he still had a fiery side. In one case he took the law completely into his own hands acting as constable, witness, prosecutor and judge. In early July 1904 on what would have been a warm day, he was travelling to the court in his horse-drawn buggy from his house at 2 Love Lane, just next to the Shanghai Country Club off Bubbling Well Road. His buggy had just turned into the Bund when as the *North China Herald* reported it, "a somewhat sensational incident" occurred after his carriage driver (called a mafoo), caused a collision with another

14 The *Straits Times*, February 28, May 1903, p3.

15 *North China Herald*, June 4, 1903, p 1109 et seq (British Court) *North China Herald*, June 11, 1903, p1184 (Mixed Court).

16 H.P. Wilkinson Reminiscences, *North China Herald*, October 31, 1925, p200-1. Satow's diaries confirm that Harrie Wilkinson was offered a permanent position of judge in Siam.

carriage. According to the *North China Herald*:

> "The mafoo backed the vehicle to free it and in doing
> so either upset, or frightened the coolie so much that
> he upset a rickshaw containing a foreigner, Frederick
> Penfold. Penfold was so enraged at this that he leapt
> into Sir Hiram's carriage and hit the mafoo on the back
> of his head. Sir Hiram sat Penfold down in the carriage
> and drove straight to the British Consulate, where he
> tried him in the Police Court and fined him $5 and
> costs. The whole affair from start to finish did not oc-
> cupy more than five minutes."[17]

The court reports for July 6, 1904 listed the case as *R v Frederick Penfold* in the Police Court "before Sir Hiram S Wilkinson, Chief Justice." Penfold was "charged with assaulting the mafoo of Sir Hiram Shaw Wilkinson, Chief Justice of the Court, in the presence of the said Chief Justice on 6th July." Penfold admitted the charge. Wilkinson, cooling down somewhat – and perhaps remembering one of the golden tenets of English justice, that a man should not be a judge in his own cause - said that since the offence had been committed so recently Penfold could have the case finalized the next day. Penfold, surely somewhat sheepishly, said he was happy to get the

The Bund where HS Wilkinson and Penfold collided.

---

17 *North China Herald*, July 8, 1904, p63.

matter over with. Wilkinson then passed sentence and at the
same time gave Penfold a lecture on the treatment of locals:

> "You jumped in my carriage and hit my mafoo. There
> is too much of that. I think the offence is a great one
> for two or three reasons. You are fined $5 and $3 costs.
> Now allow me to say to you that it is a very great
> mistake for you to do a thing of that sort. You know
> that the Chinese must be protected. You don't know
> whose servants they are or whether they are foreigners'
> servants or not. Englishmen have no right to go about
> striking them."[18]

Wilkinson may not have been in the best of moods. Less
than a week before the incident with Penfold he had arrived back in Shanghai from Canton where, after the jury in
a murder case had returned a verdict of guilty, he had had
the unpleasant duty of sentencing an Indian, Abdul Khalik,
to death.[19]

The whole case was a travesty of justice. A former British consular officer in China, P.D. Coates, commented that the
verdict "would never have been tolerated had the man been
white." The five-man jury over their one and half days of
jury service racked up massive expenses including the cost of
two bottles of champagne, two bottles of claret, one bottle of
sherry, one bottle of port, 20 whiskies and soda, five brandies
and 32 cigars. They must either have been drunk or severely
hungover when considering their verdict. The Foreign Office
paid the bill but asked that charges be kept lower in the future
and said that cigars could not be charged. There appears to
have been no suggestion that juries should be sober.

Wilkinson left Canton immediately after passing sentence

---

18 *R v Frederick Penfold*, North China Herald, July 8, 1904, p92.

19 P.D. Coates, *The China Consuls*, p368-369; *North China Herald*, June 24,1904, p1314
(short report of trial); September 9, 1904, p606 (date of hanging).

without even discussing with the Acting Consul-General, C.W. Campbell, how Khalik should be hanged. The consular jail was a single room on the ground floor of the constable's quarters to which two toilets were attached. There were no gallows and nowhere else to hang Khalik. It took two months to work out how it could be done. An executioner was brought from Hong Kong and gallows jury-rigged for the occasions. A hole was cut in the floor of the verandah in the constable's quarters leading to one of the prisoners' toilets directly below. A trap door was installed. Khalik was hanged by being dropped through the verandah into the toilet.

This was all deemed to be so unseemly that the British Minister, Ernest Satow, recommended that in future all hangings be conducted in Shanghai. The only redeeming feature of the case was that Khalik confessed just before his hanging to the murder for which he had been tried as well as to another murder. At least, an innocent man did not go to an unseemly death.

Wilkinson cannot have felt good about Khalik's trial or sentence. This may have brought pent-up anger to the fore, which he then vented on Penfold.

Wilkinson may also have been frustrated at the treatment his son Harrie had been receiving. Two months before, he had tendered his resignation to take effect between August 1904 (when he would have been in service for 40 years) and 13 June 1905 (when he would be 65).[20] Harrie had wanted to come back to Shanghai on holiday in 1904 but been told he must resign as Crown Advocate first. Wilkinson complained and received a response from W.G. Jackson of the Foreign Office:

"So far as I could understand the objection to your son's going to Shanghai was that he could not divest himself from his office, ie. could not stay in Shanghai

20 PRONI D1292/M/25 Letter from Wilkinson to Mr Cockerell, dated April 18, 1904.

in mufti, and that the technical objection would remain even if he exercised no functions. We trust that he will not resign his Siam judgeship until he has found something better and more to his liking."

Wilkinson made clear in his resignation letter that he was not happy with Harrie's treatment: "While I am very grateful to the consideration which has been shown him, I feel that my advancement to my present post has entailed loss enough upon him already."[21]

Satow and Wilkinson, however, remained close. In November 1904, Wilkinson stayed with Satow in Peking for four days. Satow's residence in Peking was quite literally palatial. In 1860 the British had taken over a Chinese palace for their legation. The Minister's quarters were fitted out in luxurious style. Photos from the time Satow was Minister show his quarters as having numerous rooms, all grandly decorated. These included a drawing room, dining room, morning room, smoking room, billiard room and, of course, bedrooms.[22]

Satow was going to miss Wilkinson. On his departure from Peking he wrote: "Wilkinson went off by the afternoon train. During his stay, he has helped me with several knotty questions, such as Hankow Bund frontages, Haimun port-dues &c. I am sorry he is going to retire."[23]

A stand-off in court

Just days before Wilkinson's formal retirement, a commercial case produced some real fireworks in court. Duncan Mc-Neill, the former Acting Crown Advocate, and a fiery Scot, challenged Wilkinson's sense of justice. McNeill was acting for a company, Moller & Co in a claim against Wheelock & Co for £350 as money owed under the lease of a ship that

---

21 PRONI D1292/M/25 Note from Jackson to Wilkinson, July 1, 1904.

22 WORK 55, 17

23 I .Ruxton (ed) Satow, Peking Diaries, Vol 2, p129.

Moller had arranged. During the trial Wilkinson clearly said he was concerned that the £350 was in fact a secret commission. It was illegal for Moller, as a broker, to receive secret commissions. If it were illegal, British courts would not enforce its payment. Wheelock did not, however, rely on this defence. They would not have wanted to admit in court that they had agreed to pay a secret commission.[24]

Following the trial, Wilkinson asked the jury to make findings on certain issues of fact. The jury found mostly in favour of Moller. Wilkinson asked McNeill and the Wheelock's lawyer, R.N. MacLeod, if they wished to make submissions as to the legality of the contract. McNeill did. MacLeod, clearly wanting to avoid being asked by Wilkinson if the money was a secret commission, said that he did not. A few days later, Wilkinson gave a long judgment where he found the transaction to be illegal and not enforceable at law. He dismissed Moller's claim. He then had to deal with the question of who should pay the costs of the case. If the transaction was illegal then the fairest would be

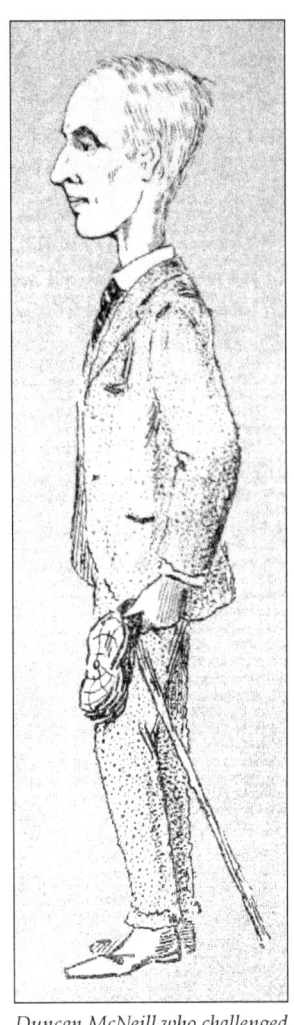

Duncan McNeill who challenged HS Wilkinson's sense of justice

24 *Moller v Wheelock, North China Herald* March 31, 1905, p680; The exchange between Wilkinson and McNeill was reported in the third person. I have changed this to the first person. The English Court of Appeal case is *Scott v Brown, Dering , McNab & Co* [1892] 2 QB 724.

to order that neither party have to pay the other costs. They were both equally at fault. However, following an English Court of Appeal precedent, Wilkinson ordered that Moller pay Wheelock's costs of defending the action. This was a harsh decision. Wheelock had been part of the transaction and did not challenge its legality. Wilkinson's order that the Moller pay Wheelock its costs certainly would have been painful to McNeill. McNeill was not going to take this lying down. He rose to his feet and told Wilkinson:

"I do not believe that any instance would be found in the records of the Court of costs being awarded to a defendant who had no honest defence to the action, and who had only succeeded on a point of law raised by the judge himself, and decided by him in opposition to the general feeling of the jury regarding the merits of the case."

Up to this point, he was within his rights as an advocate. But then he crossed the line, making a direct accusation against Wilkinson:

"I think under the circumstances a great injustice had been done to my clients."

One can imagine MacLeod, who most likely had been thinking that he needed to buy McNeill a drink to commiserate with him, freezing in his seat as he waited for a train crash to occur. Wilkinson, already in a benign pre-retirement mood, decided to let it go:

"In the course of my experience on the bench this is the first time that I have ever been accused of willfully doing an injustice. Had I been staying here I would have had to take some notice of it."

McNeill would not let go and, as he would later regret, pushed the matter. He responded steadfastly, "I desire that your Lordship would take some notice of it."

"I am quite content to leave the matter to the feeling of the Bar," responded Wilkinson softly.

McNeill was not going to back down: "I consider that a serious injustice had been done to my clients," he repeated.

The seconds must have ticked by slowly as Wilkinson contemplated the situation with McNeill standing before him and refusing to back down. MacLeod was offering no assistance, most likely sitting with his head down trying his best to pretend he was not there. Wilkinson responded with finality as he stood and left the courtroom, "Under those circumstances I should decline to hear you on any matter until you apologize."

To a non-lawyer a storm in a teacup, one may think. But this is not the way things work in higher British courts. Civility is the catchword. If you think you have been done an injustice, you appeal. If you cannot appeal, you put on your happy face to the court and complain (sometimes bitterly) in private afterwards over a few drinks.

News of McNeill's stand travelled fast. The Chairman of the Municipal Council spoke out in support of Wilkinson. The *North China Herald* published an editorial about the "regrettable incident," saying that anyone who read the case report could not come to "to any other conclusion than that substantial justice was done, and under any circumstances his well earned reputation for fairness and carefulness should of itself have protected him from the charge that was made against him, obviously without time for consideration having been taken, just as his career on the bench was coming to a close." The editorial continued that Wilkinson could be assured "that he has public sympathy with him" and that certain appreciatory remarks by the Chairman of Municipal Council "are the true echo of popular opinion in Shanghai."[25]

McNeill also knew that he could not leave things as they stood and wrote Wilkinson a personal note (which Wilkinson kept for the rest of his life) saying:

> "With reference to what took place in Court on Monday last I beg to say that in protesting against your decision I had no intention of imputing to you any willful unfairness or injustice in the conduct of this case.
> "I sincerely regret and apologize for anything said by me which may have led to a different understanding of my intention."[26]

This was not quite a full apology. That would come soon.

Farewell to H.S. Wilkinson

Wilkinson certainly was popular. Exactly one week after his run-in with McNeill, a farewell hearing was held for him. Wilkinson was retiring as the last "Chief Justice" of the British Supreme Court in Shanghai. The year before, a new Order in Council has been enacted consolidating and updating the various orders that had been enacted over the years. As part of this process, the Foreign Office had decided to bring the Supreme Court for China and Corea in line with the other extraterritorial courts it ran around the world. From the retirement of Wilkinson, the title of Chief Justice reverted to Judge and the Judge became Assistant Judge. This was strongly opposed by the local community. The *North China Herald* in an editorial fumed against the change adding that "the fact that the chief judicial authority had the title and standing of Chief Justice

---

25 *North China Herald*, March 31, 1905, p638.
26 PRONI D1292/C/9 (Wilkinson Papers).

has added proper dignity and lustre to the appointment."[27] Questions about the change were asked a number of times in the British Parliament.

John Douglas, the Registrar, who was sitting as Acting Judge in Bourne's absence, sat on the bench with Wilkinson.[28] Fittingly, before the farewells were made, Wilkinson delivered a judgment which broke the *North China Herald's* record for the longest judgment ever read out in the court: one and half hours.

After the judgment was read, W.C. Platt, the acting Crown Advocate rose to farewell Wilkinson on behalf of the bar. He recounted Wilkinson's service in Japan, his time as Crown Advocate and his appointment as Chief Justice then finished with a fitting eulogy:

> "Your predecessors in that office were men who had so ably carried out the duties entrusted to them that his court had come to be universally regarded by Chinese and foreigners alike where Law and Justice was administered impartially, and where a litigant knew that the merits of his case would be thoroughly gone into and justice administered. Such as the reputation which this Court had when you were appointed Chief Justice, and you leave it with that reputation higher if possible than ever, and with its prestige unimpaired."

Vernon Drummond as the oldest member of the local bar and who had known Wilkinson from when he first came to Shanghai in the 1870s then spoke. He noted the workload of the court that had increased markedly in recent years, which had made Wilkinson's time on the bench very busy. On top of this Wilkinson, as Chief Justice, had presided over the "annu-

---

27 *North China Herald* December 30, 1904, p1457.

28 *North China Herald*, April 7, 1905, p19. Douglas became Registrar in 1901 when Eustace Burrows resigned.

al meeting of our local parliament" (the Municipal Council),
something he had done with "readiness and cheerfulness."

Finally and simply, Drummond wished Wilkinson: "God
speed."

Now, it was time for Duncan McNeill to eat some humble
pie. He rose to address Wilkinson. All eyes in court would
have been on him to see how he dealt with his outburst of a
week before:

> "I desire at the moment, with your Lordship's permis-
> sion, to allude to a recent event which no person now
> regrets more sincerely than myself. I hope your Lord-
> ship will see your way to accept the written apology
> I have thought it my duty to write to you, but I now
> desire to express my own concurrence in the remarks
> that have fallen from Mr Platt and Mr Drummond."

Wilkinson accepted McNeill's apology. He said he knew
McNeill would regret the incident and that he was glad that
McNeill had mentioned it publicly because the incident had
occurred publicly.

Wilkinson, obviously feeling the moment, then directed
some words to the bar. He said, "it is not without emotion
that I bring to a close a career of 40 years in the east. Nearly
thirty-three years of these have been in connection with the
Bench and Bar." Referring to the decision to change the title
of Chief Justice to Judge, he said he regretted "very much that
the office which I now hold is about to be shorn of some of its
outward dignity," and hoped the decision would be reversed
soon. He finished with a simple farewell:

> "I thank you, gentlemen, most sincerely and I say to
> you what Mr. Drummond has said to me, "God speed."

The *North China Herald* then recorded: "His Lordship, whose emotion had been evident without his own allusion to it, then bowed to the court and withdrew."

The next week, the bar gave him a dinner at the Shanghai Club and formally requested that he sit for a portrait to be hung in the court after he returned home. A few days later on April 14, 1905, Wilkinson bid his final farewell to Shanghai, leaving on the *Bremen* from the French Bund. He was headed to the townland of Moneyshanere, just outside Tobermore in Northern Ireland, where he had purchased a sizeable country estate. The *North China Herald* reported that there was "an unprecedented concourse there of all nationalities, and the din and bombs of crackers was almost terrifying."[29] It continued with an almost hagiographic farewell eulogy saying, "in him we lose a good and faithful friend, and a most able, earnest and conscientious Judge" and closing:

> "Warm-hearted, kind, courteous, and obliging to all, he has made himself a home in all our hearts; he has identified himself with the best interests of Yokohama and Shanghai, and we shall long miss him; and the consciousness of this will, we hope do something to mitigate the sorrow he must feel at leaving the bench he has so adorned."[30]

Harrie Wilkinson, lost no time in getting back from his exile in Bangkok. His last sitting as Acting Judge in Siam was on March 28, 1905. Soon after that he left for Shanghai to high praise from the *Bangkok Times* which said: "he has shown himself an exceedingly able lawyer and a fearless Judge."[31]

Even after H.S. Wilkinson's departure the decision to

29 *North China Herald*, April 14, 1905, p82.
30 *North China Herald*, April 7, 1905, p9.
31 *North China Herald*, April 20, 1905, p131.

change the title of the Chief Justice continued to be challenged. A question was asked by Mr Joseph Walton in Parliament on May 23, 1905:

> "I beg to ask the Under-Secretary of State for Foreign
> Affairs whether, under an Order of Council due to
> come into effect on the 1st April, the title Chief Justice
> will be taken away from the Principal Judge of the Brit-
> ish Supreme Court at Shanghai; and, if so, whether, in
> view of the opinion of British residents that this course
> will be injurious to British prestige, His Majesty's Gov-
> ernment will reconsider the question of its retention."

Earl Percy responded, "the adoption of the nomenclature
common to all His Majesty's Extra-territorial Courts is not,
in the opinion of His Majesty's Government, calculated to
be attended with the results apprehended by the honourable
Member."[32]

In August 1905, Mr Walton again raised the topic and
said that he had received a telegram upon this matter which
ran— "Abolition of title of Chief Justice a ruinous mistake;
pray urge retention." He said the title had "a great effect in
enhancing the status and prestige of this official in the eyes of
Chinese and foreigners alike," and that as the Court was the
appellate court for the whole of China, the steps opposed to
British interests.[33]

The following year, a special ceremony was held in the Supreme Court courtroom attended by Assistant Judge Frederick Bourne, Registrar John Douglas, Crown Advocate Harrie
Wilkinson and other members of the bar to hang a portrait of
H.S. Wilkinson. All the portraits of the previous chief judges
had been moved from the Judge's room to the courtroom. The
court had been cleared of law books. Instead, on the green

32 Hansard, HC Deb 23 March 1905 vol 143 c952.
33 Hansard, Revenue Departments Estimates, 1905-6, 3 August 1905, p8.

baize of the counsel's table, white linen had been laid out with champagne and light refreshments. Bourne gave an introductory speech, saying that to be drinking tea "would be very wrong" if H.S. "Wilkinson was to be forgotten." He then asked Harrie Wilkinson to unveil the portrait, which had been covered by a red curtain. After doing so, Harrie then made a short speech where he said that nothing would make his father "more proud than of having his picture hung in this court." He added that his face

A red-faced H.S. Wilkinson offers a toast just before he leaves Shanghai. Perhaps a clue as to why all should drink a toast to him?

in the portrait was severe and there was a look of business on it. Drawing laughter from the assembled audience, he added that however, he had not had to experience it because "I have not had to appear before my father." At the end of the ceremony the party drank to the memory of all the other former Chief Justices: Hornby, French, Rennie and Hannen.[34]

Ernest Satow also retired from Foreign Office service the next year in 1906. In November that year, the China Association in London invited him as a guest of honour to their dinner at the Hotel Metropole in London.[35] H.S. Wilkinson, Harrie Wilkinson, and George Jamieson were all in attendance and seated at the same table. John Carey Hall, the husband of Agnes Goodwin and a former acting judge of both the Court for Japan and Supreme Court at Shanghai was there also, seated between the Wilkinsons.

....

34 *North China Herald*, April, 27, 1906, p198.

35 Supplement to the *London and China Telegraph*, November 12, 1906, p1-5. Photograph of the dinner from the China Association Archives held by SOAS.

Satow, in his speech in reply to the warm toast given to him, first adverted to the extreme difficulties of being Minister in Peking at the time, adding "I am not going to take you into my confidence by specifying what those difficulties are—(laughter)—but anyone who has lived six years in Peking, and some gentlemen here have perhaps been there even longer, will sufficiently know what they are." He then turned to thank the "most loyal and zealous servants to the British Government" without whom "I certainly could never have performed one half of my work." To cheers from the audience, he then said he wanted to mention "my old friend Sir Hiram Wilkinson" and gave him a fine final farewell:

"He was first of all in Japan when I was there, and afterwards Chief Justice at Shanghai, and for thirty or forty years he has been always the confidential adviser upon all legal and international questions of successive Ministers, both at Tokyo and Peking. His help I cannot too much appreciate."

CHAPTER 31

1905: A Year of Change

WHEN WILKINSON ANNOUNCED his retirement, the Foreign Office needed to find a new Chief Judge. H.S. Wilkinson had the previous year lobbied Satow for his son, Harrie, to be appointed. He had even gone so far in his own resignation letter to write: "I hope that his claims to succeed me will be favourably considered."

Satow wrote in his diary that he did not consider Harrie to be a good appointment. To his friend, H.S. Wilkinson, however, he said that there must be an interval filled by someone else and that he understood the chance of Harrie succeeding his father was small. Satow added that, in fact he had heard the bar wanted a man from Home. H.S. Wilkinson denied they would have said that. Wilkinson added that he and the former Judge for Japan, Robert Mowat, were strongly against Bourne being appointed.[1]

In the end, for the first time since the appointment of George French 28 years earlier, the Foreign Office went outside China and Japan to appoint a new full time judge. The new Judge was Havilland de Sausmarez, a career judge of the Foreign Office who had served in Africa and most recently had been the British Judge at Constantinople. De Sausmarez took up his post in April 1905 and sat for first time on the same day that H.S. Wilkinson left Shanghai, April 14, 1905. He

....

1   I. Ruxton (ed), *The Diaries of Sir Ernest Satow, British Envoy in Peking (1900-06)*, p324 and 326-327. Robert Mowat had been Assistant Judge in Shanghai from 1878 to 1891 and Judge for Japan from 1891 to 1897.

You pronounce it as you choose to do,
"SOMMERREZ" or "SAUCE-MAROO":
One reading tho' there cannot be;
SIR HEAVY-HAND DE SUMMARY

A caricature of de Sausmarez from the Eastern Sketch

did not seem to be concerned about the change of title of the Chief Justice to Judge, describing his appointment as "fulfilling one of the ambitions of my life, having reached the highest position the Foreign Office can give me."[2]

De Sausmarez was a true servant of empire. He had been born into an aristocratic family in Guernsey on May 30, 1861 to the Reverend Havilland de Sausmarez and Anne Priaulx Walters, and had been brought up in the de Sausmarez manor in Guernsey. He had no need to be travelling the world as a judge.

In early life, he studied at Westminster where he was head of the rowing club and also participated in other athletic pursuits. After Westminster, he went up to Cambridge. He graduated from Trinity College in 1883 with a Bachelor of Arts. He was admitted as a barrister of the Inner Temple in 1881 and called to the Bar in November 1884. He practiced on the Southern Eastern Circuit in England and then moved to Africa, where he practiced in Lagos, Nigeria in 1891. He was acting Queen's Advocate of the Colony of Lagos from June 1891 to January 1892.

In June 1892, he joined the Foreign Office Judicial Service when he was appointed a consul in Zanzibar. From 1893 to 1897 he was Assistant Judge of the Consular Court in Zanzibar. In 1897, he transferred to Constantinople where he was Assistant Judge until 1903 when he was promoted to Judge. He served in that position until 1905, when following in Sir Edmund Hornby's footsteps, he was made Judge of the Supreme Court for China and Corea. He was knighted at the end of 1905 after his arrival in Shanghai.

De Sausmarez was President of the Chess Club for the entire time he was in Shanghai. When he was knighted, one of the members drew a caricature of him as a knight on a chessboard.[3] He was also patron of the Shanghai Scouting troop in

2   *North China Herald* April 20, 1905, p131
3   *North China Herald*, December 18, 1920, p820.

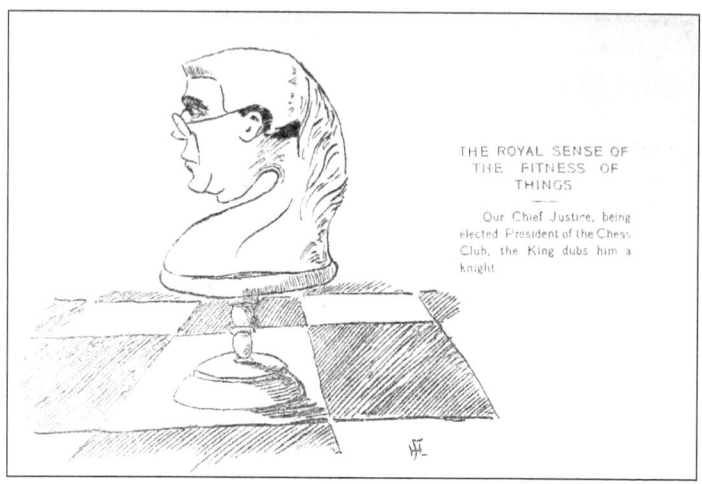

THE ROYAL SENSE OF
THE FITNESS OF
THINGS

Our Chief Justice, being
elected President of the Chess
Club, the King dubs him a
knight

1914 and 1915 and president of the Horticultural Association.

De Sausmarez appears to have been a relatively austere and wowserish person who took a dim view of immoral activity. One correspondent to the *North China Herald* complaining about night clubs just outside the concession limits said in a letter: "If my memory does not fail me I remember that when Judge de Sausmarez passed sentence on someone, not very long ago, for dishonesty caused by frequenting the famous 'Wheel,' His Honour said that he was going to approach the proper authorities with a view to having the 'Wheel' closed up, or words to that effect, and not longer after that pronouncement, we had the great satisfaction of seeing that establishment raided by the police, and its doors properly sealed up."[4]

Shanghai being Shanghai, the Wheel's doors did not remain "properly sealed up" for long. The *North China Herald* reported in September 1919 that the Wheel had re-opened in a new guise and illegal gambling was once again going on there. It was not until 1929 when Mexico withdrew consular protection for its owner that it was finally shut down.[5]

4   *North China Herald*, December 25, 1920, p877.
5   *North China Herald*, September 27, 1919, p811. Norwood Allman in *Shanghai Lawyer*

In another case, in 1911, after convicting a Mr Craig for defrauding his shareholders, de Sausmarez delivered a homily from the bench about greed and the lack of commercial morals in Shanghai. He admonished residents to show proper British character. His speech is worth repeating in full to give a flavor of his character:

"I cannot help feeling that the this crime to which you have very honourably pleaded guilty has been one of the results of folly, and more than folly, which marked the conduct of so many in this Settlement with the speculation of last year. The dire effects of that speculation on so many will point a moral of the effect of such abandonment more strongly than any words of mine can do, but there is another aspect of the case which I feel that I must speak of. It is even more serious that the former and it is this, that it has been borne in on my mind by many instances which have been multiplied recently, that there is a fatal inclination in this society here to slur over any lapse from commercial uprightness. People are content to let things drift in a course without due inquiry or care as to whether that course is right or wrong and to allow people to remain in positions which their conduct has shown them unfit to fill. In a community such as this, which exists mainly for the purpose of trade in a foreign land, I cannot but feel that such neglect in the respect for commercial uprightness must have a very serious effect upon those with whom we live, in their esteem of our character and as a commercial nation and of faith which out to be placed upon upright merchants carrying on trades in a country such as this. These are general remarks which I think I ought to make on this occasion."[6]

claims the credit for the withdrawal of consular protection in 1929. See p.96.

6 *Straits Times*, February 20, 1911, p7.

But he did have his light side. As we shall see, at an anniversary dinner for United States Court for China he gave a genuinely funny speech about his time in Africa.[7] Early on, de Sausmarez set out about improving the administration of the court, or at least reducing its costs. Soon after taking office, during the hearing of a criminal case, Harrie Wilkinson, now back as Crown Advocate, brought two matters to his attention.[8] First, a member of the Municipal Council, John Liddell, had been summonsed for jury duty. While this was allowed by the Order in Council, Wilkinson suggested that members of the council be exempted from jury duty during their term of office. De Sausmarez said that this was most likely a proper course and he would consider how to implement it. Second, Wilkinson raised the question of court interpreters pointing out that there was no interpreter in court. For many years, an officer from the consulate had usually acted as an interpreter. Wilkinson suggested that the court employ a qualified interpreter in the various Chinese dialects.

Sometimes you have to be careful what you ask for.

De Sausmarez said the question had arisen in other cases. The court was understaffed and Sir Hiram Wilkinson had been of the strong opinion that more staff were needed. He would therefore be making strong representations to the Minister to increase the staff. In the course of saying this, he dropped the bombshell on Harrie Wilkinson. "There was however, one point in connection with criminal cases; it was not the duty of the Court to provide an interpreter, but the duty of the Crown." Wilkinson protested that the Crown did not provide him with a salary for an interpreter. De Sausmarez responded, "nevertheless it was the duty of the Crown to provide an inter-

7   See Chapter 39.

8   *R v Sidney, North China Herald,* June 9, 1905, p553; FO 656/101 Letter from Harrie Wilkinson to the Foreign Office, dated May 29, 1908.

preter." From then on Wilkinson had to employ an interpreter to be "at the disposal of and necessary to the court in criminal trials," a matter he raised in a subsequent letter to the Foreign Office seeking an increase in his remuneration.

In September 1905, in a meeting with the Ernest Satow, W.C. Platt, who had acted as Crown Advocate in Harrie Wilkinson's absence, told Satow that the bar was pleased with de Sausmarez, "who does not know much law, but is a practical man." Platt added that what the bar wanted was a man fresh out from Home, but for the salary given (£2,000) no one who had any practice could be brought out. Satow told Platt that it was just the same with colonial legal appointments, and couldn't be helped.[9]

A new "appeal" procedure

The new 1904 Order in Council provided a new procedure for applying for a re-hearing of a case. In November 1905, Harrie Wilkinson made the first application for a re-hearing.[10] De Sausmarez granted the application saying that the new provision of the Order in Council was designed to "provide a means of reconsidering a judgment, without the delay and expense" of appealing to the Privy Council. He ordered that in future cases the same rules that were used to apply for an appeal to the English Court of Appeal should apply in the Supreme Court for China and Corea. He said that the motion should be heard by the Full Court (that is, the Judge and Assistant Judge) and that in appropriate cases the motion for a re-hearing could be treated as the actual re-hearing. In effect, De Sausmarez created a new simplified appeal procedure direct to a Full Court in Shanghai made up of the Judge and

9   I. Ruxton (ed), *Satow Peking Diaries*, p225.

10 *Alexandre Pavlow v TCR Ward North China Herald*, November 17, 1905, p500. The new rule of the 1904 Order in Council was Rule 114 which gave very broad powers to the court: "The Supreme Court may if it thinks fit on the application of any party or of its own motion, order the re-hearing of an action, or of an appeal, or of any arguments on a verdict or on any other question of law." An application was required to be made within 14 days.

Assistant Judge. Parties still, however, had the right to appeal directly to the Privy Council if they wished.

Wilkinson then asked if de Sausmarez would be issuing a formal rule of court, which under the Order in Council the Judge had the power to make. De Sausmarez, showing his practical side, gave a very frank reply, saying that it would be too much trouble to formally make new rules given they would need Foreign Office approval. He said:

> "It is a considered judgment and indicates the practice which I shall follow. Rules of Court require the consent of the Secretary of State and I am not anxious to embark on a set of new Rules."

Japan's victory over Russia

H.S. Wilkinson's retirement and de Sausmarez's appointment came just as Japan was about to become the first Asian country to win a war against a European power, Russia. The war had been going on since 1904 and the newspapers of the time were filled with stories of the battles. The headlines often just read "The War." Everyone knew about it and everyone was watching.

Following the trip-partite intervention after the signing of the Treaty of Shimonoseki and Russia's occupation of Port Arthur and Dalian in 1898, Japan was concerned about Russia encroaching on its own territorial gains. In particular, following the Boxer Rebellion, Russia had not withdrawn its troops from Manchuria as they had promised to. Japan felt that its own interests in Korea were under threat.

As a first step to being in a position to challenge Russia, in 1902 Japan signed a treaty with the British that obliged the other party to enter a war if a third country did not remain neutral. In 1903 Japan then commenced negotiations with Russia seeking to reach an agreement that Korea was in Ja-

Battlefields in the Russo-Japanese War

pan's sphere of influence while acknowledging Russia's interests in Manchuria.

Japan at the time had a much smaller navy than Russia and most people thought that it would be impossible for Japan, an upstart Asian country, to defeat a European power. The Russian Tsar certainly thought so and negotiated at a very slow pace. In early 1904, the Japanese navy attacked Port Arthur and landed land troops in Korea to enter Manchuria across the Yalu River. After a number of naval and land battles, the Russian

Fleet was blockaded in Port Arthur. The Japanese, at the cost of great life, captured the hills around Port Arthur and destroyed the remainder of the Russian Pacific Fleet with artillery firing from the hill tops. They then captured Port Arthur.[11] The capture of Port Arthur was effectively the end. The Japanese had demonstrated that they had the capability to defeat a European navy and army. While the war went on, for many it was a sign of things to come. One writer at the time presciently captured this mood in the beginning of a short story:

> 'Is it true Port Arthur has fallen?' asked the man ...
> 'Yes it's official,' I answered.
> 'He paused for a moment and seemed to ponder. I was silent. No doubt he was thinking upon what the news meant to the Far East, upon the effect this proof of the power of the Yellow races might have upon the future, perhaps, of the world, the magnitude of the problem which the next half century must solve overpowered him.'[12]

The only hope for the Russians was their Baltic Fleet, which had been renamed the 2nd Pacific Squadron, which was heading to Asia around Africa and via the Suez Canal. By April 1905, the fleet had arrived in Manila and then set sail for Vladivostok. In order to get there, they would either have to sail around the North of Japan or through the Straits of Tsushima between Korea and Japan. They chose the Straits of Tsushima. Based on intelligence supplied by the British, the Japanese were able to attack the fleet as they sailed through the straits on the evening of May 14, 1905. The Russians,

---

11 See E Drea, *Japan's Imperial Army: Its Rise and Fall 1853-1945*, Chapter 6 for a detailed treatment of the Russo-Japanese war. The Japanese Maritime Self Defence Museum in Sasebo also has a detailed display on the war.

12 "A City without a Soul", *North China Herald*, March 31, 1905, p660. In fact, the gentleman who was described as "having prominent nose— his English smacked a little of Israel," was pondering "I wonder how this will affect the markets?"

exhausted from months of sailing and outgunned and out-maneuvered, were convincingly defeated with the Japanese sinking all eight Russian battleships with limited loss to the Japanese side.

Only three Russian boats survived and they limped back to Manila. One of the boats, the *Aurora*, was later to be the first Russian Navy ship to support the Bolsheviks in 1917 and for this reason is still in active service in the Russian Navy. It now serves as a museum in downtown St Petersburg where it is docked. The history of *Aurora* published by the museum describes the battle in the language of heroic defeat:

> "Exhausted by the trials of an enormously long voyage, separated from their main bases and lacking combat experience, and shooting practice in the conditions of war, the Russian sailors entered the unequal battle with the Japanese ships that were faster, better armed and armoured ... The men put out fires, while doing so kept shooting to support other ships ... Many ships which sustained heavy damage and were unable to move continued to bombard the enemy with all the might they could muster."[13]

Finally, "when no ammunition was left, their crews, riddled with bullets, rejected surrender and chose to die on the sinking ships, having faithfully performed their duty without bringing disgrace on the St Andrew's flag."

After this defeat, the Russians sued for peace. United States President Theodore Roosevelt acted as a mediator and a treaty of peace was signed in Portsmouth, Maine, in 1905. Under the treaty, Port Arthur and Dalian were ceded to Japan along with the Southern half of Sakhalin Island. No indemnity was to be paid. The lack of any payment outraged Japanese

---

13 *The Cruiser Aurora*, Ego Publishers, St Petersburg.

public opinion, which considered that Japan had been treated badly in the negotiations. Japan did, however, now have its first full colonies and naval ports in China from which it was able to further extend its influence in China.

Many British were ecstatic at the Japanese victory. At the China Association dinner in November 1905, the President, Mr Gundry, hailed the victory "as of good augury for peace and successful commerce for many years." Retired Admiral Sir Archibald Douglas (father of John Douglas, the Registrar of the Supreme Court) who had in 1874 led a team of British sailors to Japan to train the Japanese Navy said:

> "The whole of the time we were there the Japanese
> were so anxious to learn that we had very little to do
> but to teach them. They wanted to learn everything,
> and subsequent events prove how well they have learnt
> it."[14]

The British lease for Weihaiwei had been agreed to last as long as the Russian were in occupation in Port Arthur. Now the Russians were gone, the British should leave as well. Mr Gundry in his speech to the China Association had said withdrawal by the British from Weihaiwei would be met with "unqualified regret." The view was obviously shared by the British government and after confirming with the Japanese that they had no objection, the British continued in occupation.[15]

Mixed Court Riot
Shanghai saw its own battles. In late 1905, rioting broke out in Shanghai originating from a fight over who had the right to

14 Supplement to the *London and China Gazette*, November 6, 1905, p1 (Grundy) and p3 (Douglas).

15 Various correspondence passed between officials at the Foreign Office about whether there should be a withdrawal. The Japanese were said to wish that the British remain in Weihaiwei. Satow recommended it as an invaluable health station and training ground. See: British Documents on Foreign Affairs: Reports and Papers from the Foreign Office Confidential Print, Series E, Volume 13, pp204-205.

detain prisoners on trial at the Mixed Court.

The Municipal Council had long been concerned about corruption in the Mixed Court as well as the filthy conditions of the cells of the womens' jail attached to the court. The Municipal Council arranged that Municipal Police should be stationed at the Mixed Court to keep prisoners in custody as well as to keep a record of the cases. The first policeman to be sent was a Sikh. The Chinese Magistrate objected to any policemen being there as an infringement of Chinese

Mr B. Twyman, the British Assessor who sparked the Mixed Court riots.

sovereignty writing to the British Consul-General, "as I have sole charge of the Court from the front door inwards, the Police have no right to interfere therewith, and I should be entitled to expel the Indian at once." Eventually, a compromise was reached where a European policeman was stationed in the court.[16]

Matters came to a head on December 18, 1905 when a Madame Li from Sichuan province was brought before the court on a charge of kidnapping girls for unlawful purposes. The case was adjourned to be heard on another day. Magistrate Kuan ordered that Madam Li and the girls be detained in the cells of the Mixed Court and instructed the Chinese runners accordingly. The British assessor, Mr Twyman, ordered that the

16 See, F. Hawks Pott, *A Short History of Shanghai*, pp166-169; G. Keeton, *The Development of Extraterritoriality in China*, 368-375 for details of the Mixed Court riot.

Municipal Police keep Madam Li and the girls in custody. This
led to an all-in brawl between the police and the runners. The
police won. They then put Madam Li and the girls in a police
van. The Magistrate ordered the doors to the court to be locked
and said that the police would have to kill him if they wished
to leave. The police broke the door down and left.

The incident inflamed Chinese sentiment against foreigners. Chinese merchant associations encouraged a boycott of
foreign businesses and products. Riots broke out around the
city. Louza Police Station, which was located at the western
end of Nanking Road at the corner with Kweichow Road
(Guizhou Road), was attacked. The police, who had orders
not to use weapons, were overpowered and the building
burnt down. The Town Hall, a few hundred metres back towards the Bund on Nanking Road was also attacked. At the
Town Hall, the police did use their weapons. They fired into
the crowd and killed two rioters and three bystanders. The riots were finally put down after landing parties from gunboats
in the harbour were called upon to help restore order.

As a result of the riots, it was agreed with the Viceroy that
Chinese prisoners would be kept in the Mixed Court cells, but
that their conditions would be improved. It was also agreed
that Municipal Police could be stationed in the court. However, as a result of the riots the Chinese magistrates were able to
recover some of the power they had been losing to assessors.
Foreign assessors were instructed to comply with the original
agreements whereby the assessor was there to observe, but
not try, cases.

The Chinese authorities also agreed to pay compensation
for British losses caused by the riots. Crown Advocate Harrie
Wilkinson was appointed sole commissioner to determine the
claims. He commenced sitting almost exactly two years after
the riots and he dealt with the claims with dispatch, complet-
ing the work in two days. Showing his independence, he refused a claim from the British Consulate for the costs of coal

The Eastern Sketch's view of the Mixed Court Riots.

for extra guards because it was too indirect. He also refused a
claim from the Race Club for converting stables into kitchens

to feed the police and troops, for the same reason. In total
he awarded compensation of $42,000, the largest being 10,000
taels for the Annex Hotel that had been trashed by the riots.[17]
At the end, he commented on the goodness of the human
spirit and a clear message for those with complaints to keep
them to themselves:

> "Someone has said: 'There is more kindness and less
> honesty in the world than anyone has a right to expect.'
> After two experiences as a Claims Commissioner, I am
> glad to say that there is more honesty than I expected.
> There is a great deal of loose talk and irresponsible
> criticism, however. I have been told that Mr So-and-
> so's motor car was a rattle-trap, that Mr So-and-so's hat
> costs less than $8 and that Mr So-and-so's best watch
> was really a Waterbury. If these things are so it is the
> duty of those who know to admonish the claimants – in
> private."

The rise of Yuan Shikai
The Mixed Court riots had helped the Chinese magistrates to
recover some lost rights in Shanghai. Another more powerful Chinese, Provincial Governor Yuan Shikai, could see that
only a far more organized force stood any chance of making
China strong. In 1905, British consuls were invited to watch
military exercises by Yuan's new army. The reports impressed
the British Minister, Ernest Satow, immensely. He wrote back
to the British Foreign Secretary, Lord Landsdowne, that Yuan
and Tieh-liang, a Manchu general, instead of being carried
around in a sedan chair had been "on horseback in European military costume and wearing swords. Such a thing was
never before seen in China." The troops had been trained by
Japanese "professors" and organized on the Japanese model

---

17 "British Claims for the 1905 Riot", *North China Herald*, January 3, 1908, p25 and January 10, 1908, p100.

Foreign observers watch Yuan Shikai and his new army

and were intended to be nucleus of a modern army. One of the consuls estimated that a foreign force fighting this army would need at least half its strength "with plenty of guns."[18]

Satow thought the days of foreigners being able to intimidate Chinese into ceding portions of territory were over. He commented that:

"if the present numbers are only doubled and if the Yangtze is held by troops disciplined like Yuan's, with an uniform armament, it will be difficult for any European Power to invade either North China or the Yangtze valley. Our only means of coercion then will be attacks on coast ports, and on the occupation of islands."

He added two caveats:

"One difficulty is that of finance, and the second the

18 I. Ruxton (ed), *The Semi-Official Letters of British Envoy Sir Ernest Satow from Japan and China*, p551-552.

jealousy naturally felt of the commander in chief of such a national army, who would be all-powerful."

He was right about finances and jealousy. He was also right about the days of European power being almost over. Only the Japanese were much later able to invade North China and the Yangtze valley.

As Satow's note suggested, change was coming to China, but not quite yet. For Americans in China, however, a new court was about to be established and, while no riots broke out, the court and its judge would go through a baptism of fire.

PART SEVEN

THE UNITED STATES COURT FOR CHINA

CHAPTER 32

Taming the Wild East

SHANGHAI AND THE OTHER treaty ports in China were the Wild East. In a report to President Roosevelt, Elihu Root, Secretary of State, called the behaviour of Americans in China a "disgraceful condition of affairs" that was "discreditable to the United States and humiliating to American self-respect." The problem was, Root explained, that under extraterritoriality there was not one court with power over all the residents of Shanghai.

"As a result of this peculiar arrangement the vice which seems to thrive in the atmosphere of the Orient has long tended to seek shelter under the flag of the country whose administration is the most lax and ineffective. American administration in Shanghai had long been notoriously lax and ineffective, and the gamblers and prostitutes of Shanghai generally flourished under the claim of American citizenship and the protection of American indifference. To such an extent had this gone that prostitutes generally in Shanghai, and, to a considerable extent in the other cities, whether American or not, were called American girls and the two expressions were practically synonymous."[1]

1   Charges against Lebbeus R Wilfley Judge of the United States Court for China and petition for his removal from office, Letter to the President from Mr Root dated February 29, 1908.

The problems were attributed to the weakness of the American consular courts, and indeed, they were not very effective. An American writer in 1904 gave this colourful description of consular court hearing held at the US Consulate on Whangpoo Road (Huangpu road) just north of the Bund:

"The US Consular Court at Shanghai 'happens' in a back room of a brick building in the Whangpoo Road. The furniture is Quakerishly simple. Item, a plain table and with two rows of wooden chairs. In one corner a metal stove. Across one end of the table is a dais, and upon that a narrower table, with three chairs beside. Opposite the stove, a new looking 'stand' for witnesses, with a chair in which they sit upon the 'stand'."

After describing how witnesses were sworn almost inaudibly and how an official had noisily stoked the stove during the course of the hearing, the writer recounted the rough-and-tumble behavior of the lawyers:

"Both advocates are in ordinary Shanghai attire. While one is speaking, the other tilts back his chair upon its hind legs, and winks at the official aforesaid. Official spits in the stove. First advocate puts a leading question. Crash! The tilted chair finds its level, and the other forensic champion is on his feet. 'No! no! I object! I object! My boy, only seventeen knows better'n that. You can't do it.' Then follows a dispute in which 'the Court' is temporarily ignored. During the resumed pleading, advocate Number Two saunters over to the stove and warms his hands. Occasionally he wrangles with the Plaintiff while his learned friend continues to address the Bench. When his turn comes to speak, and an interruption is made, he advances to the Judge, places the palm of his hand on the judicial blotting pad, and truculently demands to know if the Court is going to allow him to be 'cheeked' in this manner within these 'holy precincts.' A witness is peremptorily bidden to 'shut up' and the irate advocate further warns his learned brother that he (the speaker) has 'been too long at this game to learn anything from him.' Beyond a mild suggestion that the Court's time is being wasted, the President of the Court takes no step to vindicate the dignity of the Law."[2]

An increasingly strong and proud United States of America could not let this situation continue. In the 1880s, the State Department had tried to get a bill passed to establish a United States Court for China and Japan, but the proposal died in committee. In 1906 Root revived the idea and found a strong backer in Congress, Edwin Denby, whose father had been American Minister in Peking. Denby had himself lived in Peking from 1894 to 1895. Denby went to a lot of effort to get the bill through Congress, pushing for the bill to be passed by the Senate in the last hour of the last session of June 1906.[3]

The new law established the United States Court for China at Shanghai and provided that it would also sit at Tientsin, Hankow and Canton and elsewhere in China as necessary. Given the rush, a number of defects were left in the bill to be sorted out later. The new law established the United States Court for China with one judge, a clerk and a district attorney. The court was to act as the peak court for American consular courts in China. The law provided that the court would apply United States Law and Common Law in China. There was no provision for jury trials or other constitutional protections; nor was there provision for the appointment of acting judges. If the sole judge was not available for whatever reason, the

---

2   *North China Herald*, February 5, 1904, p264-5.

3   See letter from Denby to Charles Lobingier dated May 3, 1916, reproduced in 1916 U.S. Ct. China Decennial Anniversary Brochure 1 at pp14-17.

court could not sit. Over the years, many defects in the court structure would be fixed by legislation but this was a labourious process. To get legislation through the US Congress requires a sponsor, but no member of Congress represented overseas Americans, meaning that bills would often fall by the wayside.

The bill did provide one substantial improvement over the old system. A proper appellate procedure was provided for, with appeals going from the United States Court for China to the Ninth Circuit Court of Appeals in San Francisco.

The US Court for China was itself given appellate jurisdiction over decisions of the US consular courts in China and Korea. This included the Consular Court in Shanghai. Unlike the case with the British Consular Court in Shanghai, the United States Consular Court in Shanghai was not subsumed into the US Court for China. Instead, the Court for China took over all serious criminal cases, where the penalty exceeded 60 days in jail or a fine of $100 and civil cases where the amount claimed was more than $500. US consular courts in China, including the Shanghai Consular Court, continued to hear smaller cases.

Sherriff Wilfley rides into town

With the court established, President Theodore Roosevelt needed to appoint a judge of the court. After the bill was passed, Denby met with Roosevelt to tell him what he hoped for in the court and "begged him to make certain that the first judge should be a man of calibre and character and vision sufficient to attempt to realize the dream." Denby, it seems, wanted an Edmund Hornby as the new judge. Denby was asked for a recommendation; he had none. Roosevelt said that he had received a recommendation from Mr William Taft, then Secretary of War, who had previously been Governor-General of the Philippines that Lebbeus Wilfley, the Attorney-General of the Philippines, be appointed. Roosevelt, a Republican, made the point that he would be appointing a Democrat, "thinking to accomplish the best results thereby."[4]

Wilfley was a native of St Louis having been born in Mexico, Missouri in 1866 and a graduate of Yale Law School. He had been admitted to the bar 13 years before in 1893. In 1901, just after the United States had colonized the Philippines, he was appointed as a judge of the Philippines Court of First Instance, but very soon after, at the very young age of 35, was promoted to become the Attorney-General of the Philippines. He was 40 when he was appointed as Judge of the US Court for China and was clearly a young man in a hurry.

Wilfley was formally appointed in July 1906 and travelled immediately to Shanghai from Manila. Finding that the statute creating the court had not yet arrived in Shanghai, he went to Washington DC to meet with the State Department. He returned to Shanghai in December. At a dinner held by the American Association just before the court was formally opened, Wilfley told the American Association that the Court had been created for them. He said:

> "This Court was their Court. It had been established at their behest and in their behalf. It would be largely what they made it. The success of this Court was largely in their hands; the standard of this Court would not permanently rise much higher nor sink much lower that the standard of good Americans in Shanghai."[5]

He continued that the court was not a district court of the United States created according to the Constitution, but was rather a court created by a treaty between the United States

---

4 Letter from Edwin Denby to Charles Lobingier dated May 3, 1916, reproduced in 1916 U.S. Ct. China Decennial Anniversary Brochure 1 at pp14-17.

5 "The American Dinner", *North China Herald,* December 21, 1906, p669.

and China. As such, there would be no jury trials or trials with assessors. Wilfley then set out his intended philosophy for presiding over the court, saying that Americans were in China "at the sufferance of the Chinese Empire and this made it more incumbent that they should be more orderly governed, conduct themselves in a most orderly way." For Wilfley, just as it had been for Hornby, this was particularly important. He wanted to set an example to the Chinese and show them what "the reign of law" meant. He added that "it was more incumbent upon Americans here than at home to be always law abiding under all circumstances and conditions."

Wilfley said that court would operate in a very similar way to a court in the United States. Then, perhaps with a nod to the Assistant Judge of the British Supreme Court for China and Corea, Frederick Bourne, who was in attendance, he added, "it came naturally to members of the Anglo-Saxon race that they should have purity of administration, secondly fearlessness, and thirdly common sense." Saying that these characteristics were common to Anglo-Saxon courts everywhere, he continued, to applause from the audience: "Wherever the English flag or the American flag floated they found the symbol not only of power but of justice."

Wilfley then turned to his first major task: improving the local bar. He said, again to applause, that it was his "purpose to raise the standard of professional ethics in the Court of the United States for China so that they would be such as America would be proud." To a further round of applause, he continued that "it was highly important that the lawyers should be well grounded in the law, but of the two he laid more stress on character." In conclusion, he said that his hope was that the US Court would achieve the "high standard of repute" of the British Supreme Court for China and Corea.

The Court officially opens
The United States Court for China held its first hearing at 10.30

am on December 17, 1906 sitting in the
court room of the Consular Court at the
American Consulate.[6] Wilfley declared
the court officially open and then requested the new District Attorney,
Clerk of Court and Marshal to all present their commissions. The Hon Arthur
Bassett, Dr Frank E. Hinckley and Mr
O.R. Leonard all did so. Hinckley took
charge of the commissions. Bassett who
was only 28 had been Assistant Attorney-General in the Philippines under
Wilfley while Dr Hinckley had just
published a book on extraterritoriality
in China. He had been appointed Clerk
of the Court on the strength of this.

Lebbeus Wilfley

Wilfley then asked if Hinckley had
the Seal of the Court. Hinckley replied
in the affirmative and produced the
seal. Hinckley, in his new capacity as

Arthur Bassett

Clerk of the Court, announced that the first term of the court
would commence in the New Year on January 2, 1907 at 10
o'clock in the morning. The court would sit in the American
Consulate and the procedures to be adopted would be the
same as that used in the American consular courts in China to
date unless changed or modified by order of the court.

Wilfley, having thrown down the gauntlet at the American
Association dinner a few nights before, then turned to the expected qualification of lawyers to appear before the court. He
announced that American attorneys who wished to be admitted to the bar of the United States Court for China would be
required to produce a certificate of good moral character as
well as taking an examination in eight legal topics, namely,

6   "The United States Court for China", *North China Herald*, December 21, 1906, p676.

The New Broom - Wilfley forces US lawyers to take an examination
Thomas Jernignan and Striling Fessenden, the only two to pass,
are standing at the back of the courtroom.

Equity, Evidence, Contract, Torts, Conflicts of Laws, Criminal Law, the law creating the US Court for China and Wills and Probate. Certificates of moral character were to be filed within five days, before December 22, 1906, and the first examination would be on December 24, 1906.

Wilfley was effectively locking out American lawyers from appearing before the court unless they passed an exam on seven days notice. What must have been most galling to the American attorneys was that Wilfley ordered that foreign practitioners would be allowed to practice before the United States Court as a matter of courtesy.

First day at work
On January 2, 1907, the first formal session of the United States Court for China was called to order.[7] On his very first day sit-

7   *North China Herald*, January 4, 1907, p27.

ting as a judge, Wilfley notched up the first strike that would lead to his downfall as a judge. He also had, as the very first case before him, a case that would lead very soon to the second strike.

The first strike came with the announcement that of eight practitioners who had taken the examination, only two had passed. These were Mr Thomas Jernigan, a former US Consul-General, and Mr Stirling Fessenden. Fessenden, as we shall see, went on to become a pillar of the Shanghai community when he became the Chairman of the Shanghai Municipal Council. Wilfley described the testimonials he had received for Jernigan and Fessenden as having come from leading citizens of both Shanghai and their

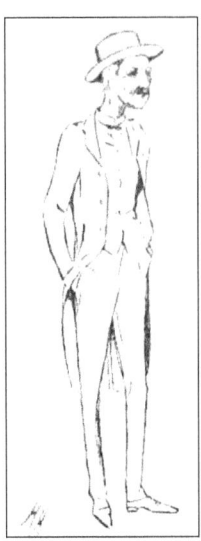

Thomas Jernigan - one of only two lawyers to pass Wilfley's examination

home jurisdictions and of being of the highest order. Wilfley also admitted Mr Noel Home, a British barrister, and Mr Musso of the Italian court. Bassett, as the District Attorney, was also allowed to practice without taking the exam. Those who had failed included, Lorrin Andrews, who had formerly being the Attorney-General of Hawaii. In the end, after other rounds of exams sixteen American lawyers in Shanghai took the exam and six failed.

Wilfley announced that he had received communications from a number of members of the bar who had failed the exam asking for permission to finish cases that they had in hand. He acknowledged that these requests "were not without merit." However, given that the number of outstanding cases was not significant, he said it was better to observe the new rule from the outset and denied the requests. He finished by saying that "no lawyer would be permitted to practice in this court except those who have complied with the rule with reference to admission to practice."

Wilfley's rush to disbar those lawyers he considered unsuitable was overzealous and unnecessary. He created enemies who would, as we shall see, strike back.

Criminal and civil cases within the jurisdiction of the US Court were then called for directions. The very first case was to become, a few days later, Wilfley's second strike. Wilfley, himself, admitted later that he made a "grave error in judgment." This was the case of the *United States v R.J. McCord*. McCord was charged with obtaining $301.50 by false pretences. Stirling Fessenden appeared on behalf of McCord and the case was adjourned until the following Tuesday.

Wilfley then gave directions in a number of other criminal cases involving an assault that had occurred on an American boat; assault with a deadly weapon; and, theft. One defendant had to find a new lawyer because his lawyer, Lorrin Andrews, had not passed the examination.

Civil cases were then called. As with the British Crown Advocate, the District Attorney was allowed to handle civil cases that did not conflict with his duties as District Attorney. Mr Bassett appeared in some of the cases. In a number of cases, the defendants said they needed to find new lawyers because their lawyers had failed Wilfley's examination.

McCord sows discord
The McCord case was a very simple case that was to take on extraordinary importance in the short career of Judge Wilfley.[8] McCord, who had previously lived in the Philippines, worked on commission for an American company, Mustard & Co. His job was to sell goods to ships, mainly navy ships, of foreign countries. He was not meant to collect money from the ships. Instead, the money was to be paid to Mustard & Co who

8   *United States v RJ MCord, North China Herald*, January 11, 1907, pp77-78; references to Wilfley's views of the McCord case are from his testimony in *R v O'Shea*. See the next chapter.

would then pay commission to McCord. On a number of occasions, McCord did collect money directly from the ships and did not pass the money on to Mustard & Co. In October 1906, McCord sold some goods to the compradore of a ship, the *Alhambra Gardens*. The compradore paid McCord $301.50 directly. Mustard & Co sought payment from the *Alhambra Gardens*. The ship said they had already paid McCord. District Attorney Bassett prosecuted and Fessenden defended McCord.

First, Wilfley had to deal with the question of what the "common law of the United States" was. McCord had been charged with the common law offence of obtaining money by false pretences. At the outset of the trial, Fessenden on behalf of McCord applied for the indictment to be quashed on the basis that it charged an offence that was not indictable under common law.

Fessenden argued that the common law, as received in the United States, could only be judge-made law. Under judge-made law, the offence of obtaining money by false pretences required that the person obtaining the money use some false symbol or token to obtain the money. This had been the common law in England until 1758. However, by an English statute of 1758 (32 George II), the common law had been amended to remove the requirement for a token to be used. Fessenden argued that the statute had not been received as part of the common law of the United States. Bassett, on the other hand, argued that all English statutes that amended the common law prior to independence of the United States were received in the United States as common law, even if that statute had subsequently been repealed in England.

Wilfley said he needed some time to consider the matter and adjourned to the afternoon. In the afternoon, Wilfley ruled that the common law as amended by the English statute was the common law of the United States and that the trial should proceed. There followed a short trial where witnesses from the *Alhambra Gardens* and Mustard & Co were called. McCord admitted that he owed money to a third party and had taken the money due to Mustard & Co to pay that third party in order "to avoid any trouble."

Wilfley found the offence was proved beyond any reasonable doubt and convicted McCord. He said he would sentence McCord the next day at 9.00am. He then, in a decision he later described as "a mistake," continued McCord's bail allowing him to be free until sentencing. Not surprisingly, McCord did not appear the next morning. He had taken a ship out of Shanghai the night before. Wilfley ordered that his bail be forfeited.

What is not mentioned in the record of the court is that the last person in court that day to see McCord was Judge Wilfley. After the hearing, McCord had come to the Astor House Hotel the night before to see Wilfley. Wilfley met him in the lobby and told McCord: "If you are here in the morning I will give you a heavy sentence."[9]

Heavy sentences

While Wilfley was not able to impose a heavy sentence on McCord, he did impose them on others. He also stopped the practice of granting bail even to those who were appealing against a conviction.

The first case where a defendant was to suffer the wrath of Judge Wilfley was *United States v Biddle*.[10] Biddle, who was the manager of the Metropole Hotel, had rented out a house in Mohawk Road (now Huangpi North Road) next to the racecourse for 3,000 taels to some Chinese on the basis that the municipal government would allow gambling at the house

---

9   Wilfley's evidence in *R v O'Shea*. See the next chapter.

10 *United States v Biddle*, Lobingier, *Extraterritorial Cases*, Vol 1, p84 (first instance), *Biddle v United States* (Appeal) Lobingier, *Extraterritorial Cases*, Vol 1, p120. For more on Biddle as a man or "gangster" as Jarvis calls him, see: Robert M. Jarvis, "Charles A. Biddle, Gambling, and the U.S. Court for China", 17 Gaming Law Review and Economics 728 (2013).

during the autumn races. Gambling was illegal in Shanghai and there was no chance that such approval would be given. The Chinese in a civil case had sued Biddle. At the conclusion of the civil case, Wilfley said Biddle should be charged with a criminal offence. District Attorney Bassett then charged Biddle with the criminal offence of obtaining money by false pretences under the common law.

At his trial, like McCord, Biddle argued that there was no common law offence of obtaining money by false pretences. It was not a federal crime and should be dealt with by state law. Wilfley disagreed and found Biddle guilty, but gave him the opportunity to refund the money. Biddle appealed the decision to the Ninth Circuit in San Francisco which nine months later allowed the appeal on a technical ground that at common law, the crime of obtaining money by false pretences was not made out where the promise made related to some future fact. The statement that the council would allow gambling in the future was not sufficient to make out the offence of obtaining money by false pretences.

Most importantly, the decision of the Court of Appeal was groundbreaking because it redefined the entire basis of United States extraterritorial jurisdiction in China in two significant ways. First, the court found that there was a "common law of the United States." This common law was, as Wilfley had found, the common law in force when the United States "separated from the mother country," England. Second, and far more importantly, the court ruled that the "laws of the United States" included the laws of the District of Columbia and Alaska, both federal territories at the time. The United States Court for China, could therefore, as necessary, apply the statutes that Congress had passed for Alaska and the District of Columbia. This principle became the bedrock for the future jurisprudence of the US Court.

The next case to bring problems for Wilfley was the prosecution of S.R. Price for assault with a dangerous weapon.[11] Price had been tried, and acquitted, in the Shanghai Consular Court before the Consul-General on related charges. He had then been brought before Wilfley and pleaded "double jeopardy"; that is, that he had already been acquitted and could not be tried again for the same offence. Wilfley rejected this on the basis that the Consul-General did not have jurisdiction to try a charge of assault with a dangerous weapon. Price also argued that because the gun was unloaded the offence of assault with a dangerous weapon was not made out. Wilfley rejected this too and convicted Price, sentencing him to six months imprisonment. Price appealed to the Ninth Circuit in San Francisco. His lawyer, Lorrin Andrews who had by now passed Wilfley's examination, applied for bail pending appeal. Wilfley refused bail, partly because of his experience of McCord jumping bail. Later, the Ninth Circuit found that Wilfley was right in rejecting Price's double jeopardy plea but wrong in holding that pointing an unloaded gun at a person was assault with a deadly weapon. They remitted the case back to Shanghai for a new trial.

Wilfley's strict enforcement of the law and in one case, at least, convicting US citizens where the British Court acquitted British citizens on the same facts was welcomed by some and not by others. Secretary of State Root, in a letter to President Roosevelt, said that "the lawyers whose most liberal clients have been the gamblers and prostitutes of Shanghai never complained of the old order of things, but they are now full of bitterness against the Judge, who has driven their clients out of business, but the decent and virtuous Americans in Shanghai were indignant and humiliated over the former conditions, and are now grateful and approving."[12]

Secretary for War William Taft, who had recommended

---

11 *United States v Price*, 9th Circuit Decision, Lobingier, *Extraterritorial Cases*, Vol 1 p129.

12 Root letter to Roosevelt, in Charges Against Lebbeus E Wilfley, Judge of the United States Court for China and Petition for his Removal from Office p6.

Wilfley for the position, in a public speech during a visit to Shanghai added support for Wilfley saying the US government had been "fortunate in the selection as the first judge of that court" of Wilfley who had intimate knowledge of Asia. Taft fully supported Wilfley's policy of "raising high the standard of admission to the bar and in promoting vigorous prosecutions of American violators of law" as to cause the "elimination from this community of undesirable characters who have brought disgrace upon the name of Americans in the cities of China."[13]

He then praised Wilfley further, saying:

"it involves no small amount of courage and a great deal of common sense to deal with evils of this character and to rid the community of them. Interests which

Wilfley presiding in the US Court for China

13 Quoted in Root's letter to Roosevelt, p9.

have fattened on abuses cannot be readily disturbed without making a fight for their lives, and one who undertakes the work of cleansing and purifying must expect to meet resistance in libel and slander and the stirring up of official opposition based on misinformation and evil report."

A Tibetan tragedy

Wilfley did not convict everyone who came before his court. In late 1907, he tried a very difficult case where Henry De Menil, a medical doctor from a wealthy family in St Louis, Missouri (Wilfley's home town),[14] while travelling in Tibet had shot and killed a Tibetan Lama. The lama, Pu Keng-lung, had been walking on a hill nearby. De Menil whose behavior had become erratic due to altitude sickness had become angry with one of his guards, Li Yu-shan, and had fired two shots in his direction to warn him. One of the bullets had hit the Lama. De Menil was brought back from Tibet to Shanghai for the trial. One of the Chinese guards who had been travelling with him was also brought to Shanghai to give evidence.

This was the first time a case involving a killing of a Chinese by an American to come before the US Court for China. The Shanghai Taotai asked Magistrate Li to watch the case. Magistrate Li was given a place on the bench next to Wilfley. District Attorney Bassett prosecuted the case and William Fleming defended.[15]

Magistrate Li must have found the whole proceeding bizarre. Fleming objected to almost every witness and piece of evidence. On a number of occasions Wilfley had to admonish Fleming for going too far and in one case said he had transcended "the bounds of professional ethics"[16] for accusing

14 The Chatillon-DeMenil mansion may be visited in St Louis.

15 *United States v De Menil*, The trial was reported in the *North China Herald* November 22, 1907, p472 and November 29, 1907, p538; Wilfley's judgment was not reported, but the key part is reproduced in Foreign Relations of the United States, 1909, p55 onwards.

16 As we shall see, this was not the last time Mr Fleming was accused of transcending

Bassett of improper conduct and violating his oath of office. On another occasion, an "animated discussion" between Wilfley, Bassett and two witnesses could be heard from the backroom of the court during the lunch break.

The witnesses were not much better. De Menil had given an interview to the *Shanghai Mercury* on his arrival in Shanghai. Bassett wanted to rely on what De Menil had told them. One witness, Mr R.D. Neish, the deputy editor, was British. Bassett first had to get a subpoena from the British Supreme Court to compel Neish to give evidence. Neish refused to produce documents. He said he had only received a subpoena from the British Court to give evidence. Bassett went back to the British Supreme Court to get an order that Neish produce the notes that he had been given by De Menil.

Once this order was obtained, the editor of the *Shanghai Mercury*, John Clark, came to court to say that despite a search having been conducted, the notes were missing. Neish then told the court that he could not remember what had been written. He then gave such evasive answers that Bassett took the extraordinary step of asking that the evidence of his own witness be struck out. Wilfley decided to take matters into his own hands and cross-examined Neish himself. At the end, Wilfley said that Neish had changed his answer on a key question. Bassett said he would not rely on Neish's testimony. He said: "I don't care to offer this testimony to the Court. I would not ask for

John Clark, editor of the Shanghai Mercury

the bounds of professional ethics. See, in particular, Chapter 42.

a man to be convicted on the evidence of such a witness."

Neish was most likely being evasive because he did not want to see De Menil convicted on what he had told him. De Menil had effectively admitted to manslaughter in his diary where he had written:

"May 30 – I am light headed, that is I must be out of my head or what is called almost crazy, and what some people call mad. I am looking about trying to find a cause for the deed that happened this morning, for I have killed a Tibetan warrior, partly carelessness, partly accidental.

".... weak after a restless bad night's sleep, with worse breakfast, irritated and angry at one of my good-for-nothing Chinese soldiers from the day before, I thought to intimidate all of them, so fired my rifle twice into air, once to right and once to left. It was left shot which struck Tibetan young man right in the left eye, passing into brain, and I saw him just as I pulled trigger coming, and I tried to put muzzle up higher but too late. Alas, I saw him disappear, but did not know if I had hit him or not, but rushed forward to see, hoping against hope. Now although my bullet had to pass over two houses, and at least two feet above second house from me and he was over fifty feet away and two trees intervened, yet a sad sight met me, which I could hardly believe, -- lying full lengthwise on his back in all his gay coloured clothes, with sword in belt and boots on, and fine turban fallen off head, with red life's blood streaming form gape where his left eye ought to have been, I felt his pulse – there was still a small feeble beat – his nostrils still breathed a little. I rushed away hardly believing it could all be true. I pressed his palm between mine and spoke to him, 'For God's sake, man, speak, speak and forgive me,' but all in vain. And my next thought was, could medical skill save him? I rushed back and on my knees beside him — no — pulse still, nostrils stopped breathing for ever, coldness coming over hand and body, stream of blood on hard stone increased and clotted, with sweet smile on his face. Now he had passed into Buddhist's heaven."

This was damning evidence. Fleming tried to exclude the diary on the basis that it had been taken off De Menil by the American Consul in Chungking after an improper search. After an argument about whether US constitutional or English common law protections against illegal search applied in China, Wilfley ruled that the diary was admissible.

With the diary in evidence, De Menil had no choice but to testify in his own defence. He said he had been arrested in Artunza in Tibet. The Chinese authorities there had found the killing to be accidental. He denied seeing the bullet in the Tibetan's eye and any suggestion the shooting was not accidental. To explain away the diary, he suggested it was an embellished account he had written after the fact with the intention of getting it published. He said he had incorporated a number of suggestions from Chinese onlookers into the diary.

Wilfley was not impressed. He said that De Menil's testimony was "peculiar to say the least." De Menil was asking him to believe all the statements that showed he did not intend to kill. But on the other hand he had made statements that were "highly improbable and lacking in frankness."

Nevertheless, after reserving judgment for three weeks, Wilfley acquitted De Menil. He accepted that De Menil was in a bad physical condition at the time. He also accepted that De Menil had not intended to kill anyone when shooting; the question was: was what he did so careless to be criminal in the eyes of the law? Wilfley found that, given the area was sparsely populated, it was not so careless. He, therefore, acquitted De Menil.

Wilfley then said that De Menil had already suffered much inconvenience and pain in the case, including being detained by the Chinese authorities, and he "did not feel the ends of justice would be subserved by imposing further punishment on the accused." This was a strange point to make. The question of the deprivations De Menil had suffered before his trial should not have affected his guilt or innocence. It may have been relevant as to what punishment to impose if he found him guilty but not as to whether he was guilty or not. One can only suspect that De Menil's station in society and the fact he was was from the same home town swayed Willfley's judgement.

It was an unsatisfactory conclusion to an unsatisfactory case.

The Chinese authorities certainly thought so. A full report on the case was prepared by Magistrate Li, which was passed on by the Taotai to the Superintendent of Trade.[17] In August 1908, the Chinese Ministry of Foreign Affairs sent a formal protest in the name of Prince Ch'ing over the acquittal to the American Minister, W.W. Rockhill. The protest complained that in shooting at his guard, De Menil clearly "had murder in his heart" and as such should be liable for the killing of Pu and that "the great wrong done the murdered man is not in the least atoned for ... In this case justice does not shine, and the good name of America suffers."

Then, in a direct challenge to the independence of the US Court for China, Prince Ch'ing wrote to Rockhill that he "must refer this case to your excellency that your excellency may think of a way to straighten this affair out, determining the crime of which the aforesaid criminal is guilty, or the fine which he ought to pay, so that angry passions may be calmed and justice displayed."

The note's request that the American Minister overturn the verdict was not made due to a lack of understanding of

---

17 Correspondence regarding the De Menil case is in Foreign Relations of the United States, 1909, pp55 et seq.

the American concept of judicial independence. On the contrary, it is clear that the Chinese had studied in detail the law establishing the United States Court. The Chinese protest noted that the act that had created the court had granted the court the powers "now exercised by consuls and ministers" and that the judge was appointed at "the pleasure of the President."

"From this it appears that the status of the court is different from that of an independent judiciary. Although the term 'judge' is employed it is evident that he is only an official of the executive department appointed for the conduct of foreign relations."

Because of this, the Chinese note concluded:

"The American minister at Peking will be regarded as having ultimate appellate jurisdiction in all matters concerning the exercise of judicial power over foreigners within Chinese territory."

This was a very sophisticated analysis and in many ways correct. The act did not create an independent judiciary. The independence only came from the common law and the practice of the judges and lawyers.[18]

The State Department could not let this direct challenge to the independence of the court pass. Secretary of State Root in early 1909 replied to Rockhill that the note from Prince Ch'ing "uses certain language in expressing its understanding of the functions and status of the court which is so incorrect that the department deems it advisable not to allow these observations to pass." Rockhill was instructed to explain the indepen-

---

18 Ironically, it is also an analysis that can be applied to the current legal system in China. The term "judge" is employed but the people who hold that position are officials of the executive department, are employed at the pleasure of the executive and have no real independence.

William Rockhill, US Minister to China. The Chinese insisted he had executive authority over the new US Court.

dence of the court and that the act establishing it had created appeals to the Ninth Circuit in San Francisco. The treaties with China and the act establishing the court required trial "according the laws of the United States" and that both statutory and common law rules should apply.

Rockhill was also instructed to inform the Chinese that De Menil could not be retried under American rules and that the lama's family could bring a claim for compensation in the court if they wished.

The Chinese complaints about the handling of the De Menil case went no further. However, Wilfley was at the same time facing serious complaints by American lawyers about his handling of other cases.

CHAPTER 33

The Wild East Fights Back

WILFLEY IN HIS SHORT time on the bench had made a lot of enemies. Lorrin Andrews, in particular, was not going to take Wilfley's refusal to admit him and treatment of his client, Mr Price, lying down. In the Price case Andrews filed a writ of *habeas corpus* in San Francisco. He was quoted in the press as calling Wilfley a "czar," suggesting he was like a king controlled by no one. He then went on to Washington DC where, on November 17, 1907 he filed a petition to President Theodore Roosevelt seeking to have Wilfley removed from office.[1]

Andrews' charges against Wilfley were a bucket list of complaints. He alleged that Wilfley had prevented six lawyers in Shanghai from practicing before the court by requiring them to take an examination; that he allowed Bassett, as Attorney-General, to practice without taking an examination; that Wilfley had libeled those who had failed the exam; that Wilfley had commenced proceedings to disbar Andrews; that Wilfley abused his power in certain cases by ordering an American to appear before the British court and refusing to grant adjournments in two cases; and, finally, that he refused to grant Price bail.

Secretary of State Root sent a formal opinion to the President on February 29, 1908, rejecting all the charges as ill-founded and explaining the difficult situation that Wilfley had found in Shanghai. Root concluded:

---

1 See Charges Against Lebbeus E Wilfley, Judge of the United States Court for China and Petition for his Removal from Office.

"My opinion is that Judge Wilfley is entitled, not to condemnation but to commendation and high credit for his conduct in office, and that the charges against him should be dismissed."

Roosevelt replied on March 2, 1908 agreeing with Root's recommendations, adding:

"I cordially concur in your finding, which is to the effect that Judge Wilfley is not only innocent but is attacked solely because of the fearlessness and integrity with which he has stamped out vice and crime in Shanghai."

Roosevelt attached to his letter a letter from Robert E. Lewis, the secretary of the International Committee of the YMCA praising Wilfley. Roosevelt added after reading this letter that "it is clear that Judge Wilfley has been attacked not because he has done evil, but because he has done good," and that "if the attack were to succeed, the beneficiaries would be every keeper of a house of prostitution, every swindling lawyer, every man who lives by blackmail and corruption, in the cities of the Far East." Roosevelt concluded that: "It is not too much to say that this assault on Judge Wilfley, in the interest of the vicious and criminal classes, is a public scandal."

Perhaps suspecting that he would not get very far with his petition to the President, Andrews through Congressman Waldo filed a further petition seeking that Wilfley be impeached directly to the Senate Judiciary Committee. This petition, in addition to the charges put to President Roosevelt, included an allegation that Wilfley was anti-Catholic. The petition was signed by Andrews and eight other Shanghai residents including W.W. Dowdell, the President of the Catholic Sodality of Shanghai and, the "Shanghai Liar", Henry O'Shea, the proprietor of the *China Gazette*.

Wilfley's anti-Catholicism was alleged to have been shown by a decision he had made in a probate case involving a Captain J.P. Roberts. The petition alleged that "in violation of the duties and oath of his high office, he has condemned the Catholic clergy as the Popish clergy, guilty of robbing the poor, the widows and the orphans under the name of the Church, which slanderous statements, if made in print, other than in a decision of one of the court of the United States would be a criminal libel."[2] He was also alleged to have applauded at a conference when a Protestant priest made an attack on the Catholic Church and to have also have made public statements questioning Catholicism.

Wilfley was required to give evidence before a small sub-committee of three. He arrived in Washington in mid-January 1908. Andrews was there as well as some members of the press. In the course of the hearing, Wilfley was asked about the *China Gazette* which Henry O'Shea, one of the petitioners, published. He responded that it "did not enter the best homes in Shanghai."

The committee found that there was no case for impeachment but after doing so delivered what Wilfley later described as "hypothetical rebuke." The committee said:

"It is obviously true that an aggregation of entirely legal acts may develop into a system of tyranny and oppression; and that an inequitable exercise of judicial discretion may convert the machinery of justice into an engine of despotic and autocratic power. This may be accomplished without the taint of individual corruption and with a laudable purpose of purifying a community and of inaugurating civic reform.

....

2   *New York Times*, November 10, 1907, p8.

"Terror to evil-doers, if purchased at the price of judicial fairness and overstrained legal authority, is achieved at too great an expense, for it defeats its own high aim and warps the very fabric of the law itself.

"The temptation of an honest judge to 'Bend once the law to his authority: To do a great right—do a little wrong,' is fraught with such danger to our whole system of remedial justice that it merits the condemnation of every legal mind."

The sub-committee continued that "such acts of legal oppression and of abuse of judicial discretion" lay at the base of the charges against Wilfley, but said they were dismissed because they fell short of an impeachable offence.

Then, in a strange passage, the sub-committee first noted that because of the dismissal of the petition Wilfley did not have an opportunity to defend himself:

"he can file no answer; make no denial; nor explain to the House the legality or necessity for his action."

All fair enough and a worthwhile point to make. The sub-committee report then undid the fairness of this comment, by adding that:

"if Judge Wilfley's judicial acts in the future are marked by the rigorous and inflexible harshness imputed to him they will hang as a portentous cloud over this new Court, impairing his usefulness, impeding the administration of justice, and challenging the integrity of American Institutions."

The report was sent to the full committee, made up of 24 members, who in the normal course would have adopted the recommendation of the sub-committee. However, given the clear rebuke in the report, the committee asked for all the evidence to be published. Ultimately, the Committee issued a final report stating:

> "Adopted unanimously that no impeachment proceedings be instituted at all."

The Shanghai Liar attacks

Henry O'Shea was outraged by Wilfley's evidence before the sub-committee and published a number of articles attacking Wilfley, each article becoming more and more virulent. O'Shea admitted later that he published the reports

Wilfley returns from Washington, vindicated

because "I wished to expose Judge Wilfley. I did not consider that he was a proper man to be head of the American Court. In the public interest I thought Shanghai deserved a better judge and one who made fewer blunders."[3]

O'Shea's attacks culminated in an article in the *China Gazette* on August 4, 1908 that was scathing in its comments on Wilfley. The attack read:

> "An exhibition of greater indecency, of more venomous mendacity, of meaner innuendo, a greater contempt for the truth and justice, and a wilder desire to simply revenge himself by besmirching the name of everyone who dared to criticize his methods, has surely never been presented in any country by a Judge than has been given in this case by this coarse, unscrupulous,

3 O'Shea's evidence in *R v O'Shea*, *North China Herald*, November 14, 1908, p394.

ignorant and vulgar mountebank, whom the grim irony of corrupt American politics has entrusted with the discharge of judicial functions -- functions that he is intellectually, mentally and morally unfitted for and incapable of exercising. The miserable tactics of Mr. Wilfley while before the Committee remind us only of the tactics of the squid, the creature which when pursued hopes to escape by darkening and poisoning the waters all round it by the discharge of the noxious fluid concealed in its glands. When Mr. Wilfley made the above statements he not only was lying, but we say it deliberately, he knew at the time he was lying, his only object being to mislead the members of the House Committee as to the standing and record of his critics in Shanghai. It was surely a poor role for a Judge to plead in order to excuse his own protection of notorious swindlers, that the British Court and British Law in China are parties to like swindles under the Hongkong Ordinances as Mr Wilfley falsely and audaciously pleaded."

The British authorities could not let such a venomous attack on the Judge of the court of a friendly power go unnoticed or unpunished. O'Shea was prosecuted for criminal defamation. The trial commenced in November 1908 before Frederick Bourne sitting with a jury of five.[4] Crown Advocate, Harrie Wilkinson, prosecuted the case and F. Ellis, J. Hays and C.W. Godfrey appeared to defend O'Shea.

Wilfley reading the China Gazete and asks "What is a Squid?"

O'Shea, from his own experience in the Shanghai Liar case,

4   R v O'Shea, North China Herald, 14 November 1908, p387 et seq; The jury was made up of E.R. Morriss, F.E. Glanville, K.D. Stewart, H. Veicht and H.E. Campbell.

knew how hard it was to prove that defamatory words were true. However, he also knew how damaging a defamation case could be for a plaintiff's reputation even if he won. After all, after the case against him, who could think of O'Shea as anybody but "the Shanghai Liar"?

O'Shea therefore pleaded "Not Guilty" to the charges and sought to justify the words that had been written. He sought to prove that Wilfley was a liar, was "intellectually mentally and morally" unfit to be a judge and that he protected notorious swindlers. For good measure O'Shea in his pleadings added that the holder of a judicial office such as that of Judge of the United States Court for China should "is one which should in the interests of the whole community, both Chinese and foreign, of Shanghai, be filled by a person of integrity, of unbiased mind, of scrupulous fairness, truthfulness and honesty, and of unquestioned legal ability."

This, as can be imagined, made for a sensational trial that lasted four days.

Because O'Shea had admitted the defamation and sought to justify it, the normal order of a criminal trial was reversed. O'Shea was required to call his witnesses first to justify the statements with the prosecution witnesses to be called afterwards.

O'Shea's counsel, Ellis, objected to Wilfley being present when the witnesses were giving evidence. Wilkinson, however, argued that even though the prosecution was being conducted by the Crown Advocate, effectively Wilfley was the complainant in the case and thus should be entitled to be present. Bourne allowed Wilfley to be present, subject to the defence being able to object to his presence for specific evidence.

Mr Ellis opened O'Shea's case. He framed it is a question of the liberty of the press and the responsibilities and duties that members of the press have in society. O'Shea, he said, was attempting to fulfill these responsibilities and duties in publishing the article.

Ellis then told the jury how O'Shea proposed to justify his statements about Wilfley. The charge of indecency related to a lack of judicial decorum which would be proved by the way he treated members of the American bar when refusing them admission as well as his anti-Catholic comments in the Roberts' case. The charge of mendacity related to statements Wilfley had made to the House sub-committee being untrue. These were that a man called Crozier had been to prison; that a man called Trissel was a fugitive from justice; and, that Wilfley did not know a man called Black. That Wilfley had made mean innuendos would be proved by his handling of the Biddle and Price cases as well as his treatment of Lorrin Andrews. Evidence would be introduced to show that Wilfley was ignorant of the law as shown by the Biddle and Price cases and that he was a mountebank (or conman) because he needed help with his judicial duties. That he was a "squid" would be brought out by his remarks about Mr Black and the *China Gazette*. Evidence that Wilfley protected swindlers would be proved by his dealings with Black and McCord as well as comments he had made about the British Supreme Court and Hong Kong companies.

O'Shea called seven witnesses on his behalf, including himself, Dr Hinckley, the clerk of the United States Court, Mr Trissel, Mr Davis, the manager of the Astor House Hotel and Mr Holcomb and Mr Brooks, two of the lawyers who had been refused admission by Wilfley.

O'Shea gave evidence about his background and how he had been surprised by the results of both the McCord and Biddle cases and that the appeal court had overruled Wilfley in the Biddle case. He gave other evidence regarding Crozier, Trissel and Black and a "pyramid scheme" known as the Shanghai Watch Club, of which Black had been a part.

He was particularly upset that Wilfley had stated that the *China Gazette* did not enter the best homes, saying:

"The statement that the *China Gazette* did not go into the best homes was equally false. I inferred from that statement that Judge Wilfley intended the Committee to understand that the *China Gazette* was a paper of an inferior character, which was not read by respectable people, and was generally taboo amongst people whose good opinion he wished to have; that it was not the kind of paper people would put into the hands of their family to read."

Mr Hays asked O'Shea if he was an intimate friend with anyone in Shanghai. O'Shea was able to pull an ace from up his sleeve. He had been a good friend of one of the leading members of the British community in Shanghai for many years. He answered: "Mr. Wilkinson's father was one of my oldest friends, and best friends, and I hope he is still." He then added, referring to the Crown Advocate, "I even consider Mr. Wilkinson as one of my friends." Wilkinson immediately confirmed this to the court with a "That is so."

And indeed, it was true. In the small extraterritorial world of China, Harrie Wilkinson was being called upon to prosecute a good friend and business partner. A few years prior to this, the Wilkinsons had formed a venture with O'Shea, the Desmond Telegraph Agency, to transmit cheap telegraphs to Europe by sending them to the Chinese border with Russia and then re-sending them from Russia, taking advantage of much lower rates for domestic telegraphs in both countries. Harrie Wilkinson and O'Shea had travelled together for months up the Amur River from Vladivostok to Aigunula, where Cossack horsemen could still be seen, to set the venture up.[5]

Despite this friendship, Wilkinson was willing to cross-

5   HP Wilkinson Reminiscences, *North China Herald*, October 31, 1935, p200.

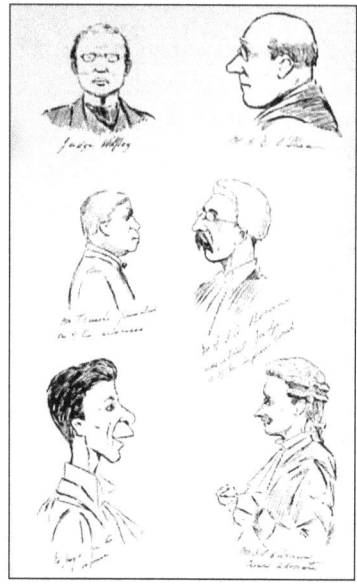

Sketches from the O'Shea trial

examine O'Shea aggressively. He put it to O'Shea that he had been willing to change sides whenever it suited him: that back in Dublin he had switched from the Nationalist to Unionist sides as a journalist; and, then during the Russia-Japan war he had switched from supporting the Japanese to supporting the Russians. O'Shea said that as a working journalist he was like a barrister. He had to do what it took to make money. One newspaper in Dublin was paying better so he switched. With regard to the war he said he was "tired of supporting the Japanese," because it was clear they were feeding his reporters propaganda. He added later that it was also partly "because I did not desire to support Asiatics against a European Race."

As to the British court protecting notorious swindlers, O'Shea pointed to a passage in Wilfley's evidence before the sub-committee where he suggested it was hard to prosecute Americans involved in companies set up under the Hong Kong ordinances.

The next witness was Sam Trissel, a newspaper correspondent. Wilfley had alleged in his testimony that Trissel was a fugitive from justice because he was wanted in the Philippines. Trissel gave evidence that he had left the Philippines voluntarily, had been back a number of times and had, in Shanghai, seen Wilfley socially on a number of occasions. The matter for which he might have been wanted in the Philippines had related to an article in the *Manila American* for which its publisher Mr Crozier had been tried, convicted and sentenced to jail. Crozier had, however, been pardoned, so it as untrue to say Crozier had gone to prison. Trissel said that he had, in fact, written the article.

With regard to the McCord case, Trissel said that Wilfley had lived in a boarding house with McCord for some time in the Philippines. Frederick Davis, the manager of the Astor House Hotel was then called and said he saw McCord come to the hotel the night he had been convicted and send his card up to Wilfley's room. Wilfley had then come down and talked to McCord briefly.

Two American attorneys who had both failed Wilfley's examination, Messrs Brooks and Holcomb, were then called. Both gave evidence that they had been given short notice of the exam; believed they had passed, but had not been given the results; and, suspected that the real reason for not passing was questions regarding their character. Brooks said that he had been indicted in Hawaii in a matter where his Japanese interpreter had implicated him in an immigration fraud, but the charges had been dropped. Holcomb also said that he had seen Wilfley with McCord the night before he disappeared and at another time Wilfley said McCord's disappearance was "good riddance to bad rubbish."

J.D. Ellis of the *Shanghai Mercury* was then called and he gave evidence that the judgment in the Roberts case had subsequently been amended to add quotation marks. A Reverend Ellis was then called and said that he considered the judgment in the Roberts case to be anti-Catholic.

This marked the end of the defence case. Wilkinson said that he proposed to call, Mr Bassett, the US District Attorney and then Wilfley. He asked that Wilfley leave the court while Bassett gave evidence. Bassett said that he was in charge of instituting prosecutions in the US Court and that when he came to Shanghai he found the problem of prostitution by Americans was very serious. He said that the McCord case was the first criminal case to come before the United States Court for China. The sureties had forfeited the bail they had put up. With regard to Trissel, Bassett said Wilfley had met Trissel a number of times when they arrived in Shanghai. Trissel had asked for a reference for a job, which Wilfley had refused. This had embittered Trissel. With regard to the Shanghai Watch Club, he said that Black was not a special friend of his. He had received advice from the Philippines (then an American colony) that a similar club was illegal as a lottery in the Philippines under a local statute, but after considering the matter, he considered it was not illegal in Shanghai because under the common law, running a lottery was not illegal.

As to Hong Kong companies, he said that he and the United States Court faced a particular problem because the companies were British. The United States Court did not have jurisdiction over the companies but only over the directors or managers if they were American. He had been to Hong Kong to see what could be done about the problem. He said he understood at the least to insurance companies would be required to put up deposits before doing business. He agreed that it would be possible to prosecute the American directors or managers for conspiracy but, as an American prosecutor, he had no method to get evidence from a British corporation. He was then cross-examined on a number of cases against American prostitutes where Bassett confirmed he had done deals with the women whereby if they agreed to leave China they would not be imprisoned.

The final witness was the star of the show, Judge Wilfley. The court was packed. Many spectators had to stand outside to get a view of the court. Wilfley said that he had come to Shanghai from Manila where he had been briefly a judge, then Attorney-General. With regard to the admission of lawyers, he said that as there were no rules governing admission, he, as the judge, had the power to make them and he wanted to ensure a high standard of professional ethics.

Wilfley was asked to explain the circumstances of Mc-Cord's escape. He said that the offence was a common law offence and there was no schedule of penalties so he took the case under advisement to consider the penalty. He did not know how easy it was to escape from Shanghai and that it was not possible to extradite people back to Shanghai. He had, therefore, continued McCord's bail. He had known Mc-Cord in the Philippines and that he had met McCord in the lobby of the Astor House Hotel after convicting him. He said that it was a "matter of great chagrin" that McCord had escaped. As to Price, he said he refused bail pending an appeal being filed but Price's appeal had never been perfected.

Early on in his evidence, Wilfley made reference to his speech to the American Association where he promised to clean up American Shanghai and said that he had no fault with that. Later, he flip-flopped saying that work done by the court had:

> "not been undertaken with any view to reforming the Shanghai or any other community. The purpose, the policy of the Court is simply this: to hear cases which are brought before it and determine them according to the facts and the law, and that is all."

He added that "the general policy of the Washington Government—the reason for the creation of the Court—is a different thing."

Wilfley turned to the Roberts case and said that the offending passage had been directly copied from a law reference book, Blackstone, and there had been no attempt to doctor the judgment.

Then Wilfley, obviously deciding that he needed to get in front of the jury that the Catholic representative in the US had said he understood Wilfley's position and accepted the matter fully, decided to sneak some inadmissible evidence in.

This led to some fireworks in the court.

Wilfley first said that "I called on the Papal delegate and discussed the matter with him for a few moments. He understood the matter fully."

O'Shea's counsel, Mr Hays, immediately leapt out of his seat to object. Wilfley, as he well knew, was breaking all the rules of evidence by trying to put in hearsay evidence as to what the papal delegate said.

Wilfley, ignoring Hays, went on: "The Papal delegate seemed satisfied and dismissed the whole matter as amounting to nothing at all. He recognized this, that it was an attempt on behalf of rejected lawyers in Shanghai ..."

Bourne intervened: "No, we cannot have that," he admonished Wilfley.

Hays speaking directly to Wilfley also sought to chastise him, saying: "I object to you going on this way trying to shoulder in evidence which you know must not go in."

This led to Hays himself being reprimanded by Bourne who warned him: "You must not address the witness. If you object, you must say so."

Wilkinson intervened to seek to calm the situation by asking Wilfley if he "would be on his best behaviour?"

"Yes. I shall be very glad to comply with the ruling of the Court ..." Wilfley responded. Then, presumably smiling like a Cheshire cat and just to show that he had known exactly what he was doing, he added, "... and the rules of testimony."

Turning to the lawyers who had been refused admission, Wilfley said that Brooks had not been admitted because of the Grand Jury indictment in Hawaii. Holcomb had failed the exam. He said Andrews had also failed, and that he had offered him a new examination in 30 to 40 days but instead Andrews had chosen to go to Washington and "made war on the Court." Andrews then asked for admission without an examination, which Wilfley refused, but he did offer to allow Andrews to practice until he passed. He then said that he had later sought to disbar Andrews because he had made a false affidavit in the Price case.

With regard to Crozier and Trissel, he said that when he was Attorney-General in the Philippines he had prosecuted Crozier and Crozier had been convicted. Wilfley also said that he also knew Trissel had written the article and that if Trissel had stayed in the Philippines he may well have been prosecuted. His statements concerning them had only been intended to convey to the sub-committee their personal backgrounds. With regard to O'Shea, he said he had been asked questions regarding the *China Gazette* and had made the comments he had. He had no personal animosity towards O'Shea.

Wilfley denied protecting swindlers or suggesting that the British Courts had done so. On the contrary, with regard to the British Court, he said:

> "I might state further that the estimate of the character of the work that this Court does and of the value of the laws that the British Government has extended to China is evidenced by the fact that in nearly all my decisions regarding extraterritoriality I have followed the decisions of the British Court, and that in drawing up a code for China we have followed very largely the Orders in Council of the British Government."

Wilfley was cross-examined by Mr Godfrey. The first few questions related to Trissel and Crozier and did not have much impact. The questioning then turned to McCord and here Godfrey landed some solid punches. Wilfley had said in his evidence that "McCord was one of the worst criminals who ever vexed the China coast." Picking up on this, Godfrey went on the attack:

> Godfrey: When did you find out that McCord was one of the worst criminals who ever vexed the China coast?

Wilfley: I had known that for a long time. I had not a
particle of doubt about it.

Godfrey: Yet when you had convicted McCord of embezzlement, knowing him to be one of the worst characters who ever vexed the China coast, you allowed
him out on the same bail?

Wilfley: I had no idea that he would escape (Laughter) I
had not the slightest apprehension that he would leave
the jurisdiction of the Court, or I should have put him
in gaol.

Godfrey: I should think it would be a temptation to a
man who was not a very black scoundrel to run away?

Wilfley: Possibly.

Godfrey: How much more is it a temptation to a man
who is the worst character who ever vexed the China
coast?

Wilfley: Yes.

Godfrey then turned to the meeting at the Astor House
Hotel. Wilfley agreed that it was indiscreet and admitted: "I
made a mistake in not putting him in gaol at the time. I made
a mistake in talking to him afterwards, or rather, in permit-
ting him to attempt to talk to me."

Wilfley was then cross-examined on the admission of
lawyers and asked a number of questions as to whether he
looked at the certificates as to morals first or the results of the
examinations. He gave very poor evidence, stating a number
of times that he did not remember and asking if he needed to
answer questions.

The cross examination then turned to the Roberts' will
case and was asked if he remembered quotation marks being inserted. Judge Bourne, impolitically, interjected making
absolutely clear that his view was. He said that the allegation
regarding the will case "was absolute rubbish." Godfrey re-
minded Bourne that this was a matter for the jury, to which

Bourne replied, "Certainly, they will have their own opinion," and allowed Godfrey to go on.

When questioned on his evidence regarding Hong Kong companies, Godfrey asked Wilfley:

> "Didn't it suggest the existence of companies under the Hongkong Ordinances, which were like 'the others,' swindling concerns, in Shanghai?"

Bourne could not resist adding his own view on this. To laughter from all those in court, he said:

> "Well, the suggestion was perfectly true, of course."

There were some further questions regarding the Price and Biddle cases and then Godfrey finished his cross-examination. Wilkinson had no re-examination and the court adjourned to the next day for closing submissions which repeated the evidence that had been called. The prosecution argued that the evidence did not prove the statements in O'Shea's article to be true the defence argued that it did.

Bourne then summed up the case. He emphasized the importance of the jury's role in a case such as this by first saying the case law was clear that:

> "An Englishman was free to publish anything he chose so long as a jury of his countrymen found it to be blameless. Thus there was nothing between the irresponsible, unconscientious abuse of the Press and men's sacred right to their good name and reputation but a jury."

He then went through the charges one by one. He said he would treat Judge Wilfley as a private person and that "he had every respect for the sister Court in this place, but what he thought it necessary to say he would say without the least compunction." Without dealing with every issue, Bourne told the jury that the areas where Wilfley could be criticized were in relation to the admission of lawyers where they had clearly been given "a run for their money," but even here O'Shea's criticism may have gone too far. With regard to the McCord case he said it was "quite true that he could have been more discreet," but there was no gross indecency in this. The Price and Biddle cases seemed to be purely questions of law and all judges were overturned on appeal from time to time. Turning to the Roberts case, he said that he may have spoken rather strongly the previous day, and that it was for them to judge for themselves. He reiterated that all lawyers in Shanghai knew the problems of Hong Kong companies. He finished up, with a fairly clear direction to convict, saying that the criticisms seemed to go far beyond what was required by the public interest.

The jury retired and returned with a verdict of guilty. O'Shea did not have anything to say. Wilkinson, addressing Bourne on sentencing, said that the purpose of the case was to put an end to "libels on a judge of a friendly power" and he was not pushing for a heavy sentence.

Bourne turned to O'Shea saying he agreed entirely with the verdict and then sentenced him to two months in prison.

Farewell to Wilfley

O'Shea was, however, to get satisfaction from his prison cell. Just like O'Shea's victory in the Shanghai Liar case, Wilfley's victory was a Pyrrhic one. His support in Washington was waning. Root cabled Wilfley requesting he calm things down, saying "the President and the State Department have been much disturbed by the strife and recrimination which have attended the conduct of affairs in Shanghai since you returned." Wilfley made the mistake of telling Root that he would resign whenever the President felt it necessary. Root accepted this as a resignation. Wilfley lobbied to keep his job, particularly with the incoming President-elect, William Taft, who had recommended his appointment in the first place. Root's decision, however, stood and Wilfley's resignation became effective on January 1, 1909. Wilfley wrote to Taft twice, denouncing his forced removal as "a *brutal* act and a *crime* against the case of *Decency* and *Good Government* in the Far East," and the "*most colossal blunder our nation has ever made in the Far East.*" (The emphasis is in the originals). Pitifully, he pleaded that he had been left like "a homeless dog ... seeking shelter."[6]

Bassett tendered his resignation at the same time. Root cabled back:

"Not only does the President not wish to accept your resignation tendered by telegraph on November 17, but the Department particularly desires you to retain your post and to assist the newly appointed Judge in continuing the good work of the Court and preserving what has been accomplished by Judge Wilfley in the unusual and most difficult stage of its existence."[7]

Bassett stayed in his post for one more year, resigning in 1910 and moving to Mexico City to practice law. He returned to Shanghai in 1913 to join the British American Tobacco Company.[8] Frank Hinckley, the Clerk of the court, took over as District Attorney.

Wilfley's last sitting as Judge was uneventful, dealing with formal applications in a number of matters. There were no farewell speeches or fanfare. He was, however, given a farewell luncheon at the Astor House Hotel attended by many

6   Quotes in this paragraph are from E. Scully, *Bargaining with the State from Afar*, p124-5.

7   *North China Herald*, December 19, 1908, p722. The same page also carries a cable in support of Wilfley and a reply from Root.

8   Profile of Bassett, *Men of Shanghai and North China*, p19.

dignitaries, including the British Consul-General Sir Pelham Warren, Frederick Bourne and Charles Denby, the US Consul-General (and brother of Edwin Denby founder of the court). Bishop Graves wished him bon voyage and Wilfley responded in suitable terms.[9]

Wilfley returned to practice law in New York. Publicly he stated that "his resignation was neither asked nor suggested, and that he told President Roosevelt in September last that he intended to resign."[10] He added that "Shanghai rogues" had no reason to celebrate his departure because his successor would continue his work. Wilfley was also not "a homeless dog seeking shelter" for long. In 1917, he married Ms Belle Zabriskie, the widow of Alonzo Zabriskie, the "capitalist", in Greenwich Connecticut. The ceremony was followed by lunch at the new Mrs Wilfley's country estate in Connecticut.

Wilfley's departure allowed time for renovations to be made to the courtroom of the US Court for China which continued to sit in the American Consulate. In August 1908, the *North China Herald* complained of the difficulties of reporting proceedings. The press table was located at the back of the court making it difficult to hear the lawyers and almost impossible to hear the judge and clerk. Two fans had also been installed on the walls but they played from either side of the room onto the judge's dais directing his voice away from the court as well as making the rest of the courtroom insufferably hot.[11]

The courtroom was renovated to make considerable alterations. A wooden screen was placed in front of the window behind the judge. A door was added to allow the judge to directly enter onto the dais, and a railing was added to separate counsel, witnesses and the Press from the general public gallery.[12]

------

9 *North China Herald* December 26, 1908, p468 for Wilfley's last sitting and farewell luncheon.

10 Re resignation: *New York Times*, January 11, 1909; Re Marriage: *New York Times* January 28, 1917.

11 *North China Herald*, August 8, 1908, p340.

12 *North China Herald*, March 13, 1909, p348.

The court was ready for a new judge.

That judge, Rufus Thayer, was appointed very quickly to replace Wilfley. President Roosevelt signed Thayer's commission on December 16, 1908 and Thayer took the oath of office on December 23, 1908.[13] But despite the quick appointment, it took him three months to get to Shanghai. He arrived in Shanghai in March 1909 and re-opened the court.

Thayer had been a lawyer in private practice in Washington DC in his own firm, Thayer & Rankin. He was born in Plymouth Michigan, on June 19, 1850 making him 58 at the time of his appointment. Thayer graduated from the University of Michigan in 1871 and joined the Library of Congress as an assistant librarian. At the same time he studied law and graduated in 1874. He was appointed law clerk in the Treasury Department where he remained for ten years before leaving to form Thayer & Rankin. He subsequently served as a Judge Advocate General in Washington.[14]

Thayer had not applied for the job. The main thing that appeared to recommend Thayer to the President was that he was the brother in law of the head of the New York Republican Party.[15] Norwood Allman, an American consular official and later lawyer, described Thayer as "a man of much calmer temperament than his predecessor, and being a likable and kindly soul, he soon established himself in the confidence of the better element of the American community without all the pyrotechnics that characterized the Wilfley regime." He was also "extremely popular with the British, probably because he wore a Vandyke and bore a striking resemblance to King Edward VII."[16]

At the first sitting of the court, Thomas Jernigan, the senior member of the American Bar in Shanghai, welcomed Thayer

---

13 *North China Herald*, March 13, 1909, p348.

14 Obituary, *New York Times*, July 13, 1917.

15 C.S. Carter, *History of the Class of '70*, p222 re Rufus Thayer; E. Scully, *Bargaining with the State from Afar*, p124.

16 N. Allman, *Shanghai Lawyer*, p105.

from the capital of the USA to the commercial capital of China which was run by an elected council and had a police force that for "its efficiency was not surpassed by any in the world." Thayer thanked Jernigan and then cut directly to the chase:

> "I assume my position as Judge of this Court with a great deal of concern. The court is unique in its position and its character. In connexion with the exercise of its functions, it must meet and solve a large number of difficult questions, due to the state of the law available to it as an extraterritorial court. These difficulties appear very large to one who is newly introduced to the US Court for China and who has suddenly imposed on him the duty of presiding over that court."

He then added, with humility, that he expected to make mistakes and would have to call on the indulgence of the bar. He thanked everyone for the welcome he had received and then with a nod to some of the problems Wilfley had had with the bar added, "I shall make a constant effort to maintain the cordial relations which are today inaugurated." He then made some general announcements about hearing dates and his plans to go on circuit to Canton, Hankow and Tientsin.

Thayer made no mention of Korea over which the court he had inherited had appellate jurisdiction. This is most likely because Korea was not a major concern for the Judge of the US Court. This was not true for the British courts. During the tumultuous two years of Wilfley's tenure, events in Korea had brought a number of high profile cases - all involving one man - before them.

PART EIGHT

DYING DYNASTIES
(1906 TO 1911)

CHAPTER 34

Korea's Hero - Ernest Bethell

THE UNITED STATES HAD, when establishing the United States Court for China in 1906, clearly foreseen that extraterritoriality would not last long in Korea. Unlike Britain, they had not included Korea (or Corea) in the court's name. The act creating the court provided that the United States Court for China would only have appellate jurisdiction over Korea "so long as the rights of extraterritoriality shall obtain in favor of the United States."[1]

They were correct that extraterritoriality would not last long. Two years before the court was created, in 1904, Korea and Japan signed an agreement whereby Korea agreed to look to Japan for advice over its administration. By a protocol to this agreement, they agreed to appoint a Japanese as adviser to their Finance Ministry and a foreigner as an adviser to their Foreign Ministry. Korea also agreed to consult with Japan before signing any treaties with other powers. In November 1905, a further protocol was signed making Korea effectively a protectorate of Japan and Japan took over foreign matters for Korea.[2] Hirobumi Ito, the former Prime Minister of Japan, was appointed Resident-General in Korea. Ito, as Resident-General, effectively ran the country. He was assisted by a Resident, Mr Yagoro Miura, and other Japanese officials.

Given that Korea was now effectively run by Japan, in 1905 and 1906, America and Britain withdrew their legations

1 S.2 United States Court for China Act, 1906.
2 R. Akagi, *Japan's Foreign Relations*, pp265-267 and 275 to 278.

The Korea Daily News

from Seoul leaving consulate-generals in their place.

In 1907, Ito engineered the abdication of the Korean Emperor in favour of the, presumably more malleable, Crown Prince.

The Japanese occupation of Korea led to three cases in the British courts all involving Ernest Bethell, the proprietor of the *Korea Daily* News and its Korean sister *Daehan Maeil Sinbo*. Bethell, who had been in the export business in Kobe and Yokohama, had first come to Korea as a correspondent for a British newspaper, the *Daily Chronicle*, during the Russo-Japanese war. He had stayed on to found his newspapers. The newspapers were pro-Korean which upset the Japanese. However, because of Bethell's extraterritorial rights, the Japanese dominated government of Korea could not directly take legal action against Bethell.[3]

As a result, Bethell had the singular honour of having an Order in Council enacted specifically to deal with him.

Hirobumi Ito (right) feigns surprise at the Korean emperor's decision to abidcate

In 1907 an OIC was issued which prohibited the publication of seditious materials or matters "calculated to excite tumult or disorder, or to excite enmity between His Majesty's subjects and the Government of China or Corea." The Supreme Court

---

3   See Chin-Sok Chong, "Ernest Thomas Bethell (1872-1909)", in *Britain and Japan Biographical Portraits* Vol VIII, H Cortazzi (ed), p481 for a profile of Bethell.

for China and Corea was given sole jurisdiction to try cases under this provision. The Order in Council, known locally as the
"Bethell Clause", was posted at the Supreme Court in Shanghai on September 5, 1907 and came into effect on the same day.[4]

Bethell found himself in court soon after this. In October 1907 he was prosecuted in the British Consular Court in
Seoul before the Consul-General, Henry Cockburn. He was
not charged under the "Bethell Clause" but for breach of the
peace for publishing articles that were "likely to produce or
excite a breach of the public peace given in that there was
an armed movement in Korea and conflict had taken place
between Korean and Japanese troops." The charge added,
"there was a considerable number of Japanese residents in
Seoul [and] that there was a feeling of dislike and hatred on
the part of Koreans against the Japanese."

At the hearing, Bethell asked who his prosecutor was. Mr
Cockburn told him that Mr Holmes of the Consulate was his
"nominal prosecutor" indicating that the prosecution was, in
fact, instigated by the Japanese authorities. Bethell was convicted and required to enter into a six-month good behaviour
bond.[5]

The conviction was not popular with everyone. Soon after,
in an article headed "As Others See it", the *North China Herald*
reported that the *Hartford Courant* in America had published
an editorial describing the prosecution of Bethell as an "illus-
tration of British slavish adherence to the Japanese alliance."[6]

Bethell and his newspapers did not stay quiet for long.
The following year, he found himself charged, on the complaint of Mr Miura, the Japanese Resident in Korea, with
the more serious crime of publishing seditious matter under
"the Bethell Clause." The charge related to three articles pub-

4   See *North China Herald*, September 6, 1907 pp 558-560 for the full Order in Council.

5   *North China Herald*, November 15, 1907, p414; for details of Bethell's questions as to
who his prosecutor was, see his evidence in *Bethell v North China Herald* reported in the
North China Herald December 12, 1908 at p661.

6   *North China Herald*, November 29, 1907, p553.

lished in Korean in the *Korea Daily News*. One article referred to the murder of Durham Stevens, a foreign affairs advisor to the Korean government who had been appointed at the suggestion of the Japanese government. The article called Stevens' assassins patriotic, loyal and righteous gentlemen because they had murdered a man who supported the Japanese protectorate over Korea. The second article was entitled "A hundred Metternichs could not keep one Italy in bondage," where Korea was compared to Italy in the middle of the 19th century and then went on to describe how the Italians rose up and fought for their independence. The third, "Flowers of the Educational World," about the death of 17 student activists said: "We will certainly recover out Korea ... What heroes have left glorious monuments in history except through blood?"

Bourne, as Judge, and Harrie Wilkinson, as Crown Advocate, travelled to Seoul from Shanghai, in June 1908, to try the case. A British lawyer from Kobe, Mr Charles Crosse, represented Bethell. Mr E. Holmes the British Pro-Consul in Seoul acted as Court Registrar. The *Japan Chronicle* arranged for a special correspondent to attend.[7]

Seoul at the time was still a backwater. The *Japan Chronicle's* correspondent noted that although the Japanese had issued an edict that top knots, the traditional form of hair style for married men in Korea, should be removed, "the tumble-down streets of this quaint city are as full of tall-hatted and top-knotted men as they were long before they were policed by the Japanese."

The trial was conducted in the hall of the former British Legation Guard's barracks and attracted considerable interest amongst foreigners, Koreans and Japanese. The *Japan Chronicle's* correspondent said that the hall made an excellent court room, "though it was almost unbearably hot this after-

7 The Bethell Trial: Full Report of the Proceedings, *Japan Chronicle*, Kobe, Japan, 1908 (Wilkinson Papers, PRONI D1292/L1/12). North China Herald, June 27, 1908, p841.

noon towards the conclusion of the day's proceedings." The
room got so hot that at one point Crosse asked Bourne for
permission to remove his wig, to which Bourne "perspiringly
acquiesced, at the same time removing his own." The correspondent also commented that the "first day's proceedings
were not without their amusing incidents" and the manner
in which both Harrie Wilkinson, the Crown Advocate, and
Crosse "invariably stumbled over the pronunciation of *Dai
Han Mai Il Shimpo* caused a smile in Court time after time."

The first witness was the Japanese Resident, Yagoro Miura, who gave evidence in English. Miura explained that the
prosecution had been brought because the "actual Government of Korea was under direction of the Residency-General
according to treaty." About half the country was affected by
armed disturbances and many Japanese soldiers and police
had been sent to quell the disturbances. Under cross-examination by Crosse, he explained the relationship between the
Japanese and Korean governments in very tortured logic:

> "The Korean Government was under the direction of
> the Japanese Government where Government business
> was concerned. Japan had a protectorate over Korea
> but there was nothing like annexation in the relation-
> ship between the two countries."

He said there were disturbances in many parts of Korea
but not in any organized way. There had even been fighting in August 1907 at the South Gate of Seoul. He admitted
that "unfortunately there were many cases of disorderly conduct committed by Japanese in Korea and there were some
instances in which Japanese had been guilty of misconduct
towards foreigners." One further Japanese witness was called
who described the circulation of Bethell's newspapers.

Mr Crosse opened the defence for Bethell, with an impassioned plea, which showed, at the least, despite the fact that Crosse lived in Japan where extraterritoriality had ended, he was not frightened of upsetting the Japanese authorities. Crosse argued that the Japanese Government of Korea was not in fact the Government of Korea. He said that as far as he understood the case for the British Crown was:

"That there was only one government here; that the Korean Government did not exist for all practical purposes; that the Korean Government was, so to speak, in the fatherly or grandfatherly care of the Japanese Government, which could tuck it up and put it to bed, or take it out again at pleasure."

He said that it appeared there were two governments, Japanese and Korean. The Japanese had chosen not to occupy Korea so that "it did not lie in the mouth of Mr Miura or anyone else to say Mr Bethell had excited enmity between the Government of Korea and its subjects, posing as the representative government of Korea."

The charge he argued, should be dismissed on the ground that the Government of Japan was not the Government of Korea.

Bethell was then called to give evidence. He said he did not read Korean but that he had given strict instructions to his staff of the Korean editions not to publish seditious materials and that he "had never in any way taken advantage of [his] extraterritorial privileges." He also deeply regretted the opprobrious terms used in relation to Mr Stevens, who was a personal friend. Bethell was then extensively cross-examined by Wilkinson. Bethell's Korean editor, Yang Ki Tak, also gave evidence on Bethell's behalf. However, most of Yang's evidence only confirmed that Bethell was respon-

sible for all the publications. A number of other Korean op-
ponents of the Japanese regime were also called to explain
their opposition to Japanese rule; their experiences in prison
and, most importantly, that the articles that had not incited
them to violence.

Bourne was very concerned that the Korean witnesses not
incriminate themselves and thereby be exposed to punishment by the Japanese. Wilkinson assured him that Mr Miura
had agreed that no steps would be taken against the witnesses
no matter what they said. Bourne insisted this be interpreted
to the witnesses and that a similar assurance be given to the
Korean interpreter.

In closing, Crosse said that he had been left to prove a
negative. That is, that the articles did not incite people to violence. The Order in Council was a muzzling of the press. The
proceedings were only to safeguard the interests of Japan in
Korea. In conclusion, he submitted, the articles did not cause
any tumult in Korea and the charges should be dismissed.

Wilkinson, in response, insisted that the British Government was not acting as a "cat's paw" for the Japanese government. He assured Bourne that he himself, as British Crown
Advocate, had decided to bring the prosecution. The articles
were clearly "calculated to excite" enmity against the Korean
government and Bethell should be convicted.

Bourne said immediately that he would convict Bethell,
but deferred giving his judgment until the next day.

The following morning, Bourne delivered judgment. He
said the articles were clearly seditious particularly given the
current state of affairs in Korea. Sitting as an extraterritorial judge, he must take notice of the situation. With regard
to Crosse's argument that Japanese Government was not
the Government of Korea, Bourne gave the only decision he
could in the diplomatic and political situation:

"But, if the Government of the existing Emperor, protected by the Government of Japan is not the Government of Korea, who is governing the country? Nations sometimes fall into a wretched state of organized rebellion when a *de jure* and *de facto* government, are existing in the same national territory at the same time, for instance in England in 1645 when the King ruled at Oxford and the Parliament in London. Here there is no existing body that can be called a government but the Emperor under the protection of Japan."

He then formally convicted Bethell. As to punishment, Bourne noted the mitigating factors that Bethell's intentions were fair and honest. But he had to take account of the fact that Bethell's paper was a recognized mouthpiece of Korean disaffection and that "under the shelter of our ex-territorial rights" the newspaper escaped Japanese censorship and its staff escaped the arm of Japanese law. Bourne sentenced Bethell to three weeks in prison. Because, there was no British consular jail in Seoul, he granted him bail until a suitable place could be found to imprison him.

Many Koreans had gathered outside the court to hear the verdict. When it was found out that Bethell had been sentenced to jail "there were some signs of active resentment, but Bethell and his friends urged them not to create any disorder." One of the Koreans in the crowd had brought Y4,000 to pay any fine which was imposed.

It was decided to imprison Bethell in Shanghai. Two days after his conviction on June 20, 1908 he was ordered to appear at the British Consulate at 4.00pm. He was met by the Marshal of the Court, Mr Rosser, who immediately took him to Seoul station to put him on a 5.30pm train to Chemulpo (now part of Incheon), the port for Seoul. It was originally thought that he would be put on a 10.30 pm train but in order to avoid demonstrations Bethell was whisked away without even being able to say goodbye to his wife.

Bethell was put on board a British Navy ship, HMS *Clio*, to be taken directly to Shanghai. On board, on giving his word to the Captain not to attempt to escape, he was given his freedom on the ship. He was put up in a small cabin made out of tarpaulins rigged between two deckhouses. He stayed on board for 2 and half days before reaching Shanghai. On arrival in Shanghai, he was taken to the British Consulate where he was passed from official to official. His first taste of what imprisonment was to mean was that he was no longer addressed by "the prefix 'Mr' which one gentleman expects from another." Bethell was not considered a high risk prisoner and he was escorted to the consular gaol in a rickshaw. His first night was a nightmare with his cell besieged by a horde of mosquitos. He had been given three blankets but no mosquito net. The following day, things improved and he was, as a first-class misdemeanant, allowed to purchase his own food, beer and a mosquito net from outside the gaol. "Time passed without wings and leaden feet until the day dawned that I was to be released."[8]

On that day, two and a half weeks after his arrival in Shanghai, on July 11, 1908, Bethell was brought before Bourne in the Supreme Court in Shanghai and was released on a 6-month good behaviour bond.[9]

The case attracted attention worldwide and particularly in England. Questions were asked in the House of Parliament to the Secretary of State to Foreign Affairs as to why Bethell was being prosecuted. The Secretary of State answered, in effect, that it was what the law required.[10] The *London and China Telegraph*, itself, ran an editorial on June 22, 1908 supporting the prosecution and conviction while lamenting that the Japanese may have ill-treated many Koreans, but it was no worse than what their own government had done to them. In any event,

8   Ernest Bethell, "My Sentence of Three Weeks Imprisonment", *Japan Weekly Chronicle*, September 3 (p358), September 10 (p394), September 17 (p437) and September 24 (p469), 1908.

9   *North China Herald*, July 18, 1908, p 181.

10   *London and China Telegraph*, June 28, 1908, p559 and July 6, 1908, p583.

the Japanese were clearly there to stay and "no amount of kicking against the pricks will alter the main fact."[11]

Bethell back in court

Bethell was back in the Supreme Court in Shanghai before Judge Bourne, exactly six months and one day after his release, but, thankfully for him, not for breach of his good behaviour bond. This time, he was there as a plaintiff suing the *North China Herald* for defamation.[12]

His barrister was John Douglas who had until early 1908 been Registrar of the Supreme Court. Douglas and Douglas' partner, Mr Noel Home had, in July that year while Bethell was in prison in Shanghai each won $5,000 in damages from the *North China Herald*. The *Herald* had alleged Home and Douglas had sent a warning letter to the *North China Herald* without instructions from their client. The headline had asked rhetorically if this was a "Case for the Bar Society?"[13] Douglas and Homes' victory had been reported the day Bethell was released from prison.

Bethell's claim against the *North China Herald* related to a report published in September 1908, two months after he had been released from prison. The report, which had been sourced from Japanese newspapers, said that Bethell had confessed to misappropriating money from the Korean National Debts Redemption Fund. This was a fund created by Koreans seeking to collect enough money to buy back Korean debts owed to Japan in the (mistaken) belief that this would lead to Korean independence.

Without ever having said that it would receive such money, funds were being sent to the *Korean Daily News* because it was

11 *London and China Telegraph*, June 22, 1908, p540.

12 *Bethell v North China Daily News and Herald Ltd*, *North China Herald*, December 12, 1908, pp 659 to 672. The jury members were C.M. Joyce, P.W. Massey, H.W. Daldy, R.M.C. Wallace and W.H. Jackson.

13 *Home v North China Daily News and Herald Ltd; Douglas v North China Daily News and Herald Ltd; North China Herald* July 11, 1908 pp106 to 123.

*The main characters in Bethell's case
against the North China Herald*

considered to be indepen-
dent of the government.
Bethell had at first passed
Y400 on to another organization but found they were
not the proper recipients.
In total, the *Korean Daily
News* had received Y60,000
that Bethell decided to invest until a proper recipient
could be found. Bethell's
Korean partner, Yang Ki-
Tak, was investigated, prosecuted for and acquitted of
embezzling some of these
funds in the Japanese con-
trolled courts in Korea.[14] In the course of the investigation of
Yang, Bethell provided the authorities with information on
Yang's behalf. This was misreported in Japanese newspapers
as Bethell having made a confession. The *North China Herald*
carried this report without checking. The *Herald* article was
subsequently repeated in numerous English language papers
in Asia.

The *North China Herald* offered an apology and to "do
whatever it could to correct the defamation" but refused to
pay damages. Bethell sued. The trial was only to decide if the
Herald should pay damages and if so, how much. Mr Philips
argued on behalf of the *Herald* that an apology should have
been enough for Bethell but that he was a gold digger seeking
large damages. He said:

"Mr Bethell had then determined that the only satisfac-

14 British Consul, Henry Cockburn, who prosecuted Bethell, was instrumental in getting Yang a fair trial. See: "Henry's war: One man's fight against rendition", *The Independent*, December 6, 2007.

tion he intended to get out of these proceedings he proposed was the payment to him of a large sum of money. Further apology he did not wish for. What he hoped to get and what he now hoped to get was satisfaction by means of a large payment. His character had been completely vindicated."

Phillips then took a dig at Bethell's barrister, John Douglas:

"I can only imagine gentlemen that, seeing his learned counsel here, Mr Douglas, with his pockets bulging with damages which had been obtained very properly a few months before, encouraged Mr Bethell to think that he could come to Shanghai and get his pockets filled and in an equally desirable condition. It is money and only that Mr Bethell requires to satisfy his condition."

This drew a strong response from Douglas who said Phillips should never have argued "that the Plaintiff's cupidity was aroused by his Counsel's pockets being stuffed with silver dollars."

Bourne then summed up for the jury. Bourne had only recently found Bethell guilty of sedition against the Japanese government of Korea. Now, he had to address the jury as to whether the conviction reflected that Bethell had a bad character. He went as a far as a judge could to indicate to the jury that this particular conviction should not go very far, if at all, to do so. Bourne said that he "could not say that those proceedings had in any way affected the plaintiff's character for the purposes of this suit. His conduct might have made him an unsuitable member of a 'peace at any price' Society or of a Quaker body', but nothing more."

Even though Bourne, as a judge, had convicted Bethell, it did not mean that Bourne, as a man, disagreed with him.

Judges have to uphold the law. It is rare that they get a chance to subsequently comment publicly on a case. Bourne made it clear, as clearly as a judge can in any event, what he thought. The jury returned with a verdict for the substantial sum of $3,000 for Bethell plus his costs.

Bethell did not, however, enjoy the bulge in his pockets for long. Soon after returning to Korea, in late April or early May 1909 he died of cardiac enlargement in Seoul at the age of 39. He was given the largest funeral ever for a foreigner in Korea and thousands of Koreans joined the cortege.[15] The only good to come from his early death was that Bethell was not alive to see the dream of Korea independence die.

The following year, in 1910, Japan completed its accretion of power in Korea. On August 22, 1910, Japan and Korea signed a Treaty of Annexation that was approved and promulgated on August 29, 1910. From that date, Korea became an integral part of Japan and remained so until the end of World War II.

When the treaty came into force, Japan issued a declaration that treaties by other powers with Korea were abrogated and that extraterritoriality in Korea was abolished.[16] The British Government formalized this by an Order in Council dated January 23, 1911, whereby the jurisdiction of the Supreme Court over Korea was formally abolished and the court was renamed the Supreme Court for China.[17]

The Bethell cases were not the only difficult cases Bourne and Wilkinson handled in 1908. They both had to deal with a difficult case where a Briton had killed a Chinese in Shanghai. The result attracted a vehement protest from the Chinese authorities.

....

15 *North China Herald*, May 15, 1909, p 404.

16 R. Akagi, *Japan's Foreign Relations*, pp278 to 281.

17 The Corea Order in Council, 1911, London Gazette, 27 January 1911, p688

CHAPTER 35

The Ricshaw Coolie and the Sampan Man

IN THE SPACE OF LESS than a year both Frederick Bourne in the British Supreme Court and Rufus Thayer in the United States Court had to try cases where a Briton and an American were accused of killing Chinese: one a ricshaw coolie; the other a sampan man. Both cases attracted strong attention from the Chinese authorities and in the case before Bourne a blistering protest at the decision.

Both dead men were, of course, more than a mere ricshaw coolie or a mere sampan man. They were Zung Zu-fung and Kong Shing. Zung had a father, mother and pregnant wife: his death caused them great distress. Kong's background is not available from the records but he was, at least, someone's son.

Their deaths were taken seriously.

In Shanghai, Thomas J. Stevenson was ordered to stand trial in the British Supreme Court for murder for the killing of Zung. The 1904 Order in Council had allowed for juries of between five and twelve jurors with the number for each case to be set by rules of court.[1] In this case a jury of twelve was empanelled. Harrie Wilkinson, the Crown Advocate, prosecuted and Mr F. Ellis and R.E. Gregson defended. All three had just completed the committal proceedings against Henry O'Shea for defaming American Judge Lebbeus Wilfley. In that case,

---

1   Article 32(3) China and Corea Order in Council, 1904.

A Ricshaw coolie drives into the night with a foreign customer

however, Gregson had been assisting Wilkinson to prosecute
and Ellis had been defending with Mr Godfrey.[2]

Stevenson, 40, was a marine engineer by trade but his cur-
rent job was as a travelling cinematographer. He had been
in China for 17 years. He travelled on a houseboat around
China and showed movies to audiences. While in Shanghai,
his wife had become ill and was convalescing in the Victoria
Nursing Home, the leading hospital in the city at the time.
Stevenson visited his wife daily. On the evening of Saturday 8
August 1908, he had been to the Astor House Hotel where he
had had two or three gin and sodas before visiting his wife.
After seeing her, he had gone drinking at the Metropole and
Globe hotels. He had then gone back to his boat around 11pm.
After getting some cigarettes he had then strolled down to

2   *R v Stevenson, North Chna Herald,* August 15, 1908 (Comittal) and *North China Herald,*
September 26, 1908, p786-789 (trial). Translation of letter from Tsai Taotai to Sir Pelham
Warren dated October 17, 1908. (FO file reference not available). The jury members were
J. Bottenheim, H.C. Gulland, H.P. Dudley, S.E. Lucas, J.A. Hayes, G.F.C. Dobson, C.C.A
Warn, F. Griffin, H.F. Gray, A. Samson, W.J.C. Budd and W.N.C. Allen.

the Bund. He ended up eating at the Grill Rooms in the early hours of the morning leaving around 4.00 am, about half an hour before dawn.

According to Stevenson, he then hailed Zung and got in his ricshaw. He was very sleepy and "remembered seeing Range Road ... When he took notice again he was in an entirely strange locality." Zung kept on going and then stopped on top of a culvert over a creek. He then went down a plank towards the creek. Stevenson told Zung to return to the road and Zung made as if he was doing so. Stevenson fearing Zung was planning to rob him, grabbed Zung and they both ended up in the creek. Stevenson said that Zung tried to hold him under water, so he grabbed his queue and twisted it around his neck. Stevenson then passed out and woke up with his mouth just above water. Zung was lying nearby, apparently dead. After crawling out of the creek, Stevenson asked passers-by to call the police.

Zung's father, elder brother and cousin attended the trial of Stevenson for the murder of their son. Despite being in their own country – and the judge speaking fluent Chinese, the trial was conducted solely in a foreign language - English. Magistrate Li, who had also observed the trial of Henry De Menil, was sitting on the bench. As he was there only as an "observer" under the Chefoo Convention, he had no power over the conduct of the case. Zung's father tried to speak at the trial to demand justice. He was silenced and removed from the court by the Marshal. Zung's cousin was allowed to remain but was not allowed to speak.[3]

Wilkinson prepared a very strong case against Stevenson. A full post mortem had been conducted on Zung which Wilkinson said in court was a "great step in advance." Dr C. Davis gave evidence that from his post mortem there were no

----

3   There is a conflict in the record of the case. The *North China Herald* report stated that Zung's elder brother gave evidence but did not record what it was. Zung's father later said Zung was his only son.

signs or strangulation. Numerous Chinese and western witnesses were called to give evidence as to what they had seen
including bar boys from the hotels Stevenson had been drinking at. Dr Davis who had also examined Stevenson after he
had been arrested gave evidence as to Stevenson's injuries.
One Chinese witness from village just near were Stevenson
and Zung had fought said she saw Stevenson throw the ricshaw from the road into the river.

Some of the Chinese witnesses, it appears, gave evidence
in Pidgin English. Wilkinson had not learnt Chinese, but he
had mastered Pidgin English which local Chinese used to
communicate with foreigners. The *North China Herald* wrote
of Wilkinson later:

> "There was one other thing that impressed the observer
> at the Supreme Court and that was an absolute and
> unparalleled mastery of Pidgin English. Mr Wilkinson
> whenever he wants to, can secure, the most delicate
> shades of meaning by the use of Pidgin English, an
> examining a Chinese witness in this medium he can
> get a much more coherent story. The present writer
> well remembers one morning in the Supreme Court the
> Crown Advocate called a Chinese witness and said to
> him, "Savvy English?" The man said, "No." This was
> quite enough and for the next two hours Mr Wilkinson
> led him through the story of the event in which he was
> connected, got a fine graphic account of it, and never
> once did an interpreter have to intervene, all been re-
> lated in the two or three dozen words of English which
> the Chinese knew."

Tsu Ah-Lay, a garbage coolie, was called to give evidence.
He said Stevenson had asked him to the police station. Tsu
said he had told Stevenson "No can come, no come, don't
spoil those marks made by the ricsha coolie." Ellis asked Tsu

to repeat what he had said but even then said he could not understand it. Wilkinson responded that if Ellis had been listening intently he must have heard. Ellis protested that Wilkinson did not "know how to behave himself." Wilkinson then replied, in a cryptic comment, "that he would learn in time for the O'Shea case."

Stevenson gave evidence on his own behalf recounting his evening out and how Zung and he had ended up in the river.

Bourne in his summing up told the jurors that they could convict of murder or manslaughter or acquit Stevenson. They came back twice saying they could not reach a verdict. Bourne considered ordering a mistrial but asked the jury to try one more time. The jury finally returned a verdict of guilty of manslaughter but "with a strong recommendation for mercy." This suggests the jury were strongly divided between acquitting Stevenson and convicting him of manslaughter.

Bourne then sentenced Stevenson. He said that he agreed with the verdict, but that while he believed Stevenson did not intend to kill the coolie, Stevenson had done so with a "great deal of ferocity." Other than the recommendation of mercy, he would have passed a harsh sentence. But, given the jury's recommendation, he sentenced Stevenson to one year's hard labour from the date of his arrest.

Magistrate Li wrote a report to the Taotai on the case, which included a petition from Zung's father complaining about the lack of justice in the British courts. Zung senior complained that he had been removed from the court by the Marshal and that his cousin had not been allowed to speak. Most importantly, the penalty imposed was nowhere near harsh enough to reflect that a pregnant wife had lost her husband and a father and mother had lost their only son and source of sustenance in their old age. He said:

> "It is my opinion that the British Judge reckons a Chinese life of little worth when he inflicts a sentence no

severer than that of one year on a man guilty of killing another."

He then pointed to the unequal treatment of Chinese and foreigners in China:

"Were a Chinese to accidentally kill a foreigner would this case be taken as a precedent? If not (I would remark that) the principles of justice are one, though mankind may be divided into Chinese and foreigners."

Magistrate Li was also not happy with the result. He commented harshly on Stevenson's plea of self-defence:

"Who can believe prisoner's crafty allegation that he was acting in self defence and not of design? (To account for the mud on his clothes) he says they came to blows (in the course of which they fell into the creek) because the ricshaw man tried to rob him – but brings forward no witness to prove it. But his muddy garments and money may just as well show that he took the victim's life by pressing him down in the mud when he could not possibly have kept on dry ground. Or alternatively he may have purposely besmattered himself with mud to divert suspicion."

Li went on to compare British justice unfavourably with Chinese justice. He found it difficult to hide his sarcasm:

"Such a story would not carry credence in Chinese law and I am surprised that foreign jurisprudence, which is of such high repute, should adopt the view it does ... It is not surprising that the deceased relatives smarting under a sense of injustice should address me as they do."

The Taotai wrote a protest to Sir Pelham Warren, the British Consul-General, in October 1908 requesting the case be re-considered and compensation paid to the family.[4] There is no further correspondence on the Foreign Office file, but as the case had been finalized by a jury verdict, under English law there was nothing that could have been done to re-try the case. The family could have brought an action for compensation but again would have to do so in a foreign language in a foreign court.

Another killing in Chefoo

The next year Rufus Thayer, in one of his first cases as Judge of the United States Court for China, also had to try an American for killing a Chinese in Chefoo. The case there had echoes of Hornby's Shantung lighthouse case, which had also been tried in Chefoo. A local American, Thomas Jones, had shot a sampan man, Kong Shing, at the Kaiping jetty.[5] Times had, however, moved on since Hornby's day. The Qing Emperor and the Empress Dowager had both just died and the government was in the process of its own legal reforms and there was far less opposition to the extraterritorial courts. Jones had not been put in chains and no gunboats were necessary to protect Thayer or his court.

Nevertheless, the case attracted a lot of local attention. The local Taotai and six other Chinese officials attended the trial. The Taotai had also instructed a foreign attorney, Mr Rice, to observe the hearing on his behalf.

District Attorney Arthur Bassett travelled to Chefoo to prosecute the case. Reprising his role from defending Henry De Menil, William Fleming, acted for Jones. There was no doubt that bullet from Jones' gun had killed Kong. Jones had

---

4   An English translation of the letter is part of the letter from the Taotai to Sir Pelham Warren cited above.

5   *US v Jones* - Two case reports are in the *North China Herald* May 15, 1909, p 387-388. Thayer's full decision is in Lobingier, Extraterritorial cases, volume 1, p154.

been trying to hail sampans to get out to an incoming steamer. Two sampans had not stopped and, according to the Chinese witnesses, Jones, getting angry, had pulled his gun and fired it. The bullet had hit Kong, killing him instantly. Jones' evidence was that he had been about to board a sampan and had taken his gun out to make it safe for the trip when a bullet had discharged, struck the water, ricocheted and killed Kong. Fleming arranged for Mr Kierie, a former officer in the Italian Navy, and W.E. Fairburn of the Shanghai Municipal Police, who was a qualified gunner in the marines, to give evidence about the carrying power of the Browning pistol Jones had been holding.

Fleming in a closing argument of three hours "in the course of which he went into the minutest details of the evidence" strongly attacked the evidence of the Chinese witnesses. He suggested that they had colluded in their evidence to try to defeat Jones' story that the shooting was accidental. He then made the startling submission, that of course Thayer

A sampan man

could not accept, that "the Court must not treat the Chinese evidence as it would treat that given by foreigners."

Bassett summed up in a short half hour speech.

Thayer did not have the problem that Hornby had of having to direct a jury that could deliver a "mischievous" verdict. There was no jury in the US Court. Thayer made it clear that he believed the Chinese witnesses and did not believe Jones' story. Responding to Fleming's argument he added that "while there were racial differences in the manner of giving testimony, still the Court had little doubt in accepting the evidence as a whole of the Chinese witnesses."

Nevertheless, this did not mean that Jones had intended to kill Kong and thus was guilty of murder. The Chinese witnesses may have thought that he intended to kill Kong, but he had no reason to. Thayer said that he had to give Jones the benefit of the doubt. He found Jones guilty of manslaughter for his criminal neglect in the handling of the weapon and sentenced him to three years imprisonment to be served in Shanghai.

Fleming made an application for a new trial and after "some conflict of opinion" Thayer agreed to Fleming making an application back in Shanghai.

The *North China Herald* reported that Thayer "seemed to find difficulty in repressing the emotion he felt when he was about to pronounce judgment." Thayer later conceded privately that he had imposed the harsh penalty to satisfy public opinion. No doubt Magistrate Li's protest in the De Menil case and the diplomatic furore the case had just caused were to the forefront of his mind when deciding Jones' sentence.

Thayer did support an application by Fleming for a pardon by President Taft. It seems this would have been forthcoming on the basis that Jones serve six months in jail and leave China for three years so as to not antagonise Chinese sentiments. Jones, however, died in prison, so was never released.[6]

6   E. Scully, *Bargaining with the State from Afar*, p16.

CHAPTER 36

For Better or Worse

De Sausmarez ill

Frederick Bourne had tried the Bethell, O'Shea and Stevenson cases as Acting Judge because Havilland de Sausmarez, had been seriously ill for most of 1908 and 1909 and returned to England for surgery.

With Bourne acting as Judge an Acting Assistant Judge needed to be appointed. The previous Registrar, John Douglas, had resigned in early 1908 and Gilbert King, the new Registrar who had replaced Douglas, was not senior enough to act as a judge. (He was also a solicitor so may not have been considered suitable.) Harrie Wilkinson the Crown Advocate, could have been asked to act as a judge, but given he had just spent five years out of private practice, he most likely declined an invitation to do so.

The Foreign Office was, however, able to call on judges Arthur Rose Vincent from the British Court for Siam and Lindsey Smith from Zanzibar to act as assistant judges during de Sausmarez's absence and when Bourne later went on leave. Smith also acted as Judge of the High Court of Weihaiwei.

Vincent on his first day on the bench presided over an otherwise unremarkable case involving the quality of sherry. Of note, however, the *Eastern Sketch* drew a parody of the case for its front cover. This is the only drawing (or photograph) I have been able to find of the inside of the main court room.[1]

---

1 See Chapter 8 for the drawing. *Mosley & Co v Caldbeck, MaGregor & Co, North China Herald,* June 13, 1908, p695

Vincent was later to do very well in life. On his way Home from Shanghai to England, he met an American heiress, Miss Maud Bourn and married her soon after arriving in San Francisco. He, not surprisingly, resigned from the Foreign Office Judicial Service. He later became an Irish senator and was so wealthy that he owned the Muckross Estate, a tract of land of 13,000 acres in Ireland. The estate was so big he could not keep it up and gave it to the Irish Government to create a National Park.[2]

Smith, on the other hand, was not so lucky and after serving one year in Shanghai, returned to Zanzibar as a judge. He later became Judge of Zanzibar and President of the East Africa Court of Appeals.[3]

De Sausmarez's illness gave Harrie Wilkinson and his father hope that their dream of Harrie succeeding H.S. Wilkinson as Chief Justice may come true. On April 14, 1908 Harrie telegrammed his father:

"Payuelos Soothsay refonduns after legrimato chylurie rupellary fullstop chymiati ruivaca penurious hostile fullstop inbiechi Jackson"[4]

At the time, most telegrams were sent in code to save costs. One word could replace whole sentences. There were commercial code books that could be used to decipher codes. However, it is not clear if this was a commercial code or private code. In one case in 1902, a telegram from Shanghai to H.S. Wilkinson in Canada could not be deciphered with any of the codebooks in the building.[5]

H.S. Wilkinson decoded the message from his son as:

---

2   Foreign Office List, 1911; Seanad Éireann - Volume 16 - 13 December, 1932, Bourn Vincent Memorial Park Bill, 1932—Second Stage.

3   Entry for Smith Foreign Office List 1920.

4   PRONI D1292 Telegram dated April 14, 1908 Harrie to H.S. Wilkinson.

5   PRONI D1292 (Wilkinson Papers). Note on reverse side of Canadian Pacific Telegraph Company incoming telegraph to Wilkinson dated April 21, 1902.

"It is possible the Chief Justice will not return after leave. I have consulted Sir Pelham Warren. I have not consulted Lauo Kung Mow probably hostile. Please inform Jackson."

It is not clear who "Lauo Kung Mow" was. Perhaps it was a reference to Frederick Bourne who may well have been hostile to Wilkinson being promoted above him.

H.S Wilkinson then immediately wrote a note to Jackson in the Foreign Office passing on the news and saying: "I need not say how grateful I would be for anything you can do to get him the post when it falls vacant. I think that the appointment ought to come to him but without friendly influence he runs a great risk of his claims being overlooked or disregarded."[6]

Harrie Wilkinson may have had a good chance of being promoted. By 1908 he had been in practice close to 20 years. His father had left Shanghai three years earlier and Harrie had now emerged from his father's shadow as competent, respected and "popular Crown Advocate" in his own right. When Wilkinson re-married to Miss Marjorie Dalzell in 1910, the Judges, Registrar's staff and the members of the bar made a special presentation to Wilkinson and his new wife of a large silver salver to commemorate the wedding. The wedding itself was attended by the good and great of Shanghai and followed by a party at the Consulate hosted by Sir Pelham Warren, the Consul-General, who had also given the bride away.[7]

De Sausmarez did not, in fact, retire. He returned to Shanghai in September 1909. The *North China Herald* reported that "notwithstanding the severe operation which he had to undergo at home and the slowness of his recovery, Sir Havilland

....

6   PRONI D1292 (Wilkinson Papers) Note from Wilkinson to Jackson dated April 14, 1908.

7   *North China Herald*, March 11, 1911, p534 (wedding) p566 (presentation); *Social Shanghai* Vol IX,p183 (with picture of wedding party).

de Sausmarez looked in very good health."[8] De Sausmarez remained in good health for many years, putting off Harrie's hopes of becoming Chief Judge for more than a decade.

Sikh Insubordination

Soon after his return de Sausmarez presided, in the full scarlet robes of a criminal judge, over a hearing in the courtroom of the British Supreme Court where in the best de Sausmarez tradition he was able to give a lecture on loyalty and the dangers of avarice.

At the time, the Shanghai Municipal Police faced very serious problems with insubordination by Sikh Police. At the worst, some were committing offences on purpose, so they would be dismissed, thereby allowing them to leave Shanghai to seek their fortune in America. It was decided they must be given a warning. All available Sikh policemen had been ordered to attend. It must have been a very impressive sight to look out over the court from the judge's dais to see a sea of red turbans.[9]

Eight police constables and three prisoner warders were brought into the court by an armed escort and ordered to stand in a line in front of the dock. They were: Narain Singh, P.C. 382, Jhanda, Singh, P.C. 399, Hazara Singh, Warder 71, Bhan Singh, Warder 92, Puran Singh, Warder 101, Phuman Singh, P.C. 320, Jagat Singh, P.O. 225, Huzara Singh, P.C. 106, Amar Singh, P.C. 402, Surain Singh, P.O. 427 and Badan Singh, P.C. 474. They were referred to in the hearing by their badge numbers. The fact they were all surnamed Singh probably made this necessary.

Duncan McNeill, Acting Crown Advocate, appeared for the Crown and Mr Wright appeared for the Municipal Council. De Sausmarez told the men that they had been brought into court because, as British subjects, they had been con-

---

8   *North China Herald*, September 18, 1909, p691.

9   *North China Herald*, October 23, 1909, p185.

victed of offences in Shanghai and they would need to show
cause why they should not be deported back to India.

Captain E.I.M Barrett, who was in charge of the Sikh
Branch of the SMP gave evidence. Barrett's rank in the Police was Assistant Superintendent. He had served in the British Army in the Boer War and in Malaysia rising to the rank
of Captain before joining the SMP. He continued, as was the
practice for retired army officers, to use his army rank. Many
Sikh Police were formerly in the British army and this is perhaps why he was put in charge of the Sikh Branch. Barrett,
who was eventually to rise to become Commissioner of Police, was a fine sportsman who had played county cricket for
Hampshire and on leave in 1912 resumed playing for them,
scoring at least three centuries.[10] He also had one cap for England in football.

Barrett gave evidence as to each of the offences committed
by the constables and warders. With regard to Narain Singh
he said:

"P. C. 382. Joined the Force on July 16, 1907. Enlisted
in India. He was punished on July 11 this year for being drunk, creating a disturbance and behaving in an
indecent manner in barracks, and for this he was fined
$5. On August 18 he was fined $1 for idling and gossip-
ing on duty. On October 6 he was drunk and assaulted
a sergeant and he is now undergoing sentence for that.
This man asked for permission to resign lately, but this
was prior to his conviction. When brought before me
on October 6 he was extremely insubordinate in my
office."

All the others had committed similar offences, such as being absent from duty or failing to obey an order. The maxi-

10 *The Singapore Free Press and Mercantile Advertiser*, 4 September 1912, p12.

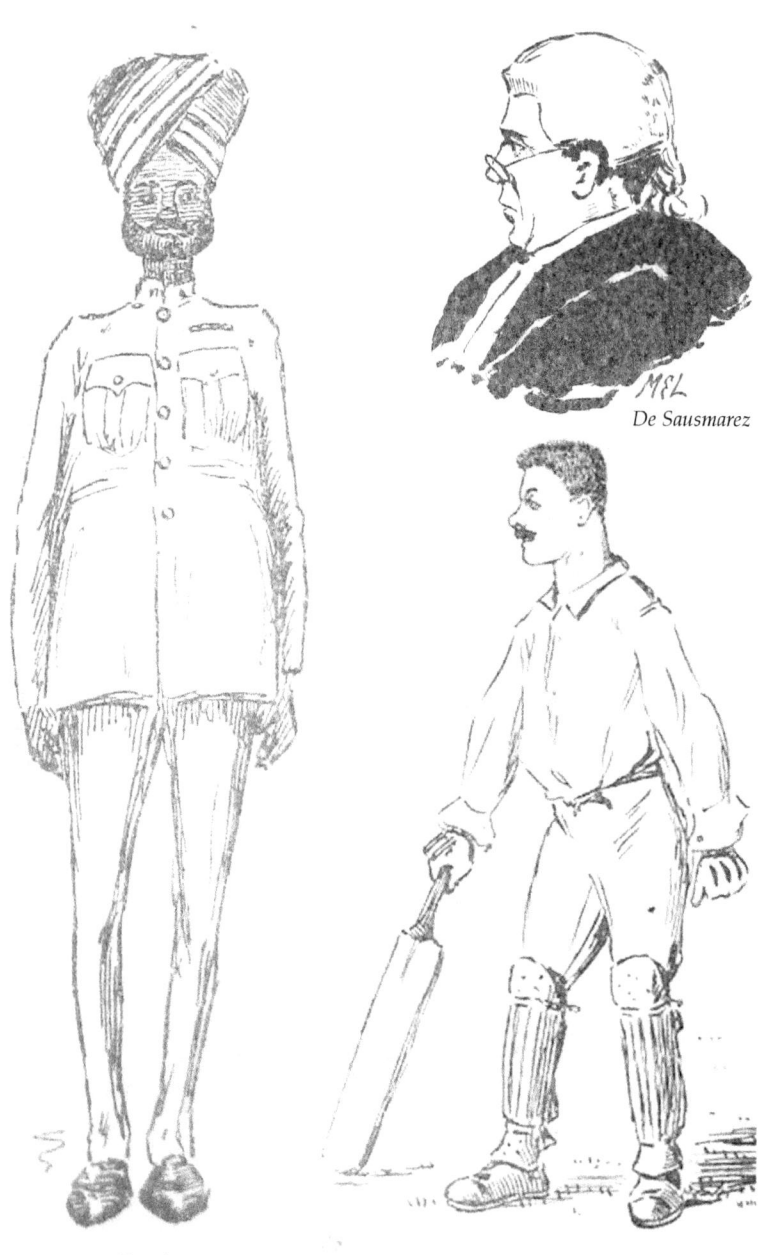

De Sausmarez

Sikh Policeman

Capt Barrett

mum fine had been $10 and some had been ordered to serve up to two weeks imprisonment. These fines were substantial. Sikh policemen were only paid $16 per month which Barrett had reduced to $13 by deducting $3 per month to pay for their passage back to India at the end of the contract or as a fine if they left early. The sum of $16 was, however, about double what they would make as a soldier in the British Indian Army. Jhanda Singh specifically complained to de Sausmarez that a fine of $10 meant that they had nothing left to buy food for the month and that when he had served in the army, the fine for being drunk was only 10 or 20 cents.

Barrett said that he believed that almost all the offences were committed with an intention to get out of the police force and go to America. He said that many Sikhs were coming through Shanghai on the way to or back from America and telling them it was the Promised Land. Barrett said that over 300 Sikhs had left Shanghai in the previous two weeks. He said they would be told "you are a lot of fools to stop here for $20 a month when you can get G$2 a day in America." G$ referred to the now gold-backed United States Dollar.

De Sausmarez asked each of the men if they had anything to say. After hearing them and questioning Capt. Barrett further, de Sausmarez decided that six of them should be ordered to be deported unless they could come up with $500 as security, an astronomical sum on the salaries they were receiving. He also asked Capt. Barrett to ensure that the authorities in India were informed of the reasons for their deportation.

Ordering the Defendants and all the other Sikhs in the court to stand to attention, he delivered a homily on duty, character and avarice as only de Sausmarez could:

> "What I have got to say to the prisoners has to do with all you Sikhs who are serving here as well. You men have neglected your duties as policemen and you have disgraced your character as Sikhs. Now what a man's

character is worth depends a great deal upon the community he lives in, and when I see many Sikhs such as you behaving in the way you have done and disregarding your good character I come to the conclusion that the Sikh community here is not as self-respecting as it ought to be. You have, come here, most of you – all those who have come here in the police – to do your duty as policemen. You are liberally paid you get twice as much as a Sepoy in India when you join the force, and you are well cared for when you are here. You chose, because you think that there is a little more money to be made, to go off to America and to disregard your honour and your word. That is a thing that cannot he tolerated, and not only that but I am not, going, if I ever get a chance of stopping it, to tolerate anyone tempting others to leave the force here and go away to America or anywhere else."

Con(fused) profession?

Noel Home, Plaintiff

The next year De Sausmarez tried a case that challenged the entire way in which British lawyers practiced before the recently renamed British Supreme Court for China.

As we have seen, from the foundation of the Supreme Court, barristers and solicitors practiced as they saw fit. Barristers practiced as solicitors and solicitors as barristers. All lawyers could form partnerships with each other. Effectively, to use modern day terminology, the professions were fused even though they had never been fused in England, where barristers were only allowed to practice as advocates before the courts after being instructed by a solicitor. In English practice, barristers were also prohibited from forming partnerships or employing assistants.

British barrister, Noel Home, who had left his partnership with John Douglas, challenged the legality of this practice. Douglas had sued Home for breach of a non-compete clause. Home had left Shanghai to return to England in 1908 soon after his and Douglas' success against the *North China Herald* on behalf of Bethell. Douglas paid him 12,000 taels to buy out the partnership and Home agreed not to practice as a barrister in Shanghai for five years, that is, up until August 11, 1913. Home found it tough going at home. He believed this was partly to do with issues that had arisen in his practice with Douglas. In 1911, he returned to Shanghai to investigate matters. He then decided to restart his practice before his five-year non-compete clause expired. Douglas sued him to enforce the agreement.

Douglas was represented by Vernon Drummond and Henry Oppe. Drummond had been forced out of retirement by the massive crash in the price of rubber shares in 1910. He was the founder and president of one large rubber company in Perak. Presumably, when the share prices collapsed, much of his wealth disappeared. Home represented himself.[11]

Home's defence was simple: the non-compete agreement was illegal. He argued that a partnership between barristers was illegal in England and therefore a contract to dissolve a partnership between barristers was equally illegal. The Supreme Court for China had to apply English Law, and under English law an illegal contract could not be enforced. As a backstop, Home also made certain allegations about the way in which Douglas carried out his practice that entitled him to

11 *Douglas v Home*, North China Herald, January 13, 1912, p130 (First Instance); *Home v Douglas*, North China Herald, December 7, 1912, p660 (Privy Council). Profile of Drummond, *Twentieth Century Impressions of Hong Kong and Shanghai*, p516.

avoid the agreement.

On the face of it, Home's defence was a powerful one, and also one that, if correct, would affect every British legal practitioner in Shanghai. Since the consular courts had been set up in China, barristers had practiced in partnership both with other barristers and with solicitors. Perhaps the only exception was the Crown Advocate who, in order to avoid conflicts of interest, practiced on his own account. If the court found the practice illegal, possibly every British lawyer in Shanghai had been breaking the law. They would not be able to enforce fee agreements and clients could potentially sue them for fees they had paid.

A judgment that the barristers practicing in partnership was illegal would be a big decision. Strangely, fusion of the profession had never been codified in any of the Orders in Council. De Sausmarez, therefore, had to consider in detail the practice of barristers and solicitors before the court in Shanghai based on his personal knowledge. He added that to guard himself against error he had consulted with the Crown Advocate, Harrie Wilkinson, and shown his draft judgment to Frederick Bourne, the Assistant Judge. He said Bourne agreed generally with it.

De Sausmarez found that the court had long recognized partnerships between solicitors and barristers and between barristers and barristers. "Barristers come to China to join these firms on salaries and on agreements in the same way as do solicitors." All those admitted before the courts in Shanghai had practiced as barristers and solicitors. He described their practice in the following way:

"They have in non-contentious matters managed business as solicitors and given advice as barristers, and in contentious matters they, have acted as solicitors in preparing cases for trial, and in the same matter the same practitioners, whether originally a barrister or solicitor, has had right of audience in Court and has conducted the case up to judgement. A 'legal practitioner' of this Court acts and has always acted as a solicitor with full right of audience in Court, and when conducting a case in Court has had the privileges of a barrister conducting a case in Court in England, and is expected to undertake the responsibilities of a barrister."

The new Order in Council had codified the practice of admission somewhat by setting out qualifications for admission. There was no distinction in these rules or any other rules between barristers and solicitors. De Sausmarez concluded:

"Such being the position of the parties is there any reason why the Court should not entertain an action between them arising out of a contract to dissolve partnership? An English Court would entertain such an action in the case of two solicitors, such a contract between two barristers in England is impossible. I can see no reason why such a contract being not only possible but usual between legal practitioners of this Court, the Court should not enforce it."

De Sausmarez also dismissed Home's other grounds which related the handling of certain transactions and one advertisement that had described "Douglas and Home" as solicitors. The latter had been wrong but had not been published by Douglas.

One of Home's allegations did require more detailed consideration by de Sausmarez. This was the payment of a percentage of fees by Douglas to his British clerk. De Sausmarez said that it was "not an entirely satisfactory arrangement." It was well known that Chinese interpreters took secret commissions. In this case, because the clerk was British and subject to the English criminal law, he was most likely not doing so. However, de Sausmarez held that a professional man should do all he can to guard against "this reprehensible practice."

Douglas was granted an injunction against Home and awarded his costs. Home appealed to the Privy Council which upheld de Sausmarez's decision, stating it was a plain a case as there could possibly be. Barristers were allowed to practice in partnership in Shanghai. They therefore could also enter into agreements not to practice for a certain amount of time. The other issues were no excuse for breaking the agreement. Home's appeal was dismissed with costs.

Douglas had, rightly, prevailed in this case. Soon, he was to win another case before Frederick Bourne that was to leave a sour taste in Bourne's mouth.

CHAPTER 37

The Law of the Land

JUST BEFORE THE END of the Qing Dynasty, Frederick Bourne and Rufus Thayer had to deal with complex cases involving perjury, and land law both of which showed the complexities arising from conflicts of laws and practice that inevitably occurred in an extraterritorial jurisdiction where the law of one land was applied in the other.

Perjury by Shekury

In 1910, there had been massive speculation in rubber shares on the Stock Exchange in Shanghai. This ended in a massive crash. We have already seen the dressing-down that de Sausmarez gave to Mr Craig for giving in to greed.[1]

One case that came before Thayer in the United States Court showed that greed in Shanghai knew no bounds. In what was a relatively simple case, Mr Gabriel Shekury, a broker and a member of the Shanghai Stock Exchange, claimed 28,000 taels from a Mr F.M. Brooks for whom he had bought shares. After the collapse in share prices Brooks had not paid Shekury.[2]

Stirling Fessenden together with Mr G.H. Wright represented Shekury. William Fleming defended Brooks. Brooks' defence was that he had been margin trading. His agreement with Shekury was not that he would buy the shares but that he would only maintain sufficient funds to pay a margin reflecting the value of the shares on the market and what had

1 See Chapter 31.
2 *Shekury v Brooks*, *North China Herald*, December 23, 1910, p736.

been paid for them. This, he argued, was a gambling contract and unenforceable.

Thayer had no difficulty accepting Brooks version of events. He said:

"Such purpose was entirely consistent with the wild speculation in rubber shares which at that time widely prevailed in Shanghai and which, as the testimony shows, affected all classes of people. Dealing in rubber shares had developed into a mania which infected both brokers and people and furnished little suggestion that many of the participants had any thought of making actual investments."

He also noted that Shekury had come out of retirement to join the mania. There could be no doubt Shekury knew the nature of the transaction. On this basis, Thayer held that the majority of the contracts were voidable by either party as gambling contracts. He found that Brooks was not liable except for two contracts that appeared to have been normal contracts for the sale and purchase of shares. Thayer granted Shekury judgment on these contracts for 2,800 taels plus costs.

Shekury must have suffered great losses in the crash or have been even greedier than all those who had been caught up in the mania of the boom. It turned out that, in at least one case, he had never bought the shares that he had sued Brooks for the price of. He had, effectively, shorted the market. Of course, you can only make money on a short if you get paid, so Shekury sued Brooks and lied in court that he had bought the shares.

Once the fact Shekury had given false testimony was discovered, Harrie Wilkinson filed a criminal case in the British Supreme Court against Shekury for perverting the course of justice. The case came before Bourne, as Acting Judge, while John Douglas, defended Shekury.

Extraterritoriality came to Shekury's rescue. Douglas filed a demurrer that it was not an offence in England to pervert the course of justice of a foreign court. It was only an offence to pervert the course of justice of a British court.[3]

Bourne was forced to agree, holding:

"Now the offence here is that of perverting the course of justice administered by the United States Court. That offence cannot be committed in England because a United States Court cannot sit there; and if committed outside the Realm, it is not by the Common Law justiciable in England."

In England, the question of committing perjury in a foreign court would not arise. British courts had jurisdiction over all those in the territory of Britain. Similarly, if Shekury had given evidence in America, a court there would have had jurisdiction over him. In extraterritorial China, the situation was different. Try as he might, Bourne could not find a legal provision that would allow him to punish Shekury. He was forced, very reluctantly, to discharge him. He concluded:

"I regret the result not only because it leaves one of the meanest, and from the point of view of the administration of justice one of the most injurious, of crimes unpunishable, but because it may appear to savour of discourtesy to the United States Court, the authority of which it is our duty and pleasure to support."

He suggested the Order in Council would need to be amended to remedy this.

Wilkinson also added that the Order in Council gave no right of appeal to the Crown in a case such as this and he

3 *R v Shekury, North China Herald*, November 4, 1911, p314.

"wanted the public and the U. S. Court to understand that his hands were tied in the matter."

Douglas then decided to try his luck and try to get his costs. This led to the following exchange where Bourne made his distaste for Shekury and the decision he had been forced to give very clear.

Douglas: My client has been put to the trouble of defending the case, and the circumstances do not leave it altogether in a satisfactory position for Mr Shekury.
Bourne: I think it is highly satisfactory for him.
Douglas: I would like to know whether any application on his behalf for costs would be entertained.
Bourne: That is out of the question.

This obviously unsatisfactory state of affairs was remedied three years later by an amendment to the Order in Council making it an offence for a British subject to commit perjury or do any act in a Chinese or foreign court in China that would be an offence in a British Court.[4]

The corrupt Tipaos

Issues around land law could not be resolved so easily. The ownership of land created a special problem in China: What law should be applied to a case involving land; the law of the defendant's country or the law of China?

This question was even more complex in the international settlements where Chinese were not allowed to own land held under consular title deeds. This problem was overcome by having a foreigner hold the land on trust for a Chinese landowner. Chinese would even seek to have land they already owned registered with a consular title, because it gave greater security of tenure and accordingly increased its value.

----

4   China (Amendment) Order in Council 1913, ss.4 and 5.

They would transfer the land to a foreigner and then get a trust deed back.

In a case just before the end of the Qing Dynasty, Thayer had to deal with the difficult and vexed question of who owned land registered under a US Consular title deed that had been fraudulently taken from its Chinese owners with the assistance of a corrupt "Tipao." In order to understand the issues Thayer faced and who a "Tipao" was, it is best to backtrack to two cases involving Frederick Bourne some years before.

Land law was an area of expertise for Bourne. When he had first been appointed Judge in 1898 he had also been appointed Consul in charge of the Land Office and had served in that position until 1901. Because of this, in one case in the late 1900s he gave an expert deposition on the process by which British citizens and other foreigners could acquire title to land in China.[5] Bourne described two systems for acquiring title. In certain concessions, such as Shameen Island in Canton, the Chinese government had leased the entire concession to the British Government, which then sub-let to tenants. However, in most concessions this had not been done and land was acquired under native title deeds. In order to give security of title to British, "who were authorised under the Treaty to lease land for certain purposes" a system of registration of title was established. In Shanghai, a formal set of instructions had been drafted covering how to register title. Bourne said, however: "Originally there was no instruction. It grew up. The Consul had to exercise his functions of protecting British property as best he could. He did it sometimes in a rather extraordinary way."

The system in Shanghai was that the British applicant for registration would bring in his native title deeds, or fangtan, to the British Consulate. The fangtan deeds were elementary

title deeds that replaced deeds destroyed in the Taiping Rebellion in the 1850s. The fangtan deeds would then be sent to
the Land Deputy of the Chinese Land Office, part of the Taotai's administration. There had also previously been another
land office, the Shengko office, which by the early 20th century was amalgamated with the Taotai's land office. The Land
Deputy would then appoint a date for meeting on the land
with the local Tipao, or if the land abutted different districts,
the local Tipaos. A Tipao was a lower level official chosen an-
nually "from amongst the people. He is generally of what we
should call the middle class, who is living in the particular
lot." Generally, his family will have been living in the area for
some time. It is the Tipao's "duty to know everybody's property and what everybody is doing as far as possible."

The Tipao took responsibility for ensuring the measurements, boundaries and ownership of the land. If the land
abutted another piece of land registered to a foreigner, the
Tipao would not involve himself with this because, as Bourne
put it, "he regards the foreigner as a different sort of being
with whom he is not concerned." Instead, a deputy from the
British Land Office would go to check the measurements. In
order to ensure that he does his job properly, the Tipao was
required to give a bond. Bourne commented that if he did not
do his job properly, "he used to be bambooed, but they have
gone beyond that now."

Anybody else with an interest in the land was allowed to
attend the meeting. The Deputy would then conduct an investigation through the Tipao as to whether the seller had the
right to sell and whether there were any rights over creeks
or roads. Then, the Deputy would report to the Taotai who
would write directly to the British Land Registry enclosing
two sealed copies of the title deed. A plan of the land would
also be sent, which would be traced, reproduced, agreed and
signed. The Vice-Consul dealing with the registration "looks
upon himself practically as counsel" for the British purchas-

er and "endeavours to protect his interest." If he is not satisfied with what the Chinese Land Office says, for example
that there is a right of way, he may write that he has been
informed there is no right of way. There would often be long
correspondence before the title deed came out.

When the title deed did come out, Bourne said, "we regard it as an indefeasible title from the Chinese government;
that, the Chinese Government has cancelled the native title of
the Chinese seller and has given out to the British subject who
bought the land, another title, in a different form altogether,
known as the Taotai's deed." Bourne explained that by issuing this deed, "the Chinese Government being the Supreme
Power has destroyed all other titles to that land and given a
new title in a new form to the British subject."

If British subjects then agreed between themselves to a
right of way over the land, this would be noted in the Consulate records without reference to the Taotai.

Other consulates registered lands for their citizens in
much the same way. If the land registered with the British
Consulate was sold to another foreigner, the owner's and the
office copy of the title deeds would be sent to that person's
consulate. The old Chinese title deeds would remain with the
British Consulate but be open to inspection.

Bourne was quite proud of the system, which he said had
originated from a "running fight" for years between "the Vice-
Consul, the Taotai, the Land Deputy, the Lawyers and the
Land Agents." The result, he said, "was that a very ingenious
system of registering land had evolved." While conceding
that the area was relatively small, he added that the system
depends "on the excellent cadastral survey which the Council
has made and is always improving." He concluded, proudly,
"I believe a better system exists nowhere in the world. One
can transfer land here as readily as Consols in London."

The question remained, however, as to which law applied
to this particular title. George French had decided that Chi-

nese law applied to leased land in the *Wushishan* case. But later in 1899 Nicholas Hannen in the case of *Hanson v Watson* ruled that English land law should apply to land leased from the Chinese authorities in Shanghai (or apply the law of the forum, called in Latin, *Lex Fori*).[6]

Soon after stepping down as Consul in charge of the land office, Bourne decided a case *McDonald v Anderson* involving land in Tientsin which the *North China Herald* described as "a landmark in the history of the Law administered by the British Courts in China."[7] Bourne decided that Chinese land law applied to all transactions in land in China and the British courts should apply Chinese land law (or apply the law of the location, called in Latin, *Lex Loci*). Bourne wrote a long and extremely well reasoned judgment to show that *Hanson v Watson* had been decided wrongly. Legally he pointed out that "to apply the law of English realty to land under the sovereignty of China is to disregard the distinction between the real and personal statutes — a fundamental principle of Private International Law," and the legislation could only overthrow this with "irresistible clearness." Practically, it produced absurd results. Land owned by British in Tientsin (and Shanghai) often abutted land owned by Germans, French and other citizens of treaty powers. If the laws of each country applied, then different land laws could apply to the same land, particularly in claims of adverse possession where German land law required 30 years possession but British only 12.

Bourne said that despite all this he should bound by Hannen's decision in *Hanson v Watson*, having been made by the Chief Justice. Bourne, however, was not going to let things go there. He found a higher authority in a recent decision of the Privy Council from Zanzibar that held that the *Lex Situs* (another term for *Lex Loci*) applied in extraterritorial courts

---

6 *Hanson v Watson*, North China Herald, June 12, 1899, p1078.

7 *McDonald v Anderson*, North China Herald, February 5, 1904, p247 and Late News Supplement (editorial).

there.[8] The only difference between the cases was that in Zanzibar there was a written land code, whereas matters "in China are thrown back on a very few written rules — the Penal code — the greater part of which cannot be applied to a Christian community—upon local customs and upon the Judge's conscience." But he emphasized, that this "is not a legal reason for applying the English feudal tenures to land in China." He therefore decided that Chinese land law was to be applied to the case.

The question then became, where to find Chinese land law? In a final paragraph to the decision, he set out that Chinese land law was made up of local customs that would need to be proved by evidence. Where there was no clear rule, a Chinese judge was required to apply "good conscience," and he suggested a British judge should apply civil law from continental codes and text writers. He added that: "If a land law so derived is thought too uncertain to support the large foreign commercial interests now in China" then "the Land Regulations would need to be amended."

The *North China Herald* praised Bourne's decision while noting that it removed the security of tenure British had felt to date in their land, the questions of land law now to be decided by Chinese Custom and that the "familiar figure of the oldest inhabitant will doubtless amuse the Courts with his personal narrative of what he remembers of local custom." However, the newspaper said Bourne was bound to decide the law as he found it and leave it to the authorities to remedy any problems if necessary.

In the case before Thayer, Mr Barchett, who had recently died, held U.S. Lot No. 1102 in his name. However, he had in fact received the land from a person named Hsu Pei Chi to hold on trust. Another Chinese, Koh Chee Wen also known as Koh Kwei Foh, challenged the title arguing that the property

---

8   *Secretary of State for Foreign Affairs v Charlesworth Piling & Co* [1901] AC 373.

was his. The executrix of Barchett's estate admitted the land was held on trust and stood neutral.[9]

Koh relied on a judgment of the Mixed Court that had found in his favour. The Mixed Court had ruled:

> "He never sold his property to anybody and did not know how the plaintiff registered it as a U. S. Lot and obtained the title deed. He found that some unlawful tipao, Chow Wen Pang, Pah Chi Tzen and Hsu Lu Yai, had intrigued one Hsu Pei Chi to deceive the authority and have the land in question shenkoed in Hsu's name. This land was apparently stolen and sold by them."

Koh sought a declaration from the US Court that the land belonged to him.

Thayer found that the land belonged to Koh because he could produce the fangtan title deeds and the tax receipts for the land. He also accepted that the judgment of the Mixed Court between the two Chinese parties was binding and ordered the land be transferred. Hsu Pei Chi had by then transferred his interest in the trust to a Woo Zung Seng.

Woo was not satisfied by the decision and instructed Shanghai's two leading American lawyers, Thomas Jernigan and Stirling Fessenden. Koh was represented by another leading lawyer, William Fleming. Jernigan and Fessenden filed a petition to have Thayer's judgment set aside on the basis that as it was a dispute between two Chinese and, therefore, the US Court had no jurisdiction. Secondly, they argued that the Mixed Court was below the Taotai in the Chinese hierarchy. The Taotai was also a judicial officer. The Mixed Court could not, therefore, make a decision contradictory to what was shown on the Taotai's deeds.

....

9   *In Re SP Barchet's Estate*, Lobingier, Extraterritorial Cases, Vol 1, P235. See also *In the Mattter of the Estate of SP Barchett (Deceased) (in Probate), North China Herald*, April 22, 1920, p219 for a report of the first hearing.

Thayer accepted on the basis of the decision in *McDonald v Anderson* that Chinese law must be applied to questions of land law. He agreed the US Court had no jurisdiction and granted the petition to set aside his earlier judgment. He noted that the Mixed Court themselves had held that:

> "In the settlement the title deed is a good and sufficient proof as to the ownership of any lot. It could not be cancelled at anytime. Otherwise, the foreign land owners in the settlement would create a serious diplomatic dispute."

He said that this must mean the Mixed Court had recognized that it had no power to enter any judgment that affected the integrity of the Taotai's deed.

All very well, but what was Thayer and the executrix to do? Thayer did the best he could in the circumstances. In order to get the land out of the executrix's hands, he ordered that the title be transferred to a third party nominated by the parties. He then ordered the parties to submit a full statement of the case to the US Consul-General with a request that he submit it to the Taotai for appropriate action.

There is no record of whether this was done. Revolution was just around the corner and the Taotai would only be in office for a few more months before the founding of the Republic of China and the abolition of the office of Taotai.

PART NINE

REVOLUTION AND WAR
(1911 TO 1920)

CHAPTER 38

The Republican Revolution

THE QING DYNASTY ended very much with a whimper. The reforms that had been introduced following the Boxer Rebellion had weakened the power of the central government substantially. Yuan Shikai controlled the strongest army in the country, the Beiyang army, and Sun Yat-sen, from his base in Canton, was travelling the world looking to raise funds for a revolution.

Numerous small-scale uprisings occurred around the country, with the largest at Hankow in mid-1911. Yuan Shikai, who had returned home nominally on sick leave, was prevailed upon to return to office and put down the revolt. After one battle where he soundly beat the revolutionaries, he changed sides to support them. He then convinced the Emperor to abdicate with promises of security for the Imperial families.

Other Manchus were not so lucky. In many cities, the Manchu Garrisons fought to maintain Qing rule and in some, such as Nanking, they were overwhelmed and killed by the Chinese. When the Qing finally fell, many Manchus were massacred around the country.[1]

The Republic of China was declared on January 1, 1912 and Sun Yat-Sen was appointed Provisional President. He only served in the role for three weeks before yielding to Yuan Shikai and his greater military power. Sun was appointed the

---

1 Massacre by Manchus in Nanking: *New York Times,*, November 11, 1911; Massacre of Manchus in Hankow, *New York Times*, October 14, 1911.

The National Review welcomes the rise of Yuan Shikai.

Minister for Railways and set about a program to build large numbers of railway lines around the country. Initially, democratic elections were held for a parliament. Yuan however, by a series of maneuvers including the assassination of the Nationalist Prime Minister at the Shanghai Railway Station in 1913, aggregated power in his hands.

Yuan served as President until 1916 when he made himself Emperor, although he was not coronated. This was the last straw for many of his supporters who still believed in a republic. Yuan only served as Emperor for three weeks before abdicating. He died soon after of renal failure.

Due to Yuan's machinations, Sun's Nationalist Party, or the Kuomintang as it is often referred to, split with the central government and formed their own government in Canton, which existed as a separate government through to 1927. The government in Peking remained the recognized government of the China but held little power over large parts of the country. Many provinces were ruled by warlords who fought for control of different areas of the country. It was not until 1927 that a unified government under the Nationalist Party was formed. The intervening 15 years gave foreigners large freedom to exercise and extend their extraterritorial rights.

The Revolution and the treaties
The Revolution brought before both British and US courts the important issue of whether the treaties granting extraterritoriality were still in force.

During the Revolution, foreigners were on high alert for attacks. On Shameen Island in Canton, Indian troops built sand-bagged defensive lines and were readied to fight. One of these soldiers, Ibrahim, an Afghani soldier serving in the 126th Regiment of Baluchistan Infantry shot and killed his superior officer. His immediate superior, the Subadar, had disciplined him for gambling and had confiscated his money. Ibrahim got his gun and killed the Subadar. The commanding officer of the unit, Major Barrett, was called. He arrived 10 to 15 minutes later. He went up to Ibrahim and asked him: "Why have you done such a senseless act?" Barrett's told the court later that he said nothing else; did not threaten him in any way. Barrett said that when he spoke to Ibrahim, he was sorry for him because he had killed the Subadar. Ibrahim replied: "Some three or four days he has been abusing me; without a doubt I killed him."[2]

---

2   *R v Ibrahim* 1913 HKLR 1; [1914]. A.C. 599; Major Barrett does not appear to have been a relation of Capt Barrett of the SMP.

A soldier of a Baluchi regiment

The British Consul in Canton considered it would be better for the case to be tried in Hong Kong. This was presumably because of the unstable situation in Canton at the time and because all the witnesses were in the British army. There would be no problem with compelling their attendance to give evidence. The 1904 Order in Council allowed for trials to be conducted either in Hong Kong or in Mandalay, Burma, provided the Judge of the Supreme Court for China agreed.[3] Havilland De Sausmarez signed a warrant transferring the case to the Supreme Court of Hong Kong.

Ibrahim's first trial was aborted when the jury could not reach a verdict. He was convicted after a second trial. The case ended up in the Privy Council and remains a leading decision on the question of voluntariness of a confession to a person in a position of authority. Both courts considered that the confession was voluntary and the Privy Council in particular considered the way in which Barrett put his question did not convey a command or inducement to Ibrahim of any kind, but rather, in truth, was "an exclamation of dismay on the part of a humane offi-

---

3   S.50, China and Corea Order in Council, 1904.

cer, alike concerned for the position of the accused, the fate of the deceased, and the credit of the regiment and the service."

The case, also, despite being a decision of the Supreme Court of Hong Kong, became a leading decision on the scope of the extraterritorial powers of the Supreme Court for China. At the trial, the Chief Justice of Hong Kong, William Rees-Davies had reserved questions of law to the Hong Kong Full Court (then like the Shanghai court made up of two judges). The questions were whether the court had jurisdiction to try Ibrahim even though he was not British and, more interestingly, whether the treaties giving extraterritorial rights were still in force? Ibrahim's counsel argued that the treaties were no longer valid following the Republican Revolution.

With regard to the first point, the Hong Kong Supreme Court and Privy Council accepted that Ibrahim as an Afghani was an alien. However, by enlisting in the Indian army, he was subject to British military law while in Shameen. The British army required service, loyalty and allegiance from its soldiers. In return, it extends to all soldiers the protection of the army. Ibrahim "enjoyed His Majesty's protection in China" and was therefore "a British protected person" subject to the jurisdiction of the Supreme Court for China.

With regard to the Republican Revolution, the Hong Kong Supreme Court took a relatively easy way out, holding that the onus was not on the prosecution to prove the validity of the treaties. No evidence had been put in to show the treaties were not valid, and thus the court would presume they were. Chief Justice Rees-Davies added that as a practical matter, the onus could not be on the Crown to prove the validity of treaties in every case saying this would be a "course pregnant with difficulty and inconvenience."

The second member of the Hong Kong Full Court, Henry Gompertz agreed in full with Rees-Davies. He added that in any event, there was no suggestion the new Chinese Government did not accept the treaties were valid:

"Treaty or no Treaty, the evidence is that the British Consular officials do assert jurisdiction at Canton over British subjects, including soldiers of the Indian Army, without apparently question or protest, from the Chinese Government."

The same issue was raised in the United States Court for China in Shanghai in the prosecution of a Mr J.F. Jordan. In that case, Jordan's counsel argued that because the Emperor had abdicated and the United States had not recognized a new government, there were no treaties that the court could rely upon to exercise jurisdiction.[4] Thayer, in fact, did not have to answer the question. Jordan jumped bail and fled China. Thayer nevertheless, considered it proper to issue a decision on the point so as to put the matter to rest for once and for all.

His first answer was that the question was a political question to be answered by the executive and not a legal one to be answered by the court. He said:

"In answer to this contention it would be quite sufficient to say that it raises questions of fact of which this Court can take no judicial notice. The making and termination of treaties and the recognition of new governments belong to the political department of the government.
"It is a well established doctrine that until the recognition of a new government by the political department, courts of justice are bound to consider the former state of things as remaining unaltered."

Despite this, he then cited a British authority on interna-

....

4   *United States v JF Jordan*, Lobingier, Extraterritorial Cases, p259.

tional law, Sir Sherston Baker, who had written that international law provided that following a revolution the state took on all the debts and obligations of the previous states. Therefore, whatever, the form of government in China at the time the treaties were still in effect.

Nevertheless, at least one American lawyer practicing in Shanghai, Mr Frost, thought that the end of the Qing Dynasty would mean the end of extraterritoriality. In 1912, in a letter to a former fraternity brother he wrote, "the revolutionists had left no court to practice in."[5]

In fact, the collapse of the Qing Dynasty meant the Shanghai Municipal Council was able to take control of the International Mixed Court. From 1911, the council employed the Chinese magistrates directly. This gave foreigners control of the court and greatly increased the power of the consular assessors.

While the United States Court and the British Supreme Court did not disappear with the Republican Revolution both of them saw some major changes after the Republic of China was established.

---

5 College and Commonwealth, and Other Educational Papers and Addresses, p336.

CHAPTER 39

New Roles and New Faces

Shanghai judges go to Hong Kong

At the beginning of 1913, British judges in Shanghai were given a new role, that of appeal judges in Hong Kong. At the time, the Hong Kong Supreme Court had only two judges, the Chief Justice and a Puisne Judge. Appeals from the decisions of the Puisne Judge or Chief Justice would be heard by the Chief Justice or the Chief Justice sitting with the Puisne Judge with an appeal to the Privy Council. Just as in Shanghai, this was unsatisfactory, particularly in relation to the Chief Justice reviewing his own decisions. The performance of Sir Francis Piggott (who was a noted expert on extraterritoriality) as Chief Justice of Hong Kong had been heavily criticized by both officials and lawyers. This included comments to the effect that "it was a matter of common knowledge that if a client wished to win his case it was advisable for him to engage a particular Solicitor, and a particular Counsel both of whom were favoured by the Chief Justice."[1]

In 1912, proposals were made to create a Full Court of three judges to hear appeals. By an agreement between the Foreign Office and Colonial Office, it was agreed that the Judge of the Supreme Court for China would sit on the Hong Kong Full Court.

This proposal was not welcomed in the Hong Kong business community on the basis that the appointment of a third

---

1 P. Wesley-Smith, "Sir Francis Piggott, Chief Justice of His Own Cause" 12 Hong Kong LJ 260, p276-7.

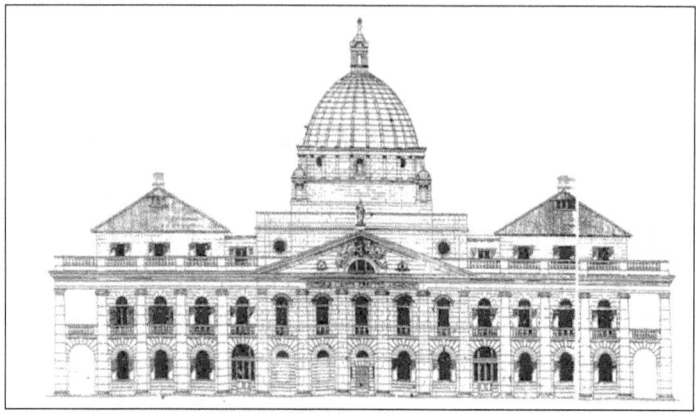

The Supreme Court of Hong Kong.
From 1913 Shanghai judges sat on the Full Court

full time judge would be much preferred compared to a judge from Shanghai visiting for 15 days every six months. The extraterritorial nature of a Shanghai judge's experience was also noted. Mr Osborne in the Legislative Council debate said:

> "Then, again, what are the qualifications of a Shanghai judge to sit in the Courts of Hongkong? Litigation in Hongkong is mostly between Chinese; cases where Chinese customs and Chinese methods of accounting are frequently involved; intricate cases which for their disentanglement may need a comprehensive knowledge of local Chinese custom and character. The jurisdiction of the Shanghai judge on the other hand is confined entirely to British subjects or where British subjects are defendants, and I submit that it is open to question whether a judge whose experience is thus limited is qualified to sit for two short periods a year upon the Bench of Hong Kong."[2]

Others in the Legislative Council also opposed the propos-

2   Hong Kong Legislative Council Debate, 6 June 1912, p49.

al, so much so that the Acting Governor adjourned the debate for the views of the Council to be passed to the Colonial Office. To no avail, it seems, as the new law was nevertheless passed. The first sitting of the Full Court was on January 2, 1913. Initially, the position of President was assigned to the judge with the greatest seniority. Sir Francis Piggott, had only recently left the bench and been replaced by William Rees-Davies. This made Havilland de Sausmarez the most senior judge. He therefore presided over the first hearing of the Hong Kong Full Court and served as President until his retirement in 1920. From then until 1941 the Judge or Acting Judge of the Supreme Court for China was entitled to sit on the Full Court of Hong Kong and until the mid-1930s when Hong Kong did appoint a third full time judge, judges from Shanghai regularly travelled to Hong Kong to sit on the Full Court.[3]

Thayer resigns

Changes were also occurring in the United States Court for China. Judge Rufus Thayer resigned under a cloud after George Curtis, a Shanghai attorney, brought complaints against him to the US Congress. The main complaints were that Thayer had been away from Shanghai for many months but certified he was in China and that he had abused his expense account for trips to Canton and Hong Kong.[4] There was probably an element of truth in the charges of being absent from office. Thayer's wife had left Shanghai in 1911, not being able to withstand the climate. Thayer was very often not

---

3 "The New Full Court: Welcome to Shanghai's Judge", *China Mail* January 2, 1913, p6. After de Sausmarez retired, other judges of the Supreme Court for China, Sir Skinner Turner, Sir Peter Grain, Penrhyn Grant Jones and Sir Allan Mossop also travelled from Shanghai to Hong Kong to sit on the Hong Kong Full Court. For cases where Shanghai judges sat, see, for example, *Ho Tsz Tsun v Ho Au Shi* 1915 HKLR 69 (de Sausmarez); *Fong Yeung Chau v Wong Lan Sang* 1920 HKLR 49 (Skinner Turner); *Chung Cheung She v The Sze Yap SS Company Ltd* 1932 HKLR 77 (Peter Grain); *Au Wing Ki & anor v Chu Yun Chi*, 1934 HKLR 66 (Grant Jones); *American Mail Line v East Asiatic Co. Hong Kong Daily Press,* 16 Nov 1935 and *South China Morning Post*, December 10, 1935 (Allan Mossop) (Mossop Law Reports).

4 *Lowell Sun*, 17 September 1913, p8.

in Shanghai.

Rather than face an investigation, Thayer resigned with effect from December 31, 1913. In mid-November, a private ceremony attended by most members of the American Bar was held in the Judge's chambers where the members of the bar presented Thayer with a silver tray. This was followed by a reception which Frederick Bourne as Acting Judge and W.C. Platt as Acting Crown Advocate also attended. Frank Hinckley, now District Attorney, and Bourne both made speeches farewelling Thayer, who responded in kind. He left a few days later on the PMS *Mongolia*. He died suddenly of apoplexy four years later in 1917 in Kingston, New York.[5]

Charles Lobingier: America's Edmund Hornby

The new judge appointed to the US court was Charles Lob-

Charles Lobingier

5 *North China Herald,* 15 November 1913, p484 (farewell); New York Times, July 13, 1917 (death).

ingier. Lobingier from his record is the man who should probably have been appointed the first judge. He was very much in the mold of Edmund Hornby and had already been a judge of a colonial court, the Philippines Court of First Instance, for 10 years. He was a good administrator, hard-working and had a passion for setting the US Court on the right footing to overcome the various legislative and administrative problems it faced. He was also well-educated, holding a PhD (and three other degrees) from the University of Nebraska.

Lobingier had been born in Lanark, Illinois in 1866, making him 48 at the time of his appointment. He had practiced as a lawyer in Omaha for 10 years from 1892 to 1902 and had also been a professor of law at the University of Nebraska from 1900 to 1903. While in the Philippines, he had been on the Commission to codify Philippines law and a member of the law faculty of the University of the Philippines. He had written nine legal books including books on Stocks and Stockholders, Constitutional Law, Equity, Foreclosure, Insurance and Evidence.

When he left the Philippines, Chief Justice Arellano wrote him a letter of praise:

"It is a great pleasure to me to tell you how estimable
and commendable are the qualities of zeal, intelligence
and rectitude which you have brought to the exercise of
your judicial functions, and of the reputation you enjoy
as a jurist by reason of your legal works. I trust they
will prove to be a happy augury of still greater successes in your new position."[6]

From his arrival in February 1914, Lobingier set out to get the United States Court for China on as strong a legal footing as possible. He also wanted to make it clear that he was get-

6 Philippine Law Journal, Vol 1, No 4, p189.

ting straight down to business. There was no formal opening of the court, as he considered this unnecessary.

In a number of early cases, he also made it clear that he would give the court the broadest legal authority as possible under the statutes that had created it. The first case where he did this was between T.H. Cavanagh and W.D. Wardem. Cavanagh was seeking a declaration of annulment of their marriage on the basis the two of them had never been legally married. Wardem opposed the application on the basis that the court had no jurisdiction to deal with annulments. Lobingier was having none of this. Using logic which he would employ in a number of cases in the future, he went back not only to the original treaties and acts establishing the consular courts but deep into the history of English common law to show that the United States Court for China had jurisdiction over almost any civil dispute. In the specific case, he held that the court had jurisdiction under the treaties; under the acts of Congress that gave power to handle cases "in regard to civil rights"; under the inherent jurisdiction of equity inherited from England; and, under the "reversionary jurisdiction" of the English Ecclesiastical Courts which had been passed to US Chancery courts.[7]

Lobingier also quickly took steps to improve the functioning of the United States Court for China. He commenced work on a bill to be put to Congress. The bill provided for, amongst other things, codification of the decision in *United States v Biddle* that the court could apply Alaskan and District of Columbia law; the appointment of a Special Judge to act when the Judge was absent; the transfer of consular jurisdiction in Shanghai to the US Court; the appointment of a Commissioner to hear smaller cases; and, for the Consular Jail to be supervised by the marshal of the court. Lobingier also sought to make the court self-funding by following the

7   *T. H. Cavanaugh v W.D. Wardem. North China Herald,* April 25, 1914, p321.

example of the British Court and charging probate fees based on 3% of the value of the estate.[8]

As well as proposing new legislation, Lobingier took matters into his own hands as far as he could. He reached an agreement with the Government of the Philippines that long-term prisoners be transferred to Bilibid Prison in Manila. The prisoners were normally transported on US Navy ships travelling between Shanghai and the Philippines. He also established the Far Eastern Bar Association in Shanghai and the Philippines for American lawyers.

Lobingier wanted to create the office of Commissioner, literally, to bring the two United States courts in Shanghai under one roof. As he told a congressional committee considering the bill in 1917:

"At the present time there are two sets of buildings. The court on one side of the street and the Consulate on the other. The United States Court is over here, with its court room and library, and over here is the Consular Court, with its court and library, presided over by a layman. I think you will agree with me that such duplication is not desirable."[9]

He also wanted the Commissioner to be able to take over as an acting judge when the Judge was absent so as to allow the court to function. Without waiting for Congress, Lobingier took matters into his own hands and appointed a member of the local bar to serve as Commissioner in Shanghai to hear smaller cases, including those that fell within the jurisdiction of the Shanghai Consular Court. Lobingier justified the appointment of the Commissioner on the basis that the statutes

8 Hearings before the Committee on Foreign Affairs, House of Representatives, 65th Congress first session on H.R. 4281. (Lobingier gave evidence at these hearings).

9 Hearings before the Committee on Foreign Affairs, House of Representatives, 65th Congress, First Session on HR 4281, p20-21.

establishing the Consular Courts since 1864 had always allowed for a Commissioner.[10]

One case challenged the right of the Commissioner to hear cases that fell within the jurisdiction of the Consular Court. Lobingier rejected this. Lobingier held that the United States Court for China had always had jurisdiction to handle any case in Shanghai. The consular courts had certain limited jurisdiction but this did not mean the United States Court for China did not have jurisdiction as well.[11] Lobingier justified this on the basis that the act establishing the Court for China gave the court exclusive jurisdiction over large cases, but only gave the Consular Courts jurisdiction over smaller cases, without mentioning that this was an exclusive jurisdiction. He pointed out that the British Supreme Court had full jurisdiction over all claims and that Mr Denby in drafting the law must have had this in mind. He added:

> "It is not uncommon for American Courts of equity to study their model, the old English High Court of Chancery, in determining any doubtful point of jurisdiction and while we do not regard this question as doubtful the doctrine seems, nevertheless, pertinent."

Finally, he held that in 1909, Congress had passed an act providing that only the Vice-Consul General in Shanghai could have judicial powers; and that in 1915, the office of Vice-Consul General had been abolished, meaning that Congress must have intended to transfer all judicial power in Shanghai to the United States Court for China. Again, he cited the British Order in Council that gave the British Supreme Court full judicial power in Shanghai and said that Congress must have had this in mind when passing the law.

---

10 *The Barkley Co., Inc. v. William E Maloney, North China Herald*, January 3, 1920, p46.

11 *In re Estate of Alberta C- K. Fitch, (deceased), Yao Sudong, v. American Food Mfg. Co., Ld., North China Herald,*, March 15,1919, p734.

The position of Commissioner was by the early 1920s formalised by an amendment to the Act creating the United States Court and the functions of the Shanghai Consular Court formally transferred to the Commissioner.[12]

Bourne retires

Soon after Lobingier was appointed, in mid 1915, Frederick Bourne went on pre-retirement leave. He formally retired on February 18, 1916 after 46 years service in China. Just before he left, Bourne published a book, Gardening in Shanghai for Amateurs. One reason for writing the book, he said, was because: "I am going home and wish to leave on record my plan of work to assist my successor in charge of the Country Club garden." In the book, he set out weekly gardening chores saying, "these notes are, I hope, so arranged that if the weekly chores are followed, the garden will be trim, and the limited number of plants given in the Index, all of which grow easily here will be forthcoming in each season." Most weeks required quite substantial work but, reflecting the spirit of Christmas for the fourth week of December, he merely gave instructions to "overhaul your tennis gear and garden tools and order new supplies."[13]

There was no special hearing to mark Bourne's retirement in the Supreme Court. Indeed, this had not been the custom when an assistant judge retired. However, in the High Court of Weihaiwei, where Bourne was Judge, Harrie Wilkinson as Acting Judge gave a farewell speech. He said that Weihaiwei and the British in China that had suffered a loss by the retirement of Bourne. He described Bourne as a "courteous gentleman, a just judge, a man with a deep and kindly knowledge of human nature and of Chinese law and custom" adding, that it would be difficult to find anyone to "fill his place, especial-

12 1902-1922, Twenty Years in the Judiciary, Far East Bar Association Bulletin VII, Shanghai, 1922, p9.

13 F Bourne, *Gardening for Amateurs in Shanghai*.

ly in this Court where the special knowledge referred to and his insight into the ways of the inhabitants of the Territory."[14]

The Colonial Office did not have to look far for a replacement. Wilkinson was now offered his first substantive judicial appointment in China. He was appointed Judge of the High Court of Weihaiwei, the position to be held concurrently with his role as Crown Advocate for China. While not the position of Chief Judge in Shanghai which he desired, he must have seen it as a stepping stone to the position when de Sausmarez retired.

A young British barrister, Allan Mossop, was appointed Crown Advocate of Weihaiwei. Mossop had that year set up a practice next to Harrie Wilkinson and acted as Crown Advocate for China when Wilkinson was not available. Wilkinson and Mossop maintained separate practices, however, they had an agreement that they would not act against each other so that Mossop could act as Crown Advocate when necessary.[15]

Mossop had arrived in Shanghai in 1908. He was the seventh son of Joseph Mossop and had born in South Africa in 1887. He was educated at the South African College, Cape Town and then went to university in England attending Pembroke College, Cambridge graduating with an MA and LLB. He was called to the Bar of the Inner Temple in 1908. Mossop moved to China soon after being called as barrister and was admitted to practice before the Supreme Court in 1909. He had first joined the former Registrar of the court John Douglas in partnership soon after Douglas' partnership with Noel Home had broken up. Douglas joined the army at the beginning of World War I and was at the time of Mossop's appointment fighting in France.[16]

Just prior to his formal retirement, Bourne was knighted

14 R v Liu Huan-Chu, North China Herald, November 13, 1915.

15 FO656/219 Letter from Mossop to Skinner Turner dated July 20, 1925 regarding Crown Advocate's position.

16 Biographical detail for Mossop: North China Herald, January 9, 1926, p 62 and October 25, 1933, p131; Obituary Times, June 19, 1965.

on January 1, 1916, making him the only Assistant Judge of the court to be knighted. Bourne's son Kenneth Bourne, who was serving in the British Army in France, returned to Shanghai after the war and stayed in the service of the Shanghai Municipal Police, rising to become the Commissioner. Sir Frederick Bourne died on August 23, 1940 in England.[17]

Skinner Turner appointed

To replace Bourne as Assistant Judge, the Foreign Office, as with the replacement for H.S. Wilkinson, again looked outside China. Skinner Turner, a judge in the Foreign Office Legal Service then based in Bangkok, was appointed in Bourne's place. Turner was born near Tonbridge, Kent on June 2, 1868 to Frederick and Marsha Turner, the eighth of nine children. In the 1871 census, his father described his profession as "farmer of 560 acres employing 20 men and 2 boys." He was named Skinner because when he was born his father was master of the Skinners Company. He became the godson of the company and was presented with a large silver tea and coffee set as a christening present by the company.[18]

Turner was educated at King's College School, Strand, and at London University. He was called to the Bar at the Middle Temple in 1890, and for some years afterwards practised on the Western Circuit and at the Hampshire Sessions.

He joined the Foreign Office Judicial Service in 1900 and served in Africa until 1905 when he was appointed Judge of the British Court for Siam, replacing Harrie Wilkinson. In 1909, on conclusion of the treaty partially bringing extraterritoriality to an end between Siam and Great Britain, he was lent to the Siamese Government as legal adviser. In this role, he sat on the Siamese Court of Appeal. In recognition of his valuable services as judicial adviser, he was awarded the In-

---

17 Knighthood, *London Gazette*, February 22, 1916, p1946; Death: *London Gazette*, June 6, 1941, p3250.

18 Email dated June 2, 2013 from John Turner, grandson of Skinner Turner.

signia of the Third Class of the Ratanabhon Personal Order by
the King of Siam.[19]

Turner as a judge was a lot of fun. He also had a very gen-
tle side to him and showed a lot of empathy for all who appeared before him or worked for him. In almost every case he
heard, he would make a joke of some kind.

When Turner was in Siam, Francis Lanchay was brought
before him for being drunk and disorderly and assaulting police, leading to the following exchange:

> Turner: Where did you get your liquor?
> Lanchay: At a Chinese shop, I met a friend.
> Turner: It is a very great pity.
> Mr Gibbons (for the prosecution): I understand that he
> knocked the Police about.
> Turner: Of Course. They always do. That is what the
> police are for. (laughter)[20]

Later when he was a judge in China, the *North China Herald* reported under a heading "British Justice: And No Waiting" that Turner was faced with a calendar that would entail a
full morning's work but actually it "amounted to very little."
In two cases, the parties did not turn up. For the remaining
two cases the NCH report went as follows:

In one case a Chinese sued Mr Smith Yates for $48 and the
following dialogue ensued (the defendant not being present):

> The Judge: This man admits that he owes the money

---

19 *The Times*, July 6, 1935 and *North China Daily News* July 7, 1935. Turner was appointed
Registrar to the British Court in the East Africa Protectorate, and in the following year
was transferred to the Uganda Protectorate to act as legal Vice-Consul. Early in 1902 he
was appointed Magistrate at Mombasa and in May of the same year was transferred to
Zanzibar as Acting Assistant Judge, receiving a definite appointment there as Second
Assistant Judge in October, 1902. In February 1904, he was promoted to be Senior Assistant Judge and also sat as one of the judges of the Court of Appeal for the Eastern Africa
Protectorates. He was granted license and authority to accept and wear his Siamese
award by the King of England on March 27, 1916 *Edinburgh Gazette* March 31, 1916, P631.

20 *Straits Times*, October 3, 1905, p1.

and he will pay $20 down and the rest in a month. Will that do?
Plaintiff: Can do
The Judge: Right. With costs.

Plaintiff failed to appear in case in which an Indian was sued for $30. Defendant admitted that he owed $2.
The Judge: Have you got $2?
Defendants: Yes. (produced)
The Judge: Judgment for $2, paid into Court.

10th Anniversary of the US Court

Turner was not the only British judge with a sense of humour. Surprisingly, de Sausmarez could also on occasions be quite funny as he showed at a dinner celebrating the tenth Anniversary of the United States Court for China.

When he arrived Shanghai, Lobingier had not thought it appropriate to have a formal opening for the court. Two years later, however, in 1916 he considered it was time to have a big party to celebrate the court's tenth anniversary.[21] The party was held at the Astor House Hotel and attended by 250 people with 150 waiters in attendance to provide service. The centre ballroom of the hotel was bedecked with the Stars and Stripes. Photographs of President Wilson and Secretary of State Elihu Root together with a portrait of former Chief Justice John Marshall were placed above the podium.

The *North China Herald* reported that it was like a "large family holding a reunion" with many small tables and a number of larger tables. The guests included US Admiral Winterhalter and various other military officers, as well as the two judges of the British Supreme Court, de Sausmarez and Turner and their wives. The guest of honour was to have been Paul Reinsch the American Minister in Peking, but he had been

---

21 1916 U.S. Ct. China Decennial Anniversary Brochure 1; *North China Herald*, July 8, 1916, p27-30.

detained in Peking and only arrived in Shanghai that evening
and then went straight into urgent meetings with the Consul-
General and later with the Admiral and his staff.

Lobingier served as toast master and gave an opening
speech recounting the history of US extraterritoriality in
China and the creation of the court. Various congratulatory
letters were read out from Presidents Roosevelt and Taft and
Elihu Root. Rufus Thayer also telegraphed congratulations.
Nothing was received from Lebbeus Wilfley. Stirling Fessenden spoke to give a history of some of the important cases
since the foundation of the court and in particular the Biddle
case that had allowed Alaskan and District of Columbia laws
to be applied. Reverend Hawks Pott then spoke followed by
Mr E.S. Cunningham, the US Consul-General in Hankow.

The *North China Herald*, in an intriguing comment, said
that de Sausmarez gave an "amusing speech" about the difficulties of extraterritoriality that was well received, but did
not print his speech. Mr Sammons, the US Consul-General,
then read out Mr Reinsch's speech saying that looking back
over the previous ten years, they should "justly feel gratified
at the work which has been accomplished by this Court in
working out problems of action and of legal theory which
confront it."

De Sausmarez's speech, which was printed in full in the
tenth anniversary brochure of the court, was indeed very
amusing and surprisingly so. All his other public pronounce-
ments gave the impression of a dour and wowserish man.
However, in his speech, de Sausmarez showed his good
breeding. After short pleasantries where he mentioned the
friendly relations between the two courts, he got down to
the subject he had been asked to talk on: "The Extraterritorial
Court." He could have given a serious talk about the British
Court, but this was an evening to celebrate the United States
Court. He was also the second-to-last speaker so he needed to

keep things light.

He, therefore, decided to talk about court buildings, but not those in Shanghai, where clearly the British had the best building, but of the "buildings" he had used in Africa. In Zanzibar, he regularly held court on a verandah with only two chairs and a table. He recalled on one island holding court on a bluff overlooking the ocean under the canopy of a mango tree – all very nice until it started to rain. One court was very small. A defendant had brought in a tame leopard to court every day. Once he had decided the defendant could lose, de Sausmarez insisted that the "noxious beast be removed." In one case, a Briton had refused to pay some native carriers. The carriers had come from inland to complain, so de Sausmarez engaged the carriers to take him inland on a pleasant one-week trip. Once there, he held court under a tree by the roadside. When the defendant did not turn up, he gave judgment for the carriers.[22]

The evening went on with music and dancing until 1am, when it was brought to a close by the band patriotically playing the Star Spangled Banner.

---

22 De Sausmarez's speech is reproduced in the 1916 U.S. Ct. China Decennial Anniversary Brochure 1.

Troops of the eight nation alliance that occupied (and then looted) Peking in 1900. Note the British solider is a Sikh. Sikhs underpinned British military power in China

Li Hongzhang in 1900. Called on, yet again, to negotiate an unequal treaty

The Entrance to the British Minister's palatial residence in Peking; restored after the siege of the legations.

The British Supreme Court for China in 1913 showing the new Police Court (down-stairs) and Second Court (upstairs)

The interior of the new Second Court

British Judges of the 20th Century

Sir HS Wilkinson

Sir Frederick Bourne

Sir Havilland de Sausmarez

Sir Skinner Turner

Sir Peter Grain

Gilbert King, OBE

Penrhyn Grant Jones, CMG

Sir Allan Mossop

Registrars, Crown Advocates, Acting Judges

John Douglas

Cyril Haines

HP Wilkinson

Victor Priestwood

John McNeill

Harold King

Arthur Rose Vincent

Lindsey Smith

Hong Kong judges who sat on the Full Court of the SCC

Sir Joseph Kemp

John Wood

Sir Henry Gollan

Sir Atholl MacGregor

Roger Lindsell

The Supreme Court of Hong Kong, where judges of the SCC sat as members of the Full Court from 1913 to 1941

US Court for China

The judge, DA, clerk and marshal of the newly established United States Court for China in 1907

The US Consulate on Whangpoo Road. The first home of the US Court for China

Judges of the US Court for China

Lebbeus Wilfley

Rufus Thayer

Charles Lobingier

Milton Purdy

Milton Helmick

Nelson Lurton (SJ)

Bertrand Johnson (SJ)

Furno Schul (Comm.)

US District Attorneys for China

Arthur Bassett

Frank Hinckley

Chauncey Holcomb

Leonard Husar

Thomas Sellett

Felthan Watson

Leighton Shields

Members of the British bar in Shanghai in 1908. R.N. MacLeod,
A.P. Stokes, W.V. Drummond, W.A.C. Platt, J.H. Teesdale

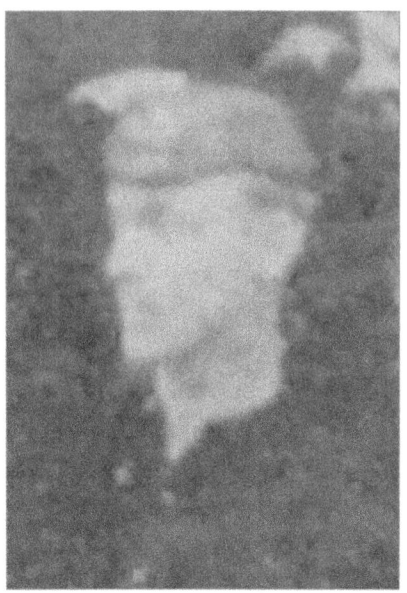

Capt. L. E. P. JONES
7th Yorkshire Regt.

Duncan McNeill, fiery Scot who
practiced in HK, Yokohama & Shanghai.

Loftus Jones, Killed in Action in
World War 1

Messrs A.B. Johnson and A.P. Stokes of Johnson Stokes & Master. The firm still
exists as Mayer Brown JSM.

Harrie Wilkinson's second wedding in 1910. A picture taken in the British consulate gardens.
1. Lady de Sausmarez; 2. Gilbert King (possibly); 3. Unknown ; 4. Sir Pelham Warren; 5. Sir Havilland de Sausmarez; 6. Mrs Wilkinson; 7. Unknown; 8. Harrie Wilkinson, 9. Unkown; 10 Loftus Jones (best man); 11. John Douglas; 12. Lindsey Smith; 13. Unknown

Charles Biddle, Defendant in US v Biddle. The appeal case defined the powers of the US Court for China

Dr Henry DeMenil, acquitted of killing a monk in Tibet in 1907

Gilbert Reid, prosecuted for Sedition in the US Court during WWI

Admiral Oskar Stark, the arrival of his flotilla of Russian refugees after WWI led to a prosecution in the US Court

HENRY D. O'SHEA,
Proprietor and Editor.

Henry O'Shea, Plaintiff in the Shanghai Liar case; Defendant in R v O'Shea for defaming Judge Wilfley of the US Court for China

THE "CHINA GAZETTE" PREMISES.

The offices of O'Shea's Newspaper, *the China Gazette*

Ernest Bethell, Korea's hero. Imprisoned in 1909 for inciting sedition against the Japanese Government of Korea

Yang Ki-Tak, Betthel's Korean co-publisher in 1918. He is carrying a sign stating he is prohibited from living in China

Thomas Jernigan

Stirling Fessenden

William Fleming

Cornell Franklin

Carl von Ingenohl. Involved in legal cases in Shanghai, HK and Manila over the seizure of his Manila factory

German Admiral Frederich von Ingenohl, Carl's brother. Ordered the bombardment of the English coast in WWI

Ingenohl's cigar factory in Mong Kong, Hong Kong located where Yin Chong St (Cigar Factory St) is today.

Lawrence Kentwell – Rebel with a Cause

CHAPTER 40

World War I

WHEN THE UNITED STATES Court celebrated its tenth anniversary, America had not entered World War I and Americans in China could still celebrate. This was not so for the British. War had started for them in 1914. While there was no fighting in Shanghai, the war had a large impact on the British Supreme Court. Most immediately, a number of the lawyers practicing before the court signed up to join the army. Others in Shanghai also wanted to go to the front, but were not allowed to. Captain Barrett of the SMP applied to be allowed to go to fight but his application was rejected. Both of Frederick Bourne's sons had signed up and were serving in the army, one in France and the other in India.

War also came home to the court when news was received at least twice of the death of members of the Shanghai bar. The first was of Loftus Jones, an Australian, who had come to Shanghai in 1899 and first practiced with Harrie Wilkinson before joining the firm of Dowdall, Hanson and McNeill. He had been best man at Wilkinson's second wedding in 1910 and had acted as in Wilkinson's place as Crown Advocate from time to time. He had signed up in December 1914 soon after war broke out and had been killed in action in France. Upon news of his death reaching Shanghai, a special ceremony was held in the Supreme Court presided over by de Sausmarez, Bourne and Gilbert King, the Registrar.[1]

---

1 "Shanghai's Roll of Honour: Capt. Loftus E.P. Jones", *North China Herald*, August 14, 1914, p434.

In late 1915, news arrived of the death of John Douglas, the former Registrar of the court. Douglas was killed in action in France just before Christmas in 1915. Douglas' death was particularly tragic; his two brothers, one serving in the navy and the other in the army, were also killed in action in 1915. Immediately after news of Douglas' death arrived, Gilbert King, in the Police Court gave a heartfelt tribute to Douglas praising him as Registrar, as an advocate and as a friend finishing with the fine tribute: "He died as he lived – An English gentleman."[2]

Two weeks later at a special memorial ceremony in the Supreme Court for Douglas, Judge Havilland de Sausmarez recalled his devotion to duty as Registrar and Coroner; the great assistance Douglas had given de Sausmarez when he arrived in Shanghai; and, especially, "his many kindly acts" particularly when dealing with probate cases. He said that:

"the widows and children of those that have died have had reason to bless the day when there interests were taken in by the late Mr Douglas."[3]

Harrie Wilkinson spoke to support what had been said by de Sausmarez, adding that he had known Douglas well and felt the loss personally. Allan Mossop, Douglas' partner in practice for six years, then spoke to farewell his old friend and concluded by saying:

"While we grieve our loss, our one consolation should

2 "The Late Capt. J.C.E. Douglas: Mr. G.W. King's Tribute", *North China Herald*, 8 January 1916, p79 ; R. Bickers, Stuck in Shanghai, describes Douglas' time in the army and his death,

3 "The Late Capt. J.C.E. Douglas: Tributes from the British Bench and Bar, "*North China Herald*, 15 January 1916, p94. Douglas is buried in the Bailleul Communcal Cemetery, Nord (France). His gravestone bears the inscription "Greater Love Hath No Man Than This." See Yorkshire Regiment War Graves. http://www.ww1-yorkshires.org.uk/html-files/bailleul-communal-cemetery-extension.htm. See the Douglas Archives (http://www.douglashistory.co.uk/history/georgedouglas12.htm#.Uu27qf0srwI) for details of the deaths of the Douglas brothers.

be that Douglas died the death that he would have chosen, a glorious death in the cause of righteousness and
of the King and his Empire."

In total, by the end of the war, one-fifth - eight out of the
approximately forty - of the British lawyers practising in China at the beginning of the war were killed in action. After the
war a memorial was erected at the foot of the steps of the
court to all eight.[4]

It was into this environment of fierce patriotism that defendants accused of disloyalty came. The war had also encouraged rebellions in other parts of the British Empire. In
1915, de Sausmarez ordered the deportation of Kesar Singh
and Ganda Singh for being members of the Sikh Revolution-
ary party.[5]

In early 1916, the most serious case involving the war
came before de Sausmarez. Wilkinson had charged Sidmond
Abbas and his son Oswald under the Defence of the Realm
Act, or DORA. DORA was enacted to allow the government
to investigate and punish crimes that would affect the war effort. The Abbases, were apparently well known in the Shanghai community and, while it was not stated directly in the
case, were of Middle Eastern descent. The case gathered a
large amount of attention because Wilkinson applied for it to
be heard in secret. The Defendants pleaded not guilty and a
jury was empaneled. After hearing the secret evidence, they
found the father guilty of the offence and the son guilty of
aiding and abetting his father.[6]

In sentencing, de Sausmarez stated for the first time pub-

----

4 "British Bar War Memorial: Unveiling Ceremony at HM Supreme Court", North China Herald, October 30, 1920, p328. The names and inscriptions read: TO THE MEMORY
OF Loftus E.P. Jones, Frederick W. Grantham, Henry Sigismund Oppe, John C.E. Douglas, Charles Gordon Kirk, Kenneth T.J. Parson, Skinner R. Sebastian, Peter S. Dixon.
Members of the Bar of H. M. Supreme Court who fell in the Great War, 1914-1918.

5 North China Herald, July 17, 1915, p191.

6 R v SH Abbas and O Abbas, North China Herald, January 15, 1916, p142.

licly what the case was about. Abbas had sold 15,000 rifles, 1,000 revolvers and about a million and a half rounds of ammunition to be delivered to India, Ceylon and the Straits Settlements to be used in a rebellion against the British Government. The sentence for this was death or whatever lesser penalty the court thought fit. In sentencing de Sausmarez gave the elder Mr Abbas a tongue-lashing:

"you allowed an utterly despicable desire for gain to overcome the sentiment of loyalty to your country which ought to have inspired you and, which, whatever your origin, were due to a country under whose government you were born, which had protected you and under whose protection you carried on a profitable business."

He then passed a very harsh sentence of 15 years imprisonment. He turned to the son and said that he appreciated that he had not been involved in the sale but had helped him to collect payment, or as de Sausmarez put it, assisted "him in obtaining the price of his villainy." De Sausmarez was much gentler on the son, sentencing him to two years in prison.

Dealing with the enemy
The outbreak of war brought a number of tricky cases before the British courts. First, there were cases that came about from a short war which Japan, with the assistance of Britain, fought to capture Tsingtao, a Germany colony, and then take over other German interests in Shantung Province. During the fighting, British Navy ships captured two ships: the *Hanametal* and the *Paklat*.[7] Both had been taken to the British territory of Weihaiwei where the crews were interned. The *Hanametal* was American owned and therefore neutral. But the Ger-

7   *Hanametal*, [1915] HKLR 3 (Gompertz ACJ); *Paklat*, [1915] HKLR 19 (Rees-Davies CJ).

man authorities in Tsingtao had insisted it take on a German crew to sail through the harbour at Tsingtao that had been mined. It had then made two suspicious voyages to Chefoo and Shanghai during which it had not taken on any cargo or passengers. It was suggested that in fact these had been spy missions to find the disposition of Japanese and British naval forces. The *Paklat* had under a white truce flag been evacuating non-combatants, principally women and children, from Tsingtao to Tientsin.

In order to formally seize (or to use the technical term, condemn) the ships an action needed to be brought before a British court in its prize jurisdiction. A prize court determines whether a captured ship should be condemned or returned to its owners. The British Supreme Court for China's jurisdiction was limited to British subjects and property and therefore did not have prize jurisdiction. The British High Court for Weihaiwei may have had prize jurisdiction but a judge from Shanghai would need to travel to Weihaiwei to try the cases. The ships were, instead, sailed by British prize crews to Hong Kong. In the case of the *Paklat*, the German engineers on board had to be forced at gunpoint to operate the engines.[8]

The prize cases were heard in the Supreme Court of Hong Kong. In the case of the *Hanametal*, the court ordered the ship returned its American owner on the basis the Crown had not proved the *Hanametal* was engaged in non-neutral activities. In the case of the *Paklat*, Chief Justice Rees-Davies ordered the ship condemned on the basis that bringing non-combatants out of a war zone was not a humanitarian mission unless permission has been granted by the besieging power in advance. He concluded with a statement that today would be considered the encouragement of war crimes or terrorism:

"Although such permission is sometimes granted,

---

8   "Sea Prizes in Port", *New York Times*, September 8, 1914.

it is in most cases refused because the fact that non-
combatants are besieged together with combatants and
that they have to endure hardships, may and very often
does exercise pressure on authorities to surrender."

The *Paklat* was renamed the S.S. *Polbain* and used as a military transport.[9]

The Japanese, after capturing Tsingtao, in early January
1915 made a set of 21 demands to the government of Yuan
Shi-Kai. These sought to confirm the Japanese occupation of
Tsingtao and other German concessions, railways and mines
in Shantung as well as Japan's special position in Manchuria.
More aggressively, the Japanese wanted China to allow Japanese advisers be appointed to its government ministries. The
demands were bitterly opposed by the Chinese people who
boycotted Japanese products. After negotiations, a watered
down treaty was signed in May 1915 giving Japan some of
its demands.

Away from the zone of actual war in Tsingtao, de Sausmarez and Wilkinson also had to deal with a number of tricky
cases regarding trading with enemy nationals and what to do
with enemy property in Shanghai. Things were made difficult because China did not join the war immediately meaning that, other than in Tsingtao, Germans were not considered
enemy nationals and British and Germans continued to live
side by side.

As soon as war was declared regulations were promulgated prohibiting trading with the enemy. These regulations had
been designed to stop money from England and its colonies
and territories being sent to fund the German war machine.
In England itself, this was a relatively easy process. Enemy
property was vested in the Custodian of Enemy Property
who held the property and any profits until the end of the

war. Depending on the treaties signed ending the war, the property would be returned or dealt with according to the treaties. But in an extraterritorial jurisdiction, this was much more difficult.

In 1915, regulations were passed requiring any British subject in China to pay any interest, dividends or profits due to an enemy national into an Enemy Dividend Account. The Registrar of the Supreme Court, Gilbert King, was designated to be the Custodian of Enemy Property in China. Towards the end of the war, Allan Mossop, was appointed the Custodian of Enemy Property when Gilbert King went on leave.

The difficulty was that while China remained neutral, Germans could freely reside and do business in China. The British Consulate in Shanghai was bombarded with questions from British banks and companies who owed money to Germans or were planning to pay dividends. In most cases, they were allowed to pay the money.[10]

Wilkinson was also asked to advise on a number of cases regarding whether trade was allowed. He submitted a number of memorandums regarding how best to put into effect the object of the legislation in an extraterritorial jurisdiction. The first set of regulations had prohibited trading with people based in enemy countries. This did not apply to Germans and other enemy nationals in China because China was neutral. New regulations were then introduced preventing trading with enemy nationals. Wilkinson suggested that it would be much better to phrase the regulations based on the court that exercised jurisdiction over a person rather than their nationality. The new regulations also, on a strict interpretation, forbade any dealings with Germans, even, for example, retail purchases from your local butcher. De Sausmarez wrote a note recommending that such transactions not be the subject of prosecution.

....

10 FO 671/371 collects the various correspondence relating to trading with the enemy.

In 1917, when China formally entered the war, the regulations prohibiting dealing with enemy property were extended to cover any balances and deposits in banks. Anyone managing property owned by an enemy was also required to report this to the Consul.

These regulations and China's formal entry into the war brought a number of cases came before de Sausmarez requiring him to decide what to do with enemy property. He was justifiably proud of the decisions he had made and collected them in a short volume of cases. The long title of the book was "The Law of Enemy Property in China: Reports of the Cases Decided in HBM Supreme Court for China in 1917, 1918 and 1919."[11] The short title de Sausmarez gave them was "Shanghai Law Reports."

The first case involved shares held by a Count Praschma in a British company. They had been pledged to guarantee a debt owed to Cathay Trust. Cathay Trust could not get the shares transferred to itself. The dividends on the shares were being paid to the Enemy Dividend Account. Cathay Trust applied for the shares to be transferred to the Custodian of Enemy Property. De Sausmarez declined to do this on the basis that the regulations likely did not cover the transfer of shares. De Sausmarez, however, suggested that it might be a case where the British Minister would consent to pay money out of the enemy dividend account to settle the debt. The Minister did consent to this and de Sausmarez made an order allowing it.

Another case involved a change of nationality from an enemy German to an ally French. Mr Gensburger had been born in Alsace, which was then French territory. He had come to Shanghai and registered as German subject. His money held with a British bank had been transferred to the Custodian of Enemy Property. After this, he registered himself with

---

11 All cases referred to in this section are reported in H. de Sausmarez, *The Law of Enemy Property in China: Reports of the Cases Decided in HBM Supreme Court for China in 1917, 1918 and 1919.*

the French authorities. The French authorities then asked the British Minister to approve payment back to Gensburger of his money. De Sausmarez approved this.

De Sausmarez next had to deal with was what to do with shares held in British companies by enemy nationals. While the companies that had issued the shares were British, they had no control over the shares. They belonged to the shareholders. De Sausmarez ruled that the court had no jurisdiction because the shares were the property of the shareholder and the court had no jurisdiction over the shareholders. He said that if the company was in liquidation, the answer may be different because then the court would have jurisdiction over the restructuring of the company. In a subsequent case involving a Mr Linke, he confirmed that once a company was placed in liquidation, the court had jurisdiction because the liquidation could not proceed unless the court could make orders affecting the shares.

The *Peking Post* prosecuted

The war also brought into the US Court for China a case that caused far greater anger amongst the public and foreign officials than the ownership of enemy property.

The ongoing civil wars in China meant that the central and regional governments in China had an insatiable need for money. Customs and salt revenue was already pledged to pay back previous loans and the Boxer Indemnity. Since 1911, the foreign-run Chinese Customs had taken over collection of customs revenue and started paying the money directly to foreign governments and bondholders. The collection of other taxes was difficult due to the unstable situation in most of the country. All regional governments and particularly the central government had to resort to taking loans from foreigners to fund their operations and ongoing civil wars.

In 1917, after America had entered the war, the Chinese government in Peking appeared to be arranging for a loan

Gilbert Reid, Missionary and publisher of the Peking Post: Accused of sedition

from American bankers with the assistance of the American Minister, Paul Reinsch. Gilbert Reid, the editor of the *Peking Post*, was outraged by this, particularly because President Wilson had denounced the giving of loans to China of a political nature. Reid had received a personal letter from Wilson thanking Reid for his support in this policy. In an article entitled "Are Chinese Loans made in the Open," Reid questioned the legality of the loans that were not being submitted to the Chinese parliament for approval and the role of Reinsch in arranging the loans.[12]

Reid, who was American, was a missionary and had been in China for many years. He had founded the Mission for the Upper Classes. When World War I first began he had been based in Shanghai. There were allegations at the time that at his mission he was showing young Chinese people films favourable to the German cause. In 1917 he had moved to Peking and taken over the *Peking Post*. The newspaper had taken a very pro-German stance and grown from a four-sheet paper to an eight-sheet paper in a very short period of time. Allegations were made that the paper was being funded by Germany as a propaganda paper.[13]

When President Wilson decided to enter the war against Germany in early 1917, Reid published a scorching editorial denouncing the decision. Reid said that the majority of the American people were not in favour of joining the war. He

12 *United States v Reid, North China Herald*, June 16, 1917, p631-633.
13 "Trail of the Serpent Reid" *Straits Times*, May 25, 1918, p3.

attacked Wilson personally:

> "And the Kaiser of Germany showed no more symp-
> toms of autocracy in getting Germany into the Great
> War than has President Wilson in getting the United
> States into the war."

He continued that the majority of the American people
may, in order to appear patriotic, acclaim the war. Only a
small minority will insist on their constitutional rights to "do
their own thinking."

Reid was arrested and charged with seditious libel against
Mr Reinsch and the American President. He was first brought
before the American Consular Court in Tientsin, granted bail
and ordered to appear for trial before Lobingier in Shanghai.

The case was prosecuted by Chauncey Holcomb who had
taken over as District Attorney from Frank Hinckley in 1915
when Hinckley's term expired. Holcomb, who had graduated
from Lake Forest Law School with an LLB in 1893, had been a
Major and assistant adjutant general in the organized militia
of Delaware from 1913 until he came to Shanghai in 1915. He
was generally referred to in court as Major Holcomb.[14]

At the first hearing in Shanghai, Major Holcomb told
the court America was at war. It is not patriotic to question
the American government when the country is at war. Reid
pleaded not guilty and said that he would make a formal objection to the charges, presumably on constitutional grounds
that his right of free speech should be protected. He was ordered to appear for trial on Monday morning, June 11, 1917.

The weekend gave Reid time to reflect and to find himself a lawyer, Dr Hua-chuen Mei, a Chinese-American. Mei,
a graduate of Columbia University with high honours, was

....

14 *Men of Shanghai and North China*, p175. Holcomb had also been a Member of the Delaware House of Representatives for several terms and speaker of the house from 1913 to
1914.

one of the first, if not the first, Chinese-Americans admitted
to practice before the federal courts in America. After being
admitted in 1915, he practiced in New York for a short time
before moving to Shanghai. Despite being Chinese and, having spent much of his childhood in China, speaking Chinese,
Mei was very much a part of the American community. He
had been a member of the Phi Beta Kappa fraternity at Columbia and was a mason.[15]

Dr Mei gave Reid some wise counsel. He advised Reid to
make a statement apologizing. So, on Monday morning, Reid
appeared with Dr Mei and read the following statement to
the court:

> "I do not occupy a pleasant position, and I believe your
> Honour will appreciate the feelings I must have when
> I stand in Court charged with libeling the President
> of my country and its accredited representative to the
> Government of China, it will be apparent to your Hon-
> our that the general public, Chinese and foreign, holds
> the one thus charged in a light far from complimentary,
> even before trial, and particularly in times of war.
> "What I wish to say, and I say it with all sincerity, is
> that I have never experienced a feeling of disloyalty to
> my country, and I do here in open Court unhesitatingly
> profess my loyalty and devotion to my country, to its
> great constitution, and to the high ideals for which our
> Republic has stood and still stands."

He continued that he never intended to libel either President Wilson or Mr Reinsch and that "if, in expressing myself
on current events, in the hurry of an editorial room, I appear
to have stepped beyond the bounds of propriety, I express my

15 Admission and fraternity membership: *Columbia Daily Spectator*, Vol LVIII, Number
188, July 8, 1915, front page; Boyhood: Oriental Economic Review Volume 1; Mason:
San Bernadino County Sun, June 18, 1940, p12. Mei eventually became a District Grand
Master.

honest regret and desire that what has been written may not be construed to possess any offensive meaning."

When Reid was finished, Holcomb asked for an adjournment so he could consider the statement (and presumably discuss it with Minister Reinsch). It was agreed the court would reconvene the following day. The next day, Holcomb said that taken at face value, Reid had "purged himself of the charges filed against him." Under American law, great latitude was given to newspapers to comment on governmental affairs and in times of peace much, even if illegal, will go unnoticed. However, in times of war, "articles of the same kind do, and it is properly so, merit and receive the attention of the prosecuting officers of the Government, especially under conditions existing in this jurisdiction."

Holcomb then asked for leave to withdraw the charges. If charges are withdrawn, they can be refiled. Dr Mei questioned if withdrawing the charges was fair on his client because the charges would "leave an axe suspended over Mr. Reid's head" that may prevent him from reporting legally. Lobingier responded that the motion was to withdraw and that was all he could deal with. He made an order that the charges be withdrawn.

Reid did not stay quiet. Once China joined the war later in the year, the Allied Powers put pressure on the Chinese not to deal with Reid. In November 1917, Reid reported in the *Peking Post* that he had been received at the Chinese Foreign Ministry on his birthday. This resulted in a strong public protest from the Allied Powers signed by John Jordan, the British Minister to Lu Chiang Hsiang the Chinese Foreign Minister. Jordan's letter read:

> "My Colleagues and I consider that it is, to say the
> least, strange that a person notoriously working in the
> interests of the enemy, and against whom precaution-

ary measures have already been adopted, should thus be favoured with special attentions on the part of high Chinese officials."[16]

In very direct language he added:

"I have been requested to warn Your Excellency against the renewal of such incorrect conduct, which, can only cause the most unfavourable comment in allied countries."

The Chinese got the message loud and clear. Within the month, they "requested" that Reid be deported. Coincidentally or not, Major Holcomb happened to be in Peking at the time and obtained an order from the Tientsin Consular Court deporting Reid. Reid was placed on the *Chingwantao* and sent to Manila.[17]

Versailles Peace Conference

World War I ended in November 1918 with an armistice and in 1919 a peace conference was held in Versailles, France. China joined as a party. As part of its requests, China sought an agreement to end extraterritoriality once China had prepared and passed new legal codes and established a new system of Western courts in all districts where foreigner resided. China undertook to have these reforms in place by 1924. It asked for an agreement that extraterritoriality would be abolished if China achieved these goals.

The Versailles Conference was, however, more concerned about sharing the spoils of victory and punishing Germany than with freeing China from the chains of extraterritoriality. China did receive some benefits under the final treaty. Ger-

---

16 "Gilbert the Filbert", *North China Herald*, December 8, 1917, p583 (re birthday party); "Officials & Dr Reid", *North China Herald*, December 22, 1917, p710.
17 "Dr Gilbert Reid Deported", *North China Herald*, December 19, 1917, p775.

many gave up all extraterritorial rights in China; agreed to return the German concessions in Tientsin and Hankow; returned to China all buildings and lands (other than diplomatic premises) it owned in China; waived claims for any more payments under the Boxer Indemnity; and, agreed to return astronomical instruments looted from Peking following the Boxer Rebellion.[18]

There was, however, a kicker. Under the treaty, all German rights and properties in Shantung (Shandong) were to be transferred to Japan. This was totally unacceptable to the Chinese government and people and triggered the first large-scale nationalist demonstrations in China. These commenced on May 4, 1919 with demonstrations by Chinese students in Peking. The protest spread nationwide. In Shanghai boycotts of foreign and, particularly, Japanese goods were organized. The movement, called "the May 4th Movement", is now considered the starting point of Chinese national awareness. Protests were also held in France by Chinese students including, it is claimed, Zhou Enlai and Deng Xiaoping to stop the Chinese negotiators signing the treaty. The movement did not stop Japan from taking over the German rights in Shantung. China refused to sign the Treaty of Versailles, becoming the only country to not sign. It therefore remained technically at war with Germany.

The American President Woodrow Wilson was instrumental in negotiating the Treaty of Versailles and pushed in addition for the creation of a League of Nations, an international body that would seek to resolve problems between countries without war. The US Senate, however, refused to ratify the treaty. The United States also remained technically at war with Germany until 1921 when a separate treaty was signed and ratified. America also did not join the League of Nations, despite Wilson receiving a Nobel Peace Prize for his role in

18 Articles 128 to 134 of the Treaty of Versailles. Articles 156 to 158 deal with the transfer of German rights to Japan in Shandong.

establishing it.

To the dismay of the Chinese, the Versailles Peace Conference left the question of extraterritoriality to a conference to be held at a later date in Washington DC. The main purpose of the Washington Conference was to discuss the reduction in navy ships by each country attending. However, given that all the major extraterritorial powers would be there, extraterritoriality was also put on the agenda.

Strangely, only after the war ended, in March 1919, China deported 2,000 Germans who were in China as enemy nationals. China had been pressured to do so during the war, but had resisted fearing reprisals from Germany. Now, the war was over they gave in to British pressure and deported most Germans under 60.

Right for an enemy to sue

The lack of a peace treaty between Germany and America brought a case before Lobingier in 1920 where he had to decide whether a German, technically still an enemy national, was allowed to bring an action in the US Court for China. The German was a partner with two Chinese in the firm Hai-Chong Hong. Hai-Chong Hong had sued the Consolidated Steel Corporation for breach of contract.[19]

Stirling Fessenden on behalf of Consolidated Steel argued that Hai-Chong Hong could not sue them, relying on a principle of common law that enemy nationals could not sue in American courts. Lobingier reviewed old English decisions as well as US decisions that had considered the common law rule during the Anglo-American War of 1812. Lobingier found that the principle relied upon by the defendant was good law. However, he also found that there was a principle that if enemy aliens were residing "peaceably" within the United States and no steps were being taken to remove them,

---

19 *Poo Shing Hing et al v Consolidated Steel Corporation*, North China Herald, November 27, 1920, p625.

then they were allowed to bring actions in court.

The problem that Lobingier faced was that the German partner was living in China. The United States government had no jurisdiction over him and could not force him to leave. The Chinese were now allowing him stay He was therefore residing "peaceably" in Shanghai but not because the US government allowed him to. Given that the war was long over, Lobingier most likely felt that this was a technical point which it would not be a good policy to enforce. He therefore held that the burden was on the American defendant to show that an enemy national was not residing peaceably in Shanghai. Consolidated Steel had not produced any evidence to show this and accordingly the case was allowed to proceed.

A few years later, an American defendant to a claim by a Russian bank made a similar argument. The defendant asserted that given that the Soviet Union was a communist country, which since the Russian Revolution in 1917 had abandoned Christianity, Russians no longer had a right to sue in US Court. Lobingier's decision was cited to defend against this argument. The Judge, Milton Purdy, rejected the argument on the basis that he had jurisdiction unless the State Department told him otherwise.[20]

American and British companies in China

Towards the end of the war, Lobingier made a very important ruling allowing the incorporation of American companies directly in China. Frank Jay Raven, an American entrepreneur, had sought to establish a banking corporation in China and filed the necessary papers with the Clerk of the Court, Mr McRae. McRae refused to register the company under the Corporations Act of 1903. William Fleming, who was also secretary of Raven's companies, then brought an action on behalf of Raven against McRae to order him to accept the

---

20 *Gromov v International Banking Corporation, North China Herald,* March 28, 1925, p536.

registration under the Corporations Act. Lobingier held that the Corporations Act did apply to China and that companies could be registered. He, however, held that banking corporations were not covered by the act and ruled against Raven.[21]

Raven lost the case, but the ruling that companies in general could be registered was in important development for American extraterritoriality in China. A few years later, the China Trade Act was passed formalizing the rules for registering an American company in China. Raven himself registered a number of companies and went on to build one of the largest financial conglomerates in China until its spectacular collapse in 1935.[22]

The ability to register American companies in China opened up the door for Chinese to register American companies in China to take advantage of extraterritoriality much as British and Hong Kong companies had been used for same reason.

Ironically, at the same time, the British were cracking down on the abuses of China companies by non-British nationals, making it harder for foreigners to register a British China company. In 1919, an Order in Council was passed that required that a British subject be the managing director of any Hong Kong company doing business in China and that the name of the managing director be registered with the British Consulate in Shanghai.[23]

The end of the war also saw a number of changes in the British Supreme Court.

---

21 *Raven v McRae, North China Herald*, June 16, 1917, p667.

22 See Chapter 55

23 China (Companies) Amendment Order in Council 1919, s4.

CHAPTER 41

Farewells and Promotions

De Sausmarez retires

The end of World War I brought an end to Havilland de Sauzmarez's long career as a judge. All long leave had been cancelled during the war. De Sausmarez was granted one of the first long leaves available commencing from March 1920. It was expected that he would not return. Just before his departure, the Shanghai Bar gave him a farewell tiffin at the Shanghai Club in what appears to have been a fairly subdued gathering. Harrie Wilkinson, no doubt wondering if the chance to succeed his father had now come, spoke on behalf of the Bar and congratulated him upon retiring, if he were retiring, at such an early stage and in sound health. Wilkinson thanked Sir Havilland and Lady de Sausmarez for their kindness to members of the bar and their wives. Wilkinson then, referring to the charitable works of Lady de Sausmarez said he hoped that "that the extensive work of Lady de Sausmarez in the public interest, especially connected with the war, and also that of Sir Havilland, would be fittingly recognized, as doubtless they would be. It was matter for regret that that recognition had not been given so far."[1]

Sausmarez replied expressing his pride in being a member of the Bar, although noting that he had not, as some of his predecessors, been actually a practising member in Shanghai. He then referred to the "high position which the British Bar

---

[1] *North China Herald*, April 10, 1920, p75. The same and previous page report de Sausmarez addressing the Church on the departure of the Dean.

in China had always held in the past, held today, and which no doubt it would continue to hold." He then wished all in attendance "a hearty farewell, if farewell it was."

His wife was recognised three months later and invested as a Dame of the Order of the British Empire, in July 1920.[2] De Sausmarez did decide to give up his post while in England and formally retired on a pension on June 1, 1921.

At that time, the opportunity arose for the Bar to recognised Sausmarez more formally. Allan Mossop, the Acting Crown Advocate, said in a hearing presided over by de Sausmarez's replacement:

"When Sir Havilland de Sausmarez left here last year on home leave, it was known to some of us that he contemplated the possibility of retiring from his judicial duties during the present year, so that the news of his retirement has not come altogether as a surprise. We members of the British Bar desire, however, in assembling here this morning, to express our great regret that we shall no longer have him with us. Sir Havilland can look back upon many years spent in the Near East and in China, in the service of his country, and his record is a distinguished one such as any Englishman should be proud of.

"In this court he presided for a long period, a longer period than did any of his predecessors in office, and that period exceeded 15 years in all. During such time, he carried out his duties with an ability and impartiality which were apparent to all. It fell to his lot to decide many cases of the greatest difficulties and importance, some of which were of such a nature as could only arise in a court exercising extra-territorial jurisdiction, and we can testify to the extreme care and conscien-

2 *North China Herald*, November 6, 1920, p63. There is also a photo of Dame de Sausmarez.

tious consideration which he always gave to such cases. Moreover, he was at all times most successful in upholding the dignity of this court and in maintaining those cordial relations between Bench and Bar which are so necessary to the smooth administration of justice in our court."[3]

Mossop added that he hoped that de Sausmarez would provide a photograph of himself, to join the portraits and photographs of Hornby, French, Rennie, Hannen and H.S. Wilkinson already hanging in the courtroom.

In reply, the new judge said first that it was "after something like 15 or 16 years' service Sir Havilland has retired." He then praised his service, saying:

"He came here and really brought our present Order in Council into force and made it a success. His legal acumen, his quick grasp of facts and principles, his energy coupled with his real kindliness of heart, made him a very difficult man to follow. He has retired in the heyday of his powers, and my wish is joined with yours to him and Lady de Sausmarez that they may live long to enjoy a well-earned rest."

After leaving Shanghai, de Sausmarez took up residence in Guernsey. As Seigneur of Sausmarez Manor and Cliatelain of Jerbourg, he held the titular office of "Third Cup-bearer to the Duke of Normandy," held by his predecessors for many centuries.

Competition for the position of Judge

De Sausmarez's retirement produced a problem for the Foreign Office that they had not faced in the past. They had two

3   *North China Herald*, June 4, 1921, p677.

equally qualified candidates for the position of Judge: Skinner Turner and Harrie Wilkinson.

Turner had, by 1920, been the Assistant Judge in Shanghai for six years and a judge for over 20 years. Harrie Wilkinson had now served as Crown Advocate for 18 years (not counting the five years when he had taken leave from the position when his father was Chief Justice); had served as Judge of the High Court of Weihaiwei for five years; and had been Acting Judge in Siam for two years. He had also sat as both Acting Chief Justice and Acting Judge of the Supreme Court and had sat as a judge on the Full Court in Shanghai with Turner.[4] While it may have been a little early to appoint him Chief Justice when his father retired, he now clearly had the qualifications.

Both Turner and Wilkinson wanted the job. The Foreign Office, however, decided to promote Turner with the announcement being made in May 1921. On hearing the news, Wilkinson went home on leave with the *North China Herald* reporting that he may not be returning while he considered his future. Turner, clearly aware of Wilkinson's ambition, said a special farewell to him.

On his appointment as Judge, a special hearing was held to congratulate Turner on his promotion. In Wilkinson's absence, Allan Mossop, was acting as Crown Advocate. He addressed Turner:

> "We are sure the pleasure we felt on learning the news of your appointment to fill the vacancy is shared by the entire community, and we feel confident that the cordial relations which have existed for many years between the Bench and Bar of this court will be maintained and continued in the future.
>
> "Today we have discovered that it happens to be by a happy coincidence, the anniversary of your Lordship's

---

4   Full Court case: *Sin Hong Chan v Low Long-Yan*, *North China Herald*, February 19, 1921, p488.

birthday, so that in offering you congratulations in connexion with your appointment, we should like to add
an expression of our best wishes that you may enjoy
many happy returns of this day."[5]

In reply, Turner said, while the members of the bar stood:

"Mr. acting Crown-Advocate and members of the Bar, I
am deeply touched and profoundly grateful to you for
what you have said this morning. You gave me, when
I came here five years ago as a stranger, welcome. You
have renewed it to me today. It is difficult for me to
say more than 'I thank you.' It is not unnatural, I think,
for me to feel very grateful when I get a welcome from
members of my own profession. Your kindly reference,
Mr. Crown Advocate, to the domestic anniversary of
my own adds personal touch to the day's proceedings
which really takes them out of the realm of formalities.
"Mr. Crown Advocate, I still have to ask you and the
Bar for that help and assistance which judges require.
It has been freely and generously given to the Bench
of this court in years past, and I do not doubt that I
shall ask for it successfully in the future; we judges do
require your assistance in the due administration of
justice in these courts. May I, therefore, refer you when
you go back to your chambers to a reference in Law
Reports, Q.B.D. on page three."

Turner then, showing his empathetic side and that he did
always stop to think of the little man:

"May I here also add my thanks to the staff of this court
who also have to play a large part in the administration

5   *North China Herald*, June 4, 1921, p677.

of justice. From one and all of them, British and Chinese, I have had loyal and willing support during the time I have been here, and I thank them for it and look confidently forward to it in the future."

Peter Grain – Assistant Judge

Peter Grain, a member of the Foreign Office Judicial Service and at the time British Judge in Egypt, was appointed as the new Assistant Judge.

Grain was born on September 25, 1864 and was aged 56 at the time of his appointment. He was the son of John Peter Grain, a well-known criminal barrister in London. He was called to the bar of the Middle Temple in January 1897. Grain was, other than Charles Goodwin, George French and Skinner Turner, the only judge of the Supreme Court to have practiced for any length of time in England before heading for overseas service. He practiced in the criminal courts, sometimes as his father's junior, in England for 10 years. He was a member of the Bar Council from 1902 until 1906.

In 1898, he defended, along with his father, a very high profile case involving Dr John Whitmarsh who had been accused of performing an illegal abortion which resulted in the death of his patient, Alice Bayly. The jury returned a verdict of guilty of murder with a strong recommendation for mercy. He could also be picky. Once when he was asked to defend a prisoner at the Old Bailey for a guinea fee, he declined to receive the fee that was offered in small change of twenty-one sixpences, eight shillings and a half crown.[6]

In 1906, at the age of 42, Grain commenced a career that followed a very similar path to that of Havilland de Sausmarez. He went from Africa to Turkey, to Egypt and finally to Shanghai. After serving in various posts in Zanzibar,[7] in 1910

6 *The Times*, May 7, 1947; *Lloyd's Weekly Newspaper*, October 30, 1898, p10 (Whitmarsh); *Western Times*, September 16, 1904 (Guinea fee).

7 In 1906 he was made Resident Magistrate at Zanzibar, and the same year he was

he was made Assistant Judge of the British Supreme Court at Constantinople; then Acting Judge in 1911. During World War I he was the Special Judge in Egypt for the trial of German and Austrian subjects and he was also Judge of the Prize Court there. In 1915, he became Assistant Judge and Acting Judge between 1917 and 1918 in the British Supreme Court for Egypt. He was appointed as Judge for British Supreme Court for Egypt in 1919.

Grain's most marked qualities "on and off the bench" were described as "his extreme courtesy, his kindness of heart and his unfailing humour." With even the "dullest or most obstreperous witness, he is patient almost to a fault." To "young and inexperienced in court before him he was ever sympathetic and patient a fact much appreciated by the bar."[8]

As a raconteur he had "no equal in Shanghai at the moment, but unfortunately he seldom exercises his gift excepts when a discerning chairman at some semi-private function calls him out of an obscure corner to respond to some toast not on the program." He also had many interests outside court and during his time in Shanghai became Chairman or President of many committees including the Cathedral Boys and Girls School Committee, President of the Shanghai Horticultural Society and President of the Shanghai Pole Club.

Some newspapers reported that he was Jewish, however, this is unlikely because he was also Chairman of the British and Foreign Bible Society and the Christian Literature Society.[9]

Registrar King called to the Bar
Around the same time as de Sausmarez's retirement, Gilbert

---

promoted to be Assistant Judge and a Judge of the Court of Appeal for East Africa. For a time he left the Bench to become Legal Member of Council and Attorney-General to the Government of Zanzibar, and he was for a short time, from August 1907 to April 1908 Acting First Minister there. He was awarded the Zanzibar Order of the Alijah, 1st class.

8   *North China Herald* October 1, 1927; *North China Herald,* May 1933, Note by "A Member of the Bar" on Grain's departure.

9   The Jewish Telegraphic Agency put out a report on March 7, 1928 when Grain was knighted headed "Peter Grain, Noted Jewish Jurist, Knighted in China."

King who had served as the Registrar of the Court for 10 years, qualified as a barrister at Gray's Inn. As a former solicitor and with his long judicial service, he was able to take advantage of a "special scheme for Foreign Service students which enabled them to advance to call after six months' worth of UK study and dining."[10] King had been planning for some time to convert to being a barrister. He had been admitted as a barrister in 1912 but had not qualified to practice. For his admission as a barrister he received strong recommendation letters from de Sausmarez, Frederick Bourne and Harrie Wilkinson. Bourne in his letter described him as "a capable and trustwor-

thy judicial official."[11] He subsequently took the Bar Qualification exams while on leave in 1914. He received a First Class and a Certificate of Honour in his Bar Final.

The intervention of World War I meant that King was unable to complete the study and formal dining at the Inns of Court that was required of pupils to be able to practice as a barrister. His first wife, Fanny, died in 1918. With the end of the war, and presumably

Gilbert King: admitted to the bar

needing some time off, he put in place arrangements to spend time at the Foreign Office so that he could complete his pupil-

10 Email from Andrew Mussell, archivist of Gray's Inn, to the author September 21, 2012.

11 Email from Andrew Mussell, archivist of Gray's Inn, to the author September 19, 2012. Bourne's letter was dated October 10, 1912.

lage. He was called to the Bar at Gray's Inn on July 2, 1919 and returned to Shanghai soon after.

As we have seen, King joined as a clerk of the court in 1903, became Chief Clerk in 1906 and, in 1908, when John Douglas resigned, was appointed Registrar.[12] His brother Harold King was in the China Consular Service and was sitting as Acting Assistant Judge when King joined in 1903. Both Harold and Gilbert were born in Bombay in India, Harold in 1869 and Gilbert in 1871. Their father Alfred King was a storekeeper and then accountant for the Great Indian Peninsula Railway. His mother, Mary, had also been born in Bombay. Perhaps because of his early years in India, King was particularly kind to Indian parties in his court.

King was educated at Brighton Grammar School and London University, where he graduated with a LLB in 1895. He then practiced as a solicitor before coming to China. In his younger years, King was a good cricketer and at all times a keen golfer and billiard player. He was also highly regarded as a judge. In particular, he was praised for his cool temperament and evenhanded way in which he dealt with even the most difficult defendants. In one case, where a defendant was obviously trying to "make as much discord as possible," "King gazed out the window at two of the consulate dogs at play, whilst a storm of invective swept over his head. During a pause he turned and said with a dry smile, said: 'Mr So-and-so, if your endeavor is to make me lose my temper, do go on, but you won't do it.'"

One hardened criminal is reported to have said to journalists after King had sentenced him to jail for seven days:

----

12 Biographical information from: FO List 1932, p304; *North China Herald*, February 14,1908; Obituary – *Times* December 24, 1937; "Promotions in the British Court", *North China Herald*, October 1, 1927; "O.B.E. for Mr GW King, *North China Herald*, July 18, 1925, p27; P.D. Coates, *China Consuls*, - biographical information for H.F. King, p521. 1911 Census information. www.family search.org Thanks for Andrew Mussell of Gray's Inn for his assistance.

"Blimey! 'E's a decent feller, 'e is. I don't mind, being
sent dahn for seven days by 'im. Did yer 'ear 'im talking to me like a farver?" And the man meant it."

De Sausmarez on extraterritoriality
De Sausmarez did not completely forget China when he retired. Five years after retirement, he gave a talk to the University of London on "The Extraterritorial Court and China." A
note of his talk reported:

> "The question of the hour and one, as Sir Havilland
> says, of great moment, is as to the maintenance of these
> invaluable British Courts, which represent the highest
> standard of British justice. The jurisdiction is as valu-
> able to China as it is to Great Britain, since the advan-
> tages of undisturbed trade are mutual. But, though
> the demand for European and American commodities
> has increased and is, despite continual disturbances,
> steadily increasing, yet there is little improvement in
> the political position. "Young China" is "quite capable
> of creating a situation as difficult as any we have had
> to face since the Treaty of Nanking. There was then at
> least a Government at Peking which could control the
> provinces and with which we could deal with. That is
> not now the case."[13]

De Sausmarez, not surprisingly, thought that the British
courts in China would be a necessity for a long time to come.
This was not a view shared by the Chinese. The next decade
was to see massive changes in China that brought the British
and American governments to agree, but only to agree, that
the time for extraterritoriality to end had come.

---

13 "The Consular Courts in China – the Extra-Territorial Court and China", A lecture
delivered in the University of London. (The China Express and Telegraph Office).

Part Ten

The Roaring Twenties
(1920 to 1927)

CHAPTER 42

Bad Behaviour at the Bar

THE 1920s, as in much of the world, were the Roaring Twenties in Shanghai. New buildings sprouted everywhere. Chinese and foreigners, in search of fortune, flooded into the city which expanded to the west and north, well beyond the French Concession and International Settlement boundaries.

Many cases and issues came before the courts, including gun running, torture and corruption. The internationalization of business also brought tricky jurisdictional cases before the courts. These stories are told in this part.

This chapter tells the story of two very badly behaved lawyers: one a story of intrigue; and, the second of unexplainable irrationality.

The strange case of Mr Levinson
The case of intrigue was that of an English barrister, William Strafford Levinson, who arrived in Shanghai at the end World War I, saying he had been wounded in battle in France in 1915. He had a scar on his face to support this. He registered at the British Consulate as a British subject. Soon after, he applied to be admitted as a legal practitioner of the Supreme Court on the basis that he had been called to the bar of the Inner Temple in 1914. He was admitted by Judge Skinner Turner in a brief hearing in August 1919 on the motion of Allan Mossop, the Acting Crown Advocate. Mossop told Turner that Levinson had served in Her Majesty's Forces during the war. Turner said that he was very glad to admit Levinson and

wished him every success in his practice.[1]

Levinson took over the firm of Ellis and Hays with Mr John Priestwood and became a name partner with the firm, changing its name to Ellis, Hays, Priestwood, Levinson. His career got off to a quick start and he appeared in many cases before the Supreme Court and other courts in Shanghai. In February 1920, he married Miss Margery Prout in a well-attended ceremony at the Holy Trinity Cathedral in Shanghai. His bride had come out from England to join him. She arrived

The increasing number of mammoth office buildings in Shanghai suggests a simple means of settling the parking question.

Sapajou's view of the growth of Shanghai

1 Details of the Levinson case are sourced from: *North China Herald*, February 21, 1920, p491; October 9, 1920, p166; November 27, 1920, p523; Inner Temple Admission records for Levinson and undated letter from SMP to Tientsin Municipal Police found at: http://btva.unilueneburg.de/T_Netz/petal/project_en/content/card/set/view/a38_m2.htm.

a few days before the wedding on the P&O ship, the *Kashmir*. The wedding notice listed his parents as Sir John and Lady Levinson of Wiltshire and Miss Prout's parents as Mr and Mrs Algernon Prout of Kensington. Presumably planning to travel with his new bride, in April 1920 Levinson applied for a new passport at the British Consulate. He made a declaration that his previous British passport had been destroyed.

Levinson, at this time, was in his early thirties and it appeared to all that a long and successful career lay ahead of him in Shanghai.

But all was not as it appeared with Mr Levinson, for he was not British, but Russian; not only Russian, but a Russian spy. He had been born in Russia in 1887 and come to England at a young age in 1891. He had not fought in the war, using his Russian citizenship to avoid call-up. In 1915, he had been running a pawnbrokers with his brother in Penrhiwceiber, south Wales. He had then moved to Doncaster where he took a job as a teacher at Doncaster Grammar School. On the side, he pretended to be an inspector of munitions and obtained access to a number of munitions factories and sought out information from employees. In July 1916, he had been caught and was prosecuted at the Doncaster Magistracy under the Defence of the Realm Act. He pleaded guilty and was fined £10.[2] The residents of Penrhiwceiber punished him further by wrecking his pawnshop.

After the war, he decided to try his luck in Shanghai. Communication was not so efficient in those days and there were no databases to check citizenship. He was issued a British passport on the basis of his declaration that he was British. The fact that he was a barrister would surely have also impressed the consular authorities. Nevertheless, after receiving an anonymous tip in May 1920, the British authorities worked out who he was. In September 1920, on direct instruc-

---

2   "Penrhiwceiber Barrister Arrested", *Cyrmu 1914*, July 1, 1916, p4.

tions from the Foreign Office in London, Levinson was struck off the roll of British subjects.

He and the new Mrs Levinson then left Shanghai very quickly for Japan, Levinson using a Russian passport. On October 2, 1920, a telegram reached Shanghai stating:

"Levinson died last night heart trouble Davis."

The next week, the *North China Herald* received a letter from a "J.W. Davis (Davidoff)" from Levinson's deathbed in Shinagawa, Tokyo. Davis described himself as Levinson's friend from Oxford; recounted Levinson's genius and philanthropy and that his grandfather had been a British soldier in the Russian army. The letter finished:

"His death at Shinagawa at the age when most men begin to live will leave a blank not easily filled. It is because he was my friend, his only one out East, and as I know he was known in Shanghai that I write this appreciation in the hope that his friends in Shanghai will know him for what he was. We Russians in Japan appreciated him, but we knew he was wasting his life in Shanghai. When the vast majority are so petty, his large vision and breadth of outlook raised him to a pinnacle. Eheu!"

It seems, however, that news of his death was premature. Mr and Mrs Levinson boarded the *Empress* bound for Vancouver on the same day the telegram was sent.

Harrie Wilkinson, as Crown Advocate, made an immediate application for Levinson to be removed from the roll of the Supreme Court on the grounds that Levinson had lied in his admission documents and that as a non-British subject he was not entitled to become a practitioner of the court. At the time, foreigners could be admitted to practice as barristers in England but not in many of the colonies.

Skinner Turner heard the case. He said he would not strike Levinson off on the basis he was a foreigner because that was a technical question that he did not need to consider.[3] Levinson had lied to obtain his registration as a British subject and passport and "lying in order to obtain the prize of British nationality is to say the least of it not a desirable quality in a man who in his professional career is rightly expected to be truthful." Turner also added that matters of a very serious nature were disclosed in an affidavit sworn by "our first British official in Shanghai," the Consul-General.

Turner was, however, concerned that Levinson, albeit due to his own fault, had not appeared to respond to the charges. He therefore suspended Levinson from practice and gave him six months to show cause why he should not be disbarred. Levinson, not surprisingly, did not appear to do so.

Three years later, Wilkinson appeared before Turner seeking Levinson's disbarment. Turner asked why it had taken so long for the application to be made. Wilkinson said that "his going on leave had had a great deal to do with it." He added that "he understood that certain actions had been taken by the Inns of Court to which Mr. Levinson belonged, and it seemed right in the circumstances that there should be a certain amount of delay. No one had been prejudiced, and it was now certain that no application had been, or would be, made to the Court by the person concerned."[4] What Wilkinson meant is unclear.

Turner made an order striking Levinson off.

Despite all this, it was true that Levinson had been a barrister in England. He was admitted to the Inner Temple in

---

3   Foreign barristers had been admitted in the past. In 1901, Mr Arthur De Mornay Bidoulac, a Dane, was admitted but "not being a British subject, ... subject to the normal conditions." *North China Herald*, December 11, 1901, p1149.

4   "The Strange Case of Mr Levinson", *North China Herald*, January 13, 1923, p.116.

1911 and called to the bar in 1914 after studying at the University of Wales (not Oxford).

Soviet Russia was only a new country in the early 1920s. Levinson would not have been a deep sleeper agent of the type the Russians planted a few decades later. More likely, he was drawn, as were many, to the idea of a socialist utopia and, as his letter (for it can only be he who wrote it) from Tokyo showed, he had grandiose dreams of glory. He had presumably offered to help the Soviet cause, which then became his undoing.

What subsequently happened to Levinson is unclear. In 1923, the Shanghai Municipal Police wrote to the British police in Tientsin providing background information on him, so presumably he was in Tientsin for a while. Inner Temple records show that he was disbarred in England in 1928. Strangely, because one would imagine his actions in Shanghai were enough to disbar him for misconduct, he was not disbarred based on information from China, but at his own request.

The United States Court – One man too powerful?
An American lawyer, William Fleming was, at the same time as Levinson was being uncovered as a spy, getting himself into very serious trouble in the US Court. Fleming launched a campaign against the clear structural weakness of the United States Court for China - the over concentration of power in the hands of one man, the Judge.

His campaign resulted in Fleming being jailed by Judge Lobingier for six months, a decision upheld on appeal and a subsequent review by the United States Supreme Court. As a result of his complaints, the United States Court was shut down for almost a year in 1922 while his allegations were being investigated. It nearly led to Lobingier's forced resignation and almost certainly resulted in Lobingier not getting the reappointment as Judge he clearly desired.

Fleming's campaign started after he lost five cases in a row before Lobingier. He took this badly, which became apparent in a number of cases he was handling.

His first outburst was in the Mixed Court where, in an opium smuggling case, Fleming ended up in a war of words with Dr Oscar Fischer, an Austrian lawyer. Fleming alleged that Fischer had asked for a special assessor.[5] Fischer told the court he had never asked for a special assessor, saying:

Dr Oscar Fischer, an Austrian, accused by Fleming of being an enemy of America and China

> "It is an absolute lie. I repeat it, an absolute lie. It is only blackmail on Mr Fleming's part."

Fleming was not in court at the time but arrived soon after. He said that he understood Fischer had accused him of blackmail. He fired back:

> "I do not understand why he should have made this statement. I do not know why he should accuse me of dealing with something that is his own principal stock-in-trade."

Completely gratuitously, he added:

> "Mr. Fischer is an Austrian. He is one of the enemies of my country, and an enemy of China."

The assessor tried to calm matters down, but Fleming insisted that Fischer be forced to withdraw his remarks, saying

5 *North China Herald*, November 20, 1920 p626-627. For the libel case see *North China Herald*, December 4, 1921, p673.

after some heated discussions:

> "It will be sufficient for me to say that Fischer is the most black-hearted scoundrel we ever had in Shanghai."

The *China Observer*, an American newspaper in Shanghai, criticized Fleming heavily. Fleming responded by bringing a criminal libel case against the editor, Mr Missemer. He instructed Stirling Fessenden, the leader of the American Bar, to represent him.

Before the case against Missemer made it to court, Fleming decided to engage in a much bigger fight: taking on the whole US justice system in China. Fleming published a paper "The United States Court for China as an Institution."[6] The paper was highly critical of how so much power had been given to one man, the judge of the court, and advocated for a jury system, as was used in the British Supreme Court, to be introduced, or, at the least, for trials with assessors. He argued:

> "The Judge of the United States Court for China exercises a jurisdiction, power and control over the affairs of his fellow American citizens in China, greater than any civil judicial officer ever appointed under our system of Government, and greater even than that exercised by the Chief Justice of the United States."

He compared the system unfavourably to the Chinese legal system; challenging the very basis of extraterritoriality. He wrote that the practices of the court were:

> "consistent with the practice under the barbarous

6　A summary of the paper was published in the *North China Herald* on March 12, 1921, p672 under the heading "US Court System Attacked."

system obtaining in
China, against which
we were attempting
to guard when we
demanded our extra-
territorial jurisdiction
and at a later date es-
tablished this Court."

Stirling Fessenden

Fleming did not at-
tack Lobingier person-
ally. But he clearly felt that Lobingier was presiding over a
court that had too much power, some of which Lobingier did
not always exercise fairly. Fleming left Shanghai soon after
this to take up his campaign directly with the Department of
State in Washington DC.

The *North China Herald* interviewed Sterling Fessenden
about Fleming's allegations. Fessenden supported the current system, saying the small size of the American community made it difficult to have a proper jury pool. He added in
an apparent dig at Fleming, "so far as I know the only people
who have urged the adoption of a jury system or anything
similar to it are defeated litigants and other persons who may
be disgruntled over the decisions of the Court." Finally, in a
clear dig at Fleming he said: "He has been a prominent lawyer practicing before the Court for more than 10 years, and it
is rather curious that after all this experience he should now
for the first time discover the great defects of the present system, as implied in his article."[7]

Despite this, Fessenden remained Fleming's lawyer in the
Missemer case. But because Fleming was in America, Fessenden could not obtain any instructions from Fleming to
advance the case. He asked Fleming's partners to take over

---

7 "The US Court and Jury System", *North China Herald*, March 19, 1921, p743.

the case, but they declined. In May 1921, Fessenden made an application to Lobingier for the case to be withdrawn because he could not get any instructions. Lobingier allowed this.[8]

The next month, Fleming was on the receiving end of some harsh criticism. Fleming had been acting for Gaston, Williams and Wigmore (GWW) in an employment dispute. GWW had brought a criminal case against a former employee, Mr Boulon and had him arrested. Boulon was granted bail in the very large sum of $10,000. Boulon filed a counterclaim seeking $300,000 in damages. Soon after this, GWW changed lawyers, instructing Fessenden instead of Fleming. The case was quickly settled by payment of a relatively small sum of money, 20,000 taels, by GWW to Boulon.[9]

When the settlement came before Lobingier to be approved, Mr H.D. Rodger for Boulon criticised Fleming in a quite extraordinary statement:

> "In withdrawing the suit for damages, my client wishes me to say that we do so in the firm belief that the action taken against him was instituted on the undoubtedly malicious, and reckless legal advice of Mr. W. S. Fleming whose attitude in this case is now difficult to understand. The charge against Mr. Boulon was fostered in Fleming's soured and vindictive mind, and he never took the trouble to ascertain, as was surely his duty, the facts connected with the issue. In conducting the criminal prosecution Mr. Fleming employed means that no other American lawyer has heretofore used and which merited a rebuke from this Court. Had this case been in the hands of the present counsel for defendant firm, Mr. Fessenden, no criminal proceedings would have been instituted. Mr. Fleming's course throughout

8   "Libel Charge Dismissed", *North China Herald*, May 21, 1921, p558.
9   *Gaston, Williams and Wigmore v Boulon*, *North China Herald*, November 20, 1920, p561 (details of suit); North China Herald, June 4, 1921, p700 (withdrawal of suit).

the proceedings, the statements he made to the Court, and in his pleadings, were not only uncalled for, but, if used by any person other than a lawyer, or at any other time, would have resulted in a prosecution for criminal libel."

More extraordinarily, Fessenden, who had until the previous month been Fleming's lawyer, agreed with this. He said that the criminal case should never have been brought and that it seemed there had been "some personal animus" on the part of Mr Fleming in bringing the case.

Fleming and Fessenden were back in court the following month, this time fighting each other. Fessenden had filed a criminal libel action against his former client, Fleming.[10] Fleming and Fessendens' firms had been competing for work from the Philippines National Bank in relation to an investigation into large losses incurred in stock market speculation the previous year. Fleming wrote a letter to the bank that clearly libeled Fessenden:

"I have a long story to tell you someday as to the reason why these unfair methods have been introduced by the members of the firm of Fessenden and I can tell you in confidence now that, since they have done these things, I have come into possession of evidence that will not only discredit them but ruin their names in the community. They realize this now and are trying to make complete retraction of what they have said and done in this matter."

The preliminary hearing of Fessenden's claim was before Commissioner Ferno Schul. H.D. Rodger, who had only recently called Fleming "sour and vindictive," acted as District

10 *North China Herald*, July 30, 1921, pp360-364 set out all details of the arguments and Fleming's conviction.

Attorney. The courtroom was packed beyond capacity and a large number of people had to stand in the lobby trying to watch. Rodger also brought a second libel case against Fleming for libeling Mr Concepcion, the manager of the Philippines National Bank. Concepcion had been sent to Shanghai from Manila at the very young age of 23 to try to fix problems with the stock exchange contracts. Fleming wrote a remarkable letter to Rodger which even for the time was extraordinarily racist:

> "The character of this young man became apparent at once during his examination before you, when he arose from his chair and, in a burst of intense anger, stated to me: 'You are a son of a gun. If you talk that way, I will stick a knife in your belly.' Thus we have an intimate view of the real nature of the man who so easily and naturally reverts to the savage type from which he so recently sprung. His proper environment is among the cockfighters and bolo-wielders of the Philippine jungle. Lying to him is an accomplishment."

Ferno Schul, US Commissioner, accused of bias by Fleming

At the beginning of the hearing, Fleming tried to file charges against Concepcion for threatening serious bodily harm, presumably for threatening to stick him with a knife. Astonishingly, he then sought to prosecute everyone involved in the case including Judge Lobingier and Commissioner Schul.

He first said: "I desire also to file complaint

against Earl B. Rose, charging him with embezzlement and also charging Charles S. Lobingier, Stirling Fessenden and Chauncey P. Holcomb."

Then, "I have another complaint charging Charles S. Lobingier, Chauncey P. Holcomb, Stirling Fessenden, Ferno J. Schul and H. D. Rodger with criminal conspiracy. And another one charging H. D. Rodger with criminal libel."

Schul told him that all these matters would be dealt with after the charges that had been pressed against Fleming were dealt with. Schul then sent Fleming for trial before Lobingier.

Ordinarily, this would all be madness. But there was a method to Fleming's madness. He was trying to show that the United States Court for China was a flawed institution. By accusing all the lawyers and judges involved with the case of various crimes, including conspiracy, he was trying to force them out of the case. In an ordinary legal system, they would have had to withdraw and the case be heard by another judge. In China, because there was no other court with jurisdiction to hear the cases, the cases should not be able to proceed.

The penalty for contempt of an American consular court was 24 hours in jail and a fine of $50. Fleming was willing to take that risk. When he appeared before Lobingier, he made an immediate application for a change of venue. Fleming read out, as the *North China Herald* reported it, "a lengthy affidavit, in which he made many allegations against various Court officials and members of the local American Bar." The exact details were not published. Lobingier in his later written decision said:

> "We shall not befoul these pages by quoting the offending affidavit. It is a tissue of falsehoods from first to last and its contents are the most scandalous and insulting which we have ever known to have been presented to any court."

In a later appeal decision, the Ninth Circuit in San Francisco summarized the allegations as that Lobingier was prejudiced against the Fleming in favor of Fessenden; that Fessenden had brought the prosecution against Fleming "with the connivance, consent and assistance" of Lobingier; that Lobingier was party to the crime of embezzlement committed by the clerk of the court Earl B. Rose in 1919; that Fleming had recently filed charges of official misconduct against Lobingier and that Lobingier conspired with others to convene a meeting of the Far Eastern Bar Association to investigate Fleming and defame him.

Rodger made an immediate application that Fleming be committed for contempt of court saying that "this is a deliberate plan to disqualify the only Court that has jurisdiction" and that it was "a deliberate attempt to discredit anyone who has anything to do with this prosecution." With regard to Fleming's affidavit he said, "he is guilty of the grossest contempt of Court. It is all misrepresentations and wild, irresponsible statements, made by a person charged with a very serious offence, in an attempt to confuse the issue and make such a muddle of it all that he will thereby escape trial."

Lobingier asked Fleming to justify why he should not be cited for contempt. Fleming asked for time to send someone to his office to collect a brief. While this was being done, Fessenden, as complaining witness, was asked for any submissions. Fessenden said he supported Rodger's arguments.

His brief having arrived, Fleming rose to give his response. His principal argument was that as soon as he had filed his application, Lobingier had no right to hear the cases against him. He said:

"I have alleged your Honour is a party to this conspiracy and that Mr. Fessenden is a party to it, to charge me with a criminal offence, and therefore your Honour is a party directly interested in the prosecution."

He said that was all he needed to do. There did not need to be evidence to prove the allegation was true, only that the allegation was made and supported by an affidavit. He continued to Lobingier:

"You cannot yourself inquire into it, because you would be judging whether you are right or wrong and no man can judge his own acts. No man can be judged by his greatest enemy, as I have shown here and, by what I have shown here, your Honour cannot sit."

His true goal then became clear when he asked rhetorically that if Lobingier could not hear the case, who could? He said:

"If there is some lapse in the law, I am not responsible. If I had made it I should have made it different to what it is."

He finished by saying that he was entitled to a change of venue and the court should give it.

Rodger responded that if he had a bona fide application for a change of venue it could have been made without adding all the scandalous materials.

Lobingier then gave his decision. He acknowledged that the Federal Judicial Code would require a change of judge in these circumstances, but that in the United States Court for China there was only one judge and no way for judges to be replaced. He added that Mr Fleming had himself told him in a conversation the previous year that there was no way for Lobingier to be replaced. Lobingier had mentioned to Fleming that a US judge had suggested Lobingier and he exchange places for a period of time. Fleming had told Lobingier that legally this was not possible.

Coming to the point, he then said that if Fleming's argument were accepted, the court would cease to function because every defendant before the court would say: "I object to the judge."

Turning to Fleming's affidavit, he said that it was clearly scandalous. In a similar case, the US Supreme Court had upheld a sentence of six months. He said that as far as the statements related to himself:

> "they are absolutely and unqualifiedly false and the product of a diseased imagination. In referring to me as his greatest enemy he has only stated something that exists in his own imagination."

He found that the offence was a "direct contempt committed in the face of the Court, deliberately, knowingly and with premeditation," by a lawyer who knowing the law who "proposed to violate the law as he apparently thought with impunity." Lobingier sentenced Fleming to six months imprisonment and ordered the Marshal take him into custody immediately.

Fleming immediately responded "under the revised statutes no Consular Court can commit any man for longer than twenty-four hours, or impose a fine of $50."

Lobingier replied simply: "This is not a Consular Court. It does not apply to this Court. That is my sentence and you are placed in the hands of the Marshal for confinement."

Fleming made himself comfortable in the consular jail. He arranged for his own bed to be brought into his cell and for it to be wired with electricity. He then had an electric fan installed, a necessity in the heat of Shanghai's summer. He also avoided having to eat prison food by having his meals brought in from the nearby Astor House Hotel.[11]

---

11 *Japan Advertiser*, August 27, 1921, p1.

Almost two weeks later, Fleming applied for a reduction in sentence and bail pending appeal. His main ground for seeking a reduction in sentence was that the United States Court for China was a consular court and did not have the power to impose a sentence of six months. In a long judgment, Lobingier rejected this and upheld the sentence. He did, however, grant bail pending appeal saying that while bail would not be granted as of right, in this case bail could have been applied for at any time and that he did not want "to put the slightest obstacle in the way of ... review by the appellate court." He added that if he were wrong, then unless bail was granted, any appeal would be a waste because the sentence would have been served before the appeal could be heard.[12]

Soon after this, Lobingier, Fleming and Fessenden all headed to the United States in a great race to Washington. Lobingier left first on the *Silver State*. Fleming and Fessenden, both not knowing of each others' plans, left on the *Empress of Russia*. Fleming boarded the boat at the last minute coming on board from the launch that had come out to the ship to collect the pilot.

Both ships passed through Yokohama, allowing the somewhat bemused *Japan Advertiser* to carry reports on the brief visits of all three and the fact that Fleming and Fessenden, perhaps not surprisingly, were not talking to each other on board. Fleming and Fessenden both told the *Japan Advertiser* they were heading to Washington; Fleming to push his case against Lobingier and Fessenden to defend him. Lobingier on the other hand put out a statement that he was heading to America for his normal holiday and to attend a number of meetings. The *Empress of Russia* was bound for San Francisco where Fleming also presumably filed his appeal against his conviction.[13]

12 *North China Herald*, August 13, 1921, p502.

13 "Fleming Following Lobingier to US", *Japan Advertiser*, August 27, 1921, p1; "2 On Way to US in Lobingier Case", *Japan Advertiser*, August 28, 1921, p1.

Fleming's complaint against Lobingier contained hundreds of pages of documents. The only person with authority to remove the Judge of the United States Court for China was the President of the United States. Fleming, therefore, filed the papers directly with President Harding. Harding passed them on to the Department of Justice to review.

Lobingier demanded a full enquiry with lawful evidence and a right to cross-examine Fleming. The case was first handled by an officer of the DOJ and then by a reviewer. Numerous lawyers gave testimony from Shanghai. The review was completed by February 1922 and a report was completed. It was however, decided to wait until the decision of the Court of Appeal in San Francisco on Fleming's appeal before making a final decision.

All this time, Lobingier, knowing what a snakepit Washington was, remained in the United States to defend himself. This led to a massive backlog in the court back in Shanghai with prisoners who could not make bail stuck in jail and no major civil cases being heard.[14] One non-British correspondent to the *North China Herald*, "A Lawyer", unfavourably compared the situation to the British Courts in the Far East, which he said were "administered in an excellent manner for which at least all British nationals should be proud."[15] He suggested that a system should be put in place in the US Court for a temporary judge to be able to sit.

The Court of Appeals heard Fleming's appeal in March 1922 and immediately handed down a decision supporting Lobingier in all respects and upholding the conviction and sentence.[16]

The Department of Justice then issued its decision. Out of all the allegations, the DOJ found that Lobingier had not properly handled a case where his clerk, Earl Rose, had sto-

14 E Scully, *Bargaining with the State from Afar*, p159-161; *North China Herald*, October 29, 1921, p311.

15 *North China Herald*, January 14, 1922, p103.

16 *Fleming v United States of America*, Reproduced in full in the *Japan Advertiser*, July 21, 1921, p2.

len a client's assets and had created an "unfortunate situation which ... which weakened the prestige" of the Court. The report stated that Lobingier had "lost his usefulness in China and [was] not conducting his office to the best interests of the Government." The Department of Justice wrote to Lobingier, with President Harding's consent, suggesting that he resign "for the good of the service in China and in order to establish that atmosphere that is so essential to a Federal Court, especially in a Foreign Country."[17]

Lobingier refused to resign. There was not enough evidence to justify dismissing him; nor to deal with the political fallout. On June 21, 1922 Lobingier met with President Harding and no doubt impressed on him the fact that the court had not been functioning for almost 10 months; that the Chinese were already questioning whether America was complying with its treaty obligations by failing to provide a forum for Chinese to bring cases against Americans; and, that the appointment of a new judge would need Senate confirmation and could take some time. He also seems to have assured Harding that he would make peace with Fleming and that quiet would be restored to the court.

The meeting was a success for Lobingier. Two days later on June 23, 1922, Harding issued an executive order completely clearing Lobingier. It read:

"A full investigation of the charges preferred by W. S. Fleming against the Judge of the United States Court for China having been made, the charges are determined to be unfounded and are, therefore, dismissed.
"The Judge of the court is hereby directed to return to his post of official duty at the earliest practicable moment. (Signed) Warren G. Harding."[18]

17 This paragraph and all quotations are from E. Scully, *Bargaining with the State from Afar*, p161.
18 "Sustains Shanghai Judge: Harding Dismisses Charges Filed Against Lobingier",

Harding also sent a personal letter to Lobingier saying that the "decision is in accord with the views" of the Department of Justice.

Lobingier returned to China via Yokohama, where he gave a full interview to the *Japan Advertiser* and provided them with copies of his letters from Harding and the decision of the Court of Appeal. The *Advertiser* published these in full together with an editorial saying:

"The considerable section of foreign opinion in China and Japan that has sided with Mr. Fleming until now must admit that confidence was misplaced, and must regret the harm to American interests which has resulted from what can only be termed the irresponsible and vindictive action of a man who thought too much of his personal animosities and too little of the reputation and interests of his Country in China."

That man, Fleming, still had a prison sentence of five and a half months hanging over him and that five and a half months was most likely not going to be served in the comfort of the Consular Jail. At the time, for sentences of over three months American prisoners were sent to Bilibid Prison in the Philippines. Even before the final decision of the Supreme Court in Washington, he decided to do what any rational man would do. Apologize. He, therefore, filed a motion applying for a reduction in his sentence on September 5, 1922. The motion included an apology and retraction, which Fleming read out in court a few days later:

....

New York Times, June 24, 1922; "Full Acquittal of Judge Lobingier", *North China Herald*, June 24, 1922, p888; "Lobingier Entirely Vindicated, Back to Shanghai Court", *Japan Advertiser*, July 21, 1921, pp1-2; *Japan Advertiser*, July 21, 1922, pp1-2 for the Executive Order and personal letter from Harding; The Decision of the Court of Appeals is reproduced in full on p2. The editorial mentioned below is on p4. The interview mentioned in the following paragraph is on p1.

"I, William S. Fleming respondent in the case of contempt against myself, respectfully appearing before the court for the sole purpose, do hereby express my deep regret for having filed and read in open court on July 28, 1921, the petition, motion, application and affidavit for a change of venue in Case No. 1431 for which I was convicted of contempt in this and the appellate court.

"I retract all statements made therein and apologize for having made and filed them, particularly the statements that the Judge of this court was a party to the crimes of Earl B. Rose or to the prosecution of myself or that he conspired with others to defame and injure me.

"I acknowledge that the language used in said petition, motion, application and affidavit was improper and disrespectful. I humbly ask the court's pardon for having used it, and I undertake never to repeat such unbecoming expressions.

"I further ask leave of the court to withdraw from its files the said petition, motion, application and affidavit that the same may be destroyed and held for naught."[19]

Lobingier said in response that "As far as I personally am concerned, I wish to say that I bear no malice whatever against the defendant in this matter." However, because the matter was before the United States Supreme Court he would have to adjourn the case until the Supreme Court made a decision. On October 23, 1922, the Supreme Court rejected Fleming's petition for leave to appeal.[20]

As if by serendipity, the day the Supreme Court rejected Fleming's petition, the American community, led by the Far Eastern Bar Association, held a dinner in Lobingier's honour at the French Club in Shanghai. The reason given for the din-

19 *North China Herald*, September 9, 1922, p767.
20 "The charge Against Mr W.S. Fleming", *North China Herald*, December 22, 1922.

ner was that the day before October 22, 1922, marked the 20th year Lobingier had sat on the bench since his first appointment as a judicial commissioner in Nebraska. No doubt, a much more important reason was for the community to show its support for Lobingier. Over 400 people attended the dinner including representatives of the Chinese government. Stirling Fessenden acted as toastmaster. President Harding sent a dispatch congratulating Lobingier and the Chinese government conferred upon him the Decoration of Chiao-Ho.[21]

After dismissing Fleming's application to appeal from the Ninth Circuit, the new Chief Justice of the United States Supreme Court, former President William Taft, issued a mandate to the US Court for China to carry out its sentence. The mandate arrived in December in Shanghai.

Lobingier now had to decide what to do with Fleming. He issued a long decision but unlike all his other decisions he did not cite numerous case authorities. In what must have been a calculated plan to show he was making a political and not legal decision, the only authority he cited was Victor Hugo's Les Miserables and the story of Jean Valjean.

Valjean had been caught by the Archbishop he had befriended stealing the Archbishop's silver candlesticks. Instead of punishing him, the Archbishop had given further assistance and sent him on his way. Lobingier in his judgment said:

> "That second act of generosity effected a transformation. It touched the latent spark of manhood and changed the offender's entire outlook on life. Thereafter he was moved by the spirit of his benefactor. From a petty criminal seeking whom he might victimize, he became a kind man of conscience who ultimately accomplished real feats of moral heroism."[22]

21 1902 to 1922: 20 Years in the Judiciary, Far Eastern Bar Association, Bulletin VII, 1922.

22 *North China Herald*, December 30, 1922, p881. The mandate dismissing his appeal is in the *North China Herald*, December 23, 1922, p821

But, Lobingier said, Fleming's offence was far more serious. Valjean "did not steal the good name of the victim." Moreover, the candlesticks were restored. A good name can sometimes never be restored.

"Indeed, the consequences already resulting are irreparable — the interruption of public business, the delay and loss to litigants, the needless waste and suffering."

Then taking into account the suffering further imprisonment would cause on Fleming's wife and daughter, he gave the family a late Christmas present. Lobingier reduced Fleming's sentence to time served. Fleming was a free man.

The wording of his judgment make it clear Lobingier did not like this. Perhaps this was the deal Lobingier had done with Harding to keep his job. That some type of deal was done is supported by the fact that none of the other libel cases against Fleming were proceeded with; nor was an application brought to disbar him. Fleming continued to practice for many years in Shanghai until his sudden death at the age of 55 in 1932. A special hearing was held for Fleming in the US Court for China. Showing that, for most, bygones were bygones, Ferno Schul and H.D. Rodger both spoke to praise Fleming. Stirling Fessenden, notably, did not attend.[23]

Lobingier was soon back into the thick of things dealing with a number of gun running cases, where he was able to write a long detailed judgment citing many case authorities.

....

23 Tribute to Mr Fleming", *North China Herald* September 21, 1932, p458. In the mid 1920s, Norwood Allman who, as we had seen started out in China as a student interpreter and had gone on to become a consul and assessor in the Mixed Court, left the United States Consular Service and joined Fleming as a partner. Allman recalls joining Fleming because of his run in with Lobingier. This, to Allman, showed his "courage, loyalty and integrity." N. Allman, *Shanghai Lawyer*, p80.

CHAPTER 43

Gun Runners

THE 1920S HAD BEGUN with some hope for China that the treaty powers might finally take steps to bring an end to extraterritoriality. The Washington Conference that was agreed as part of the Versailles Peace Treaty convened in 1922. The United States, Britain, Japan, China, Italy, Belgium, Netherlands, and Portugal all took part. The Soviet Union was not invited. The conference reached agreement on the substantial reduction in sizes of the United States and British navies and limits on the growth of the Japanese navy.

No agreement was reached, however, on an end to extra-territoriality. Instead, it was decided that a Commission on Extra-Territoriality should be established to consider and report on steps for the abolition of extraterritoriality. The commission was meant to be established immediately, but China at the time was still very unstable. No one faction ruled for any length of time in Peking. The Nationalists had established themselves firmly in Canton but had not yet expanded their power to the rest of the country.

There was one glimmer of hope for China from the conference. All countries participating agreed that that they would ban the import of arms into China. In 1922, the US Congress had passed a "Joint Resolution to prohibit the exportation of arms or munitions of war from the United States to certain countries and for other purposes."

As a result of the agreement to ban imports and in an attempt to keep crime down in the city, the Shanghai Municipal

Police constantly on the lookout for gun-runners. One case worthy of a Hollywood plot came before Magistrate Loh and Mr Jacobs in the Mixed Court.

A Serbian, Borxo B Stanoyevich, was suspected of dealing in arms. He had been arrested at the Great Eastern Hotel by Detective Sergeant Maurice Tinkler. Tinkler had arranged a sting operation where one Chinese detective of the SMP had acted as a general from the Jiangsu army, another as his attendant and a third was disguised in the uniform of a hotel attendant. Tinkler and Taubram hid in an alcove outside. Stanoyevich was very careful and it took three meetings, before he brought some sample pistols. The undercover general then asked the undercover hotel attendant to get some cigarettes, the pre-arranged signal for Tinkler and Taubram to pounce. Pounce they did; and they got their man. Stanoyevich's house was searched but no further weapons were found.[1]

Stanoyevich, because he claimed to be Serbian, was brought before the Mixed Court. Police investigations revealed he had at one time been registered as Italian and his counsel, M Lemiere requested his case be referred to the Italian Consulate. This was so ordered. The Italians rejected his claim of nationality and so he was tried before the Mixed Court where he received a sentence of two years which was reduced on a review to one year.

In the US Court, the resolve to stop the smuggling of guns to China led almost immediately to two prosecutions for smuggling munitions into China. In the first case, James Slevin was prosecuted for bringing 14 cases of airplanes into China. He was acquitted because there was no evidence the planes were for military use.[2]

The second case was bizarre. It involved a Russian Admiral, Cossack soldiers, Chinese warlords and a sea captain

---

1 "Detectives' Smart Arrest", *North China Herald,* September 6, 1924, p388.

2 *United States v Slevin, North China Herald*, February 10, 1923, p402 (trial); February 17, 1923, p474 (judgment).

with two wooden legs.

In early July 1923, the new District Attorney, Leonard Husar gave newspaper interviews to say he was investigating the activities of alleged gun-runners. He estimated that guns and shells worth millions of dollars were being sold in China. Husar believed that Shanghai was "the center of a gigantic organization carrying on an illicit trade in arms and ammunition throughout the Far East."[3]

Husar, had been appointed to replace Major Holcomb as US District Attorney for China in 1922. Before coming to China, Husar had been Chief Trial Attorney of the Prosecuting Attorney's Office in Los Angeles. Husar had been admitted to practice in California 11 years before in 1912 and then, reversing the normal order of things, graduated in law from the University of Southern California in 1914. He was at the time of his appointment very young, being only 33 years old.[4]

His investigations, he said, had found 12 prominent Americans actively involved in contraband operations and that up to 30 Americans were involved as well as British, Chinese, Japanese and Russians. He identified one deal with a Chinese warlord Chang Tso-lin as being worth US$3 million. According to Husar, one prominent American running guns was Captain Lawrence D. Kearny.

By mid-July 1923, Husar was ready to take action. He issued warrants for Kearny's arrest: one for the sale of weapons to the governor of Chekiang Province, and one for the sale of Russian ships to Kiangsu province. Kearny was not in Shanghai when the warrants were issued. Husar circulated his description and photograph to US consular authorities and police around the nation. Kearny was identified as being "just over five feet in height, stout, and about 60 years though he appears to be not more than 45 years of age. He is full faced and talks in a deep gruff voice."

3 *Logansport Pharaoh Tribune*, July 14, 1923, p1.
4 *North China Herald*, June 3, 1922, p674.

Other than his youngish looks, this was the description of anyone who has spent many years at sea. However, Kearny had one distinguishing feature that meant it would be hard for him to hide out anywhere in China. He had two wooden legs, one going above the knee; the other being shorter and joining the leg below the knee. He walked without crutches, but his gait must have been a clear giveaway as to who he was. The US Marshal, Mr van Busbick, went to Ningpo where Kearny had last been seen to arrest him, but Kearny had left the day before. Finally, Kearny was caught by the Chekiang River Police in Chinhai near Ningpo, kept on a junk for three days, and then handed over to van Busbick who had been sent to collect him.

In preparing the warrants, Husar faced a big problem: what to charge Kearny with? There was no law of the United States of America, or of Alaska or the District of Columbia, that prohibited the import of arms into China. There was no common law crime either. Husar had to fall back on the US treaties with China, all of which had prohibited the importation of weapons into China in some form. The Federal Penal Code made it an offence for persons to conspire to commit an offence against the United States or to defraud the United States. Husar framed his charges on the basis that Kearny had conspired with others to import weapons into China in contravention of the Treaty of Wanghsia and the Treaty of Tientsin.[5]

5 For details of the charge and Lobingier's decision on the objection (or demurrer), see *United States v Kearny* 1 China Law Rev 336. One of the charges read: On or about the 20th day of November, 1922, and upon several days thereafter at the City of Shanghai, Republic of China, and within the jurisdiction of the above entitled Court, did wilfully, knowingly, maliciously, unlawfully, feloniously, conspire, confederate and agree with one Admiral Stark, George A. Mayer, Harry Horowitz and Y. T. Foo, and other parties whose names are unknown, to commit an offense against the United States of America, to wit, wilfully, knowingly, unlawfully and feloniously to trade in contraband articles of merchandise, to-wit machine guns, bayonets, rifles, cartridges, pistols, revolvers field artillery pieces, and other arms, ammunitions and munitions of war, in violation of Article XXXIII of the Treaty of Wang-Hsa, entered into between the United States of America and the Government of China, in 1844; and Article XIV of the Treaty of Tientsin, entered into between the United States of America and the Government of China in 1858; and Rule III of Article I of the Treaty entered into between the United States of America and

This was a stretch and Husar probably knew it. However, with Charles Lobingier on
the bench Husar would have
known he had a judge who
would do his best to stretch
the law to prevent activities
that harmed US relations
with China.

Judge Cornell Franklin, Kearny's lawyer and later Chairman of the SMC

Kearny's lawyer was Cor-
nell Franklin, a senior American lawyer in Shanghai who
like Stirling Fessenden would
later serve as Chairman of the
Shanghai Municipal Coun-
cil. Franklin practiced law in
Hawaii before coming to Shanghai. He had been assistant attorney general for Hawaii from 1917 to 1918 and First Judge
of the First Judicial Circuit of Hawaii from 1919 to 1921[6]. He
continued to use the title Judge in Shanghai and was often
referred to as "Judge Franklin."

Franklin was prepared to fight the charges and fight
hard. He filed a demurrer to the charge, which Lobingier
acknowledged to be "exhaustive and ingenious." Franklin
argued that the treaties were not in force, or went beyond
the treaty-making power of the United States. The first argument, on the face of it, seemed weak. If the treaties were not
in force, then the Court itself would not have jurisdiction -
indeed, it should not exist. The argument was a little more
sophisticated. The argument was that each treaty had been
cancelled by the succeeding one and thus ultimately the joint

the Government of China in 1858, establishing trade regulations and tariff; and Rule III
of Annex III of the Treaty entered into between the United States of America and the
Government of China, dated October 8, 1903, which said Treaties, and each of them, are
still in full force and effect.

6 *Men of Shanghai and North China*, p139.

resolution of Congress following the Washington Conference
had cancelled any parts of the treaties that prohibited arms
smuggling. Lobingier made short work of this, pointing out
that in international law, one treaty did not supersede the
other, unless the treaty specifically stated it did so. This had
been confirmed by the Supreme Court in the Ross case. In
any event, the joint congressional resolution had nothing to
do with smuggling arms into China but with exporting arms
from America.

  Franklin's second argument was much stronger. Treaties
are made by the executive branch with the consent of the
Senate. Laws should only be made by Congress, that is, the
House of Representatives and the Senate together. The argument was that the President, by signing a treaty, could not
create an offence without Congress enacting a law to support
it. Lobingier, in an exhaustive analysis, held first that the acts
establishing first Consular Courts and later the US Court had
been passed to enforce the treaties. Under the act establishing
the US Court the court had been:

> "'expressly empowered to arraign and try ... all citi-
> zens of the United States, charged with offenses against
> law,' in China, and this grant of jurisdiction is made
> for the express purpose of carrying 'into full effect the
> provisions of the treaty.' Then, as if to meet just such a
> situation as this, the Court is authorized to supplement
> the treaty by imposing penalties at its discretion."

  Secondly, Lobingier, relying on various Supreme Court
decisions interpreting Article 6 of the United States Constitution, provided that treaties were self-executing, meaning
they became part of United States law once ratified even if
the treaty proscribed an offence. He concluded that only an
appellate court could find otherwise, saying: "If this record is
to be broken it should be by some higher tribunal." Kearny's

objection was therefore overruled and his cases came on for trial.

The two cases against Kearny were tried separately but the judgments given together. The first case heard in September 1923 related to dealings with Russian navy ships that had landed at Woosong to the north of Shanghai in December 1922 with over 3,000 Russian refugees on board. The second case was heard in October and related to an attempt by Kearny to sell a Russian ship, the *El-Dorado*, that was in Korea to Governor Chang of Chekiang Province.[7]

The ships in the first case were the remnants of a flotilla that had left Vladivostok in October 1922 when the last resistance to the communist revolution in Russia had ended. The flotilla was led by Admiral George Stark, a 72-year-old retired admiral who had been called back into service at the beginning of World War I to be based in Vladivostok. He had previously been a polar explorer. In 1904, he had been the Admiral in charge of the Russian Fleet in Port Arthur when the Japanese had launched a surprise attack at the start of the Russo-Japanese war. After the attack on Port Arthur he was relieved of duty and sent back to Europe. Admiral Stark was re-assigned to Asia in 1905 as part of the Baltic Fleet sent to relieve Port Arthur. As we have seen, they did not make it. Stark took part in the battle of Tsushima and was on one of the few surviving ships that made it back to Manila.[8]

During the Russian Revolution, the Czarist forces had built up a large stock of arms in Vladivostok to fight the communist revolutionaries. Stark had been sent to Vladivostok

---

7   Case reports: "Kearny on Trial in U.S. Court" *United States v Kearny,(No.1) North China Herald*, September 19, 1923, p942; "Outstanding Story in the Kearny Case", *United States v Kearny (No.2), North China Herald*, October 13,1923, p128; Judgment: "Arms Traffic Case", *North China Herald*, December 1, 1923, p631.

8   See *North China Herald*, December 16, 1922, pp707 and 708 for background on Stark and ships. In one of those interesting footnotes of history he was not the only Admiral Stark to be relieved of duty following a Japanese surprise attack. In 1941, Admiral Harold Stark was second in command of the US naval forces in Pearl Harbour and was also relieved of duty following the attack. See *New York Times*, "Modifies Blame for Pearl Harbour", November 11, 1948.

to take command of storing and distributing the weapons. However, due to poor transportation out of Vladivostok, most of the weapons had remained there. As the revolution turned in the communists' favour, Britain, France, the United States and Japan had intervened to land a force in Western Russia to support the White Russian forces. By 1920, all the countries had withdrawn their forces except for Japan. Japan, fearing a communist neighbor so close to it particularly on its borders with Korea, had maintained its army in the Far Eastern Provinces of Russia. By late 1922, under strong pressure for the US and also facing domestic opposition to the commitment of forces, Japan withdrew its troops. This led to the quick collapse of the White Russian resistance.

With the communists approaching Vladivostok, Stark put together a flotilla of 30 boats, some of them very old, to evacuate the armed forces and all other refugees they could take. In total about 8,000 people were on board all the boats. The 30 boats made it to Korea where 16 were declared unfit for further travel and the passengers put in care of the Japanese Red Cross. The remaining boats with about 3,000 people on board were provided with supplies and ordered to leave. They headed for Shanghai, losing one boat during the journey. The boats arrived slowly off Woosong during December 1922. Their arrival caused great concern to the Chinese authorities who were worried that the weapons or boats may fall into the hands of warlords. The arrival also caused great concern to Western residents of Shanghai that they were about to be overrun with more Russian refugees.

Kearny made deals with Admiral Stark to sell weapons from the ship to Admiral Tu of the Chinese Navy. In total 50 guns, 160,233 rifles, 564,492 rounds of ammunition and 26 field telephones were transferred from the Russian boats and taken to Nanking.

The second case involved the purchase of a ship and weapons from Gensan on the east coast of Korea from Ural-

The Saddles a popular recreation area and site of a Russian arms transfer

Cossack soldiers who had also retreated from the Far Eastern Provinces with the communist victory. They had taken five boats with them and for a period of time had been allowed to work in Korea. The work came to an end in winter. Kearny, through intermediaries, had approached the men to buy the boats and offered them passage to southern China. He had said he was acting on behalf of the governor of Kiangsu province, Chang Tsai-yang. One group of about 800 men had agreed and the boat the *El Dorado* had sailed for Chekiang Province. On the way, arms had been off-loaded in the "Saddles" a set of islands off the coast. The Chinese authorities refused to allow the men to land and stationed a police boat to ensure they did not leave their ship. In total, it was alleged that 6,000 guns, 21,000 rounds of ammunition, 28 machine guns and one field gun were sold in this transaction.[9]

At the beginning of the case involving Admiral Stark's ships at Woosong, Kearny's counsel, Cornell Franklin, applied to have the charges dismissed on the basis of a letter from Admiral Tu Shih-Kwei of the Chinese Navy explaining the background of the case. Lobingier overruled this application on the basis the letter was not admissible evidence.

A number of witnesses were called in each case to show Kearny's involvement in the deals. Kearny did not challenge this evidence strongly and at the end of the prosecution case in each case sought a dismissal because the prosecution had not proved that the arms were not for the Chinese government. Lobingier overruled the applications on the basis that on a reading of the treaties and the law, it was incumbent on Kearny to prove that the arms were for the Chinese Government.

This Kearny then attempted to do. Kearny was not embarrassed about being an arms dealer. He had obtained legal advice, most likely from Franklin, that stated there was nothing illegal in selling arms to the Chinese, and he had been happy to do so. In the *El Dorado* case, Franklin had been involved with the deal. Nevertheless, the facts of the *El Dorado* case were far murkier than the deal with Admiral Stark. In the case of his deal with Admiral Stark, Kearny chose to give evidence about what had happened. In the *El Dorado* case, he exercised his right to silence.

With regard to his deal with Admiral Stark, Kearny said

9   "Exciting Story of Gun Running", *North China Herald,* July 14, 1923, p104.

that he had been contacted by Admiral Tu of the Chinese Navy, who was concerned about the arrival of the Russian boats. The Chinese were worried that the five or six hundred refugees would land in China and cause disruption in Shanghai. They were also worried that the boats would be bought by rebels in Fukien Province to support a rebellion there. Reports had already been received that the boats were selling ammunition over the side. Kearny employed a Mr Horowitz who spoke some Russian to help him negotiate. He said he did not want a Russian to interpret because a Russian would double cross him. Kearny contacted Admiral Stark who was in charge of the flotilla and told him they would have to hand over their weapons. Some witnesses claimed that at times Kearny claimed to be an admiral in the Chinese navy. In any event, a number of meetings were held in Shanghai and on the boats, and at various times cash was paid to Admiral Stark. The refugees were apparently upper class. Horowitz said that he had purchased mink stoles and other items from them. A car was on one of the boats and Admiral Tu purchased this for his own use. A deal was done and the majority of weapons on the boat were sold to Admiral Tu. Kearny himself informed the American Consulate of his dealings relating to the boat. Lobingier did not give a decision immediately, leaving that until after the trial of the second case.

In the case of the *El Dorado* deal, the evidence was murkier and the trial far more sensational. Kearny had hired two men, Louis Roth and George Mayer, to go to Korea to negotiate a deal. Roth had failed but Mayer had succeeded in getting a deal to charter four of the boats, but the deal fell apart when Mayer was unable to cash a cheque for $5,000 to pay a deposit. Both Roth and Mayer gave evidence that Kearny had told them at a birthday party for Kearny, in front of Kearny's lawyer, Franklin, that the weapons were for Governor Chang so he could use them to launch an attack on foreigners in Shanghai so that Chang could be made President of China.

The attack would include the use of gas bombs prepared by
Russian chemists. Kearny, they said, had also claimed to have
been appointed an admiral of the Chekiang government.
Three other witnesses gave evidence regarding negotiations
in Korea supporting Mayer's evidence. There was no direct
evidence that arms had ever been imported into China nor
how the *El Dorado* had arrived in China.

Again, at the end of the prosecution evidence, Franklin
sought to have the case dismissed on the basis there was no
evidence that the weapons were not for the government of
China. This brought up the fraught question: who was the
government of China? District Attorney Husar said that the
only government that could be recognised by the Court was
the central government at Peking. Unless it could be shown
Chang was allowed to import arms, no defence could be
raised. Lobingier rejected the application.

Kearny called evidence from others present at the birthday party to challenge that he ever said that there would be
an attack on Shanghai. His only other witness was Mr Chang
Nieh-yun who said he was "adviser to the Commissioner of
Foreign Affairs in Shanghai, Counselor to General Lu Yung-
hsiang, adviser to the Chapei Tax and Works Department and
adviser to the Chamber of Commerce."

Chang gave evidence as to what powers a Civil Governor
had. Chang said that before the Republican Revolution, a civil
governor had a bodyguard and a regiment of soldiers that he
armed. There was no written law providing for this, but it
had been the custom for a long time. Chang said that the Civil
Governor of Chekiang was, in addition to that role, the commander of a division, the largest military unit in the Chinese
army. As such, and unless there was an express prohibition,
he was entitled to purchase arms and if he was bringing them
into his own province, he had complete power to do so.

Husar cross-examined and asked what provisions of the
Provisional Chinese Constitution gave the Governor the

power to purchase arms. Chang said that not all powers were express; some came from custom. Husar then asked how Kearny would be appointed to purchase arms. Chang said that he should receive an appointment with a seal on it. Mr Chang said that he did not know how the governor had been appointed but said he had not been governor for very long. Husar then asked point blank: "There exists a state of war between Peking and Hangchow?" Mr Chang replied, to laughter in the court, "I wouldn't say that, but relations have been strained for some time."

With that, the defence closed the case. Franklin asked Husar to agree to obtain from the Commissioner for Foreign Affairs a statement as to Governor Chang's position and powers. Husar offered to agree to put in evidence a letter from Chang. Franklin declined this. The hearing completed with Lobingier ordering that depositions be taken from Governor Chang.

Franklin tried to get evidence from both Governor Chang and Admiral Tu, but both being Chinese, the United States Court had no power to compel them to give evidence. After a number of hearings where it was explained it was impossible to get evidence from the Chinese witnesses, Husar and Franklin agreed to admit the letter from Admiral Tu explaining the deal with him and the letter from Governor Chang giving his explanation. Admiral Tu's letter took full responsibility for the deal and confirmed he had engaged Kearny to assist him. Governor Chang's letter on the other hand, denied all knowledge of the deal. He said he had met with Kearny once and said "My conversation with L. D. Kearny on that date, being confined to the subject of purchase of ship, had absolutely nothing to do with any other question."

Lobingier gave his decisions in both cases on November 30, 1923. Not surprisingly, given the content of Admiral Tu's letter, he acquitted Kearny of the charge relating to Admiral

Stark. Also, unsurprisingly given Governor Chang's letter, he convicted Kearny on the second charge. Franklin had argued that for there to be a conspiracy there had to be evidence of overt acts. Lobingier dealt with that by pointing to undisputed evidence of payment of money as well as the fact the *El Dorado* had arrived in China. As to punishment, he said that, "we must consider on the one hand the gravity of the offence from the public standpoint and the menace to life and property in China, from the illicit important and consequent reckless distribution of arms, and munitions" but because this was the first case under the treaties he would impose a heavy fine of $2,500 rather than imprisoning Kearny.

Admiral Stark and his crew had by this time sailed on to the Philippines, leaving 2,000 or so Russian refugees in Shanghai. The majority of the crew was then given passage to America. Stark himself went first to France and then to Helsinki where he died in 1928. What happened to the Ural-Cossacks on board the *El Dorado* remains a mystery.

After Lobingier had convicted him, as Kearny left the court, a free but poorer man, he turned to Lobingier and said "Thank you, Judge."

Soon, many others would be lining up to say "Thank you" to Judge Lobingier as well.

CHAPTER 44

A Sad Farewell: Lobingier Retires

IN APRIL 1924, Charles Lobingier became the first judge to serve his full term as Judge of the United States Court for China.

The only blot on what was otherwise a very successful term of office for Lobingier was William Fleming's attack on him and the subsequent Department of Justice investigation. He stabilized the court after a very difficult beginning and developed the court's jurisprudence fully, putting it on par with the British Supreme Court.

He retired to well-deserved accolades from the American bar and others. The *North China Herald* published a hagiography praising all that he had done to improve the US Court during his time.[1] At a presentation by the American Bar Association, he was presented a silver shield reading:

> "To Charles Sumner Lobingier, First Judge of the United States Court for China to serve a full period, and the only Judge whose decisions were never reversed, this testimonial is presented in grateful acknowledgement by the, members of the Bar of said court."

Stirling Fessenden, the Chairman of the Far Eastern Bar Association, had now also been elected Chairman of the Shanghai Municipal Council. He had intended to give a

---

1 *North China Herald*, March 1, 1924, p325; "Retirement of Judge Lobingier", *North China Herald*, March 29, 1924, p468.

speech farewelling Lobingier, but had to attend an urgent Municipal Council meeting.

Speeches were, instead given by Cornell Franklin and Paul Linebarger, a former judge from the Philippines who was now practicing in Shanghai (and also acting as an adviser to Sun Yat-sen). Linebarger credited Lobingier with having "scientifically built up and established a system of law for the Court." Franklin, who had been a judge in Hawaii, said he thought:

> "there was no judicial position in the U. S., or probably in the world, equal in difficulty with that of the U. S. Court for China. Deprived of the assistance of a jury - upon whom so much responsibility could be shifted - the Judge of that court had himself to bear the burden of unravelling intricate questions of law and fact and traverse the entire field of extra-territoriality."

Then with great praise he said:

> "Judge Lobingier had not only threaded this intricate maze without a reversal, but had plotted his course, blazed a trail for those who were follow, and as long as there, was an extraterritorial jurisdiction anywhere existing, his opinions and authority would be cited with approval."

Major Holcomb, the former District Attorney, then added that there had been a "feeling not only of regret, but almost of distress when it became known he was not going to be reappointed."

Lobingier responded by first commenting that the size of the American bar had increased substantially in the 10 years since he set up the Bar Association. He also added that he was happy to see that for new lawyers in the United States, law school training would become necessary. He ended by giving thanks for "this superb expression of your confidence and esteem."

Perhaps the highest praise for Lobingier came one month later from the man sent to replace him, Milton Purdy. Purdy was effusive in his praise of Lobingier's decisions saying:

"His decisions show a remarkable clarity of legal vision and precision, all the more significant because he had no precedent to fall back on. It is his interpretation of treaties, thought out with a marvellous clearness that has advanced the Court to its present status, ranking as it does, above the similar bodies in America. All his work was done, though it is not finished, during a formative period. We who are here must work without legal assistance on the part of our fellow jurists and one must work single-handed."[2]

After returning to the US, Lobingier was appointed an officer of the Securities and Exchange Commission.

Milton Purdy

Lobingier's replacement, Milton J. Purdy, had served briefly as a federal judge in Minnesota from July 1908 to May 1909 having been given a recess appointment, but had failed to obtain confirmation in the Senate. The President had appointed him without consulting the senators from Minnesota and they had killed the nomination by sending it to sub-committee from which it never emerged. Before that, Purdy had been a special assistant Attorney-General in the Roosevelt administration to handle anti-trust actions. He had become well known as "the chief trust buster." After his nomination for a federal judgeship failed, he re-entered private practice and

---

2   "Judge Purdy of the US Court", *North China Herald*, April 12, 1924, p55

between 1912 and 1916 he was a national committee member of the Progressive Party. In 1916, he returned to the Attorney General's office in the Harding administration. It is possible that Harding has planned to appoint Purdy to replace Lobingier in 1922, if Lobingier had agreed to resign - Purdy applied for a passport to travel to China in early July 1922. In any event, President Calvin Coolidge, who had been elected in 1923, appointed him as the Judge of the United States Court for China when Lobingier's term came to an end.[3]

Purdy took office on April 11, 1924 and was welcomed by all members of the American Bar Association in Shanghai. Stirling Fessenden began with the usual pleasantries and then got to the point, stating outright that there had been frictions at the bar before the Judge's arrival and he hoped that these could now be smoothed over.

Purdy expressed his pleasure at both being in Shanghai and for the welcome and said "it would be his constant aim and endeavour to maintain the present high standards of the Court and the excellent reputation that it had attained under his predecessor Judge Lobingier and all his predecessors in office." He welcomed all members of the bar to come to his Chambers at any time to discuss matters of importance and the administration of the law in China.

The District Attorney, Leonard Husar also welcomed the Judge. In words that he must surely have regretted later, particularly in relation to Husar, Purdy said that:

> "I have already thought many times how fortunate had been the U.S. Government in getting men of such excellent quality and ability as the officials of this court."[4]

Norwood Allman, who appeared before Purdy many

---

3 *New York Times*, Obituary, February 14, 1937; Failure of 1908 nomination: New York Times, June 2, 1908; Passport application dated 8 July 1922.

4 *North China Herald*, April 19, 1924, p94. Quote has been changed to first person.

times, described Purdy as having a very annoying habit of taking the examination of witnesses out of the lawyer's hands and examining them himself. When judges ask questions, it can some times be very effective. Witnesses who have been evasive can suddenly tell the truth. However, if done too much it can bog down a case and not help a lawyer get to an answer he is looking for.

Not everyone found this annoying. A writer in the *North China Herald* described how Purdy "had a singular faculty of getting the real truth from an awkward witness and on occasion when lawyers had finished their examination and cross examination, he would with a few very direct questions elicit the facts which the witness was only too anxious to withhold."[5]

Allman also said that lawyers "were often bored by the judge's favorite story which went something like this:

"A judge in trying a Negro asked him who his lawyer was.
'I ain't got one,' replied the Negro.
'In that case,' said the judge, 'I'll appoint one.'
The Negro shook his head. 'No suh, jedge, ah doan want to be hindered by no lawyer.'"[6]

Purdy, literally, received a baptism of fire soon after his arrival in Shanghai. In September 1924, he was driving in the countryside with Major Holcomb when his car, which was travelling on a road on the frontlines between two Chinese factions, was caught in the middle of rifle and artillery fire. The chauffer "stepped on the gas" and got them safely back to Shanghai.[7]

....

5 Purdy Obituary, *North China Herald*, February 17, 1937, p285.
6 N. Allman, *Shanghai Lawyer*, p107 and Purdy Obituary, *North China Herald* February 17, 1937 p285.
7 *New York Times*, September 7, 1924.

Purdy believed in open justice, which he made clear when he put an end to a practice that had grown up under Lobingier of not publishing details of divorce cases in the papers. Major Holcomb was acting for a Mrs Dolan in a divorce case where she alleged cruelty against her husband. The allegation was that he had hit her while she was in bed in Peking. Their maid corroborated the story. Mr Dolan did not offer any evidence. In those days there was no "no fault" divorce. Husbands and wives who wanted a divorce would often have to come up with grounds for divorce which, while they may have been true, could be exaggerated. Most courts played along with the game to allow parties to divorce. Major Holcomb asked Purdy to request the newspapers not publish details because publication was "not good for the name of the community."

Purdy had no sympathy, saying, "if people wanted their names be kept out of the papers, the best thing for them to do was to keep out of court." He did not want the courts to operate in secret and in particular "he did not want the newspapers or anybody else to consider it a Star Chamber proceeding," referring to the notorious secret courts that had sat in England until the 17th Century. Turning to the divorce itself, he played along with the game, as it had to be played. He said he found the evidence very unsatisfactory and he would prefer to have more evidence to justify his action, but "from what had been said it was clear that these two people could not get along together and in this instance he would grant a divorce."[8]

Purdy also took a practical view to extraterritoriality. Very soon after his appointment, he had to decide whether the Municipal Council bye-laws could be enforced in the US Court. This was a particular problem because the statute establishing the US Court made no mention of them or the Land Regulations they were made under. A Mr Fuller was prosecuted for carrying ammunition in the settlement con-

8   *Dolan v Dolan*, *North China Herald*, September 27, 1924, p516.

trary to municipal bye-laws. His lawyer, Nick Char, argued the Court had no power to try any cases under the bye-laws. Purdy did not bother with fine legal reasoning to deal with the issue. He said that the court had not only the authority, but also the duty to enforce municipal regulations. To not do so would create a condition of chaos, if "any one government [held] it cannot enforce the bye-laws against its own citizens." He therefore held that under the Court's common law power, it could enforce the bye-laws of the municipality in which it was existing, particularly when the Land Regulations had been enacted with the consent of the American Minister. He added that all the courts of other countries in Shanghai enforced the municipal bye-laws and that the US Consular Court and Commissioner had also done so over the years. He said that if he was wrong, the Court of Appeals in San Francisco could correct him.[9]

The following year, Purdy, however, made it clear that, if possible, he would prefer to try cases under United States law rather than municipal bye-laws. E.J. Beardsley was arrested by the French police for conducting a gambling game at 19 Avenue Edward VII (Yan'an East Road) across the road from the International Settlement, just back from the Bund and conveniently around the corner from the Shanghai Club.[10] During the raid, the French police had seized a large amount of gambling paraphernalia including a roulette wheel and gambling chips. The US District Attorney, Leonard Husar, prosecuted and Beardsley was defended by Ferno Schul.

Beardsley was charged under the French Concession bye-laws that prohibited gambling. The police had raided the premises without a warrant. Detective Sergeant J. Dulinatz of the French Police gave evidence that they had knocked on the door and been let in by the Chinese boys. They had found

9 *United States v Fuller, North China Herald*, April 25, 1925, p158.

10 *United States v Beardsley, North China Herald*, May 29, 1926, p412 and July 31, 1926, p226. Shanghai Pharmaceutical Co Ltd now occupies the building.

Illegal gambling in Shanghai

23 people grouped around a Roulette wheel with gambling chips. Beardsley had come into the room and told the police he was the occupant of the rooms.

Schul objected to the Roulette wheel and gambling paraphernalia being put in evidence on the grounds it had been obtained by an illegal search by the French Police. Similar issues had come up in the US during prohibition where the Federal Government had tried to use evidence illegally obtained by state police in federal prosecutions for making or selling alcohol. In most cases, the federal courts had ruled the evidence could not be used. (Luckily for treaty port Americans, prohibition was never extended to China, mainly it seems due to the impossibility of enforcing it in an extraterritorial jurisdiction.[11])

Schul argued by analogy that the evidence obtained illegally by the French Police in relation to gambling could not be used to support a prosecution in the US Court. Purdy agreed and ruled the evidence out. Schul then asked for the roulette

11 "The Volstead Act and China", *North China Herald*, May 28, 1921, p621.

wheel to be returned to Beardsley, "so it could not be used against him." Purdy rejected this, saying that he had no jurisdiction over the French Police and could not order them to return the property.

Husar then asked for a ruling whether it was appropriate to bring a charge under the French bye-laws. This was the first case to be brought before the court under municipal bye-laws other than traffic cases or the Fuller case. Husar said that he had brought it as a test case to see if the bye-laws could be enforced. Purdy had a bet each way. He did not rule out enforcing the bye-laws, but said:

> "I am not disposed to enforce a municipal law where
> there is a law of the United States applicable."

The District of Columbia had laws prohibiting gambling and Husar could rely on those. Traffic cases were a special type of case, because the laws of England and America were directly contradictory as to which side of the road cars should drive on. Purdy dismissed the charges. Husar said he would re-file the charges under the District of Columbia Code.

Two months later Beardsley was back in court. This time Husar had charged him under the DC Code. The previous evidence was allowed in by agreement. Schul asked for a dismissal because without the gambling paraphernalia in evidence there was not enough evidence to convict. Purdy overruled this on the basis that there was eyewitness evidence of gambling going on and Beardsley's own statement that he was in charge. Beardsley then gave evidence on his own behalf. He admitted he had leased the premises and that he knew gambling was going on. He said the real boss was a Mr Garcia who paid him to take the lease and look after the place. Schul manfully pushed on, seeking an acquittal. Purdy was having none of it and convicted Beardsley, sentencing him to a fine of G$500 or four months in jail.

In the prosecution against Fuller for carrying ammunition, Fuller had been represented by Nick Char, a Chinese American from Hawaii. As we shall see in Chapter 50, some years later, Char would find himself in trouble in Chinese courts when he was treated by the Chinese authorities as being Chinese despite being an American citizen.

More immediately, in the British Supreme Court, a British barrister who had been brought up in Hawaii by his Hong Kong Chinese mother was getting in trouble in the British courts, despite later, also claiming to be Chinese.

CHAPTER 45

Rebel with a Cause: Lawrence Kentwell

OUT OF THE MANY extraordinary judges and lawyers of the British and American Courts in China, Lawrence Klindt Kentwell, a British barrister of mixed Hong Kong Chinese, Hawaiian, American and British heritage was perhaps the most extraordinary.

Kentwell arrived in Shanghai during World War I after graduating from Oxford. He built himself a successful practice representing mainly Chinese and but also lower to middle class Westerners and Indian moneylenders in a number of the courts in Shanghai. His Eurasian blood probably made him attractive to Chinese seeking a British lawyer. It certainly made him unattractive to the upper class British society. Despite being a barrister and Oxford graduate, he was refused membership of the Shanghai Club which until the mid-1920s did not admit Chinese.

Throughout the 1920s, Kentwell was in and out of the numerous courts in Shanghai not just in his professional capacity as a barrister but personally suing and being sued in the British and American courts. The British Crown Advocate, Harrie Wilkinson, accused him in one case of being a criminal mastermind.

Kentwell was born in Hong Kong in 1882 to a Hong Kong Chinese mother and an English ship captain, Robert Kentwell, who it appears were not married. He migrated with his mother to Hawaii when young and grew up there. His mother, who taught him Cantonese, either subsequently married into or came from a wealthy family. Kentwell attended the exclusive Oahu College in Honolulu and graduated in 1897. (United States President Barack Obama also attended the same school which had by then been renamed Punahou School.) As part of his graduation ceremony, as the only student to be "born under the British flag," he was chosen to speak on Queen Victoria's reign in her 60th Jubilee year. In words that he may have regretted in later life, he praised her rule and finished by saying:

> "it is our pleasure to add one little laurel leaf to the royal crown, to the name and fame or our gracious sovereign and to offer this sentiment, dear to every British heart – God save the Queen!"[1]

He then attended Columbia University in New York and, later, Oxford University in England. While at Columbia, he made the newspapers in New York for assisting his sister, Elisa Christian, to give birth at the 3rd Avenue Elevated Station at 67th Street when accompanying her on the way to the New York Foundling Hospital. All went well and by the time the ambulance surgeon, Dr Saniel, arrived he found a baby girl "crying lustily."[2]

Despite his success in life, Kentwell's Chinese blood led him to face active official discrimination in both America and Britain. This was, justifiably, to taint his view of the world for the rest of his life.

In the early 1900s, he was working as Manager of the Hawaiian Realty and Maturity Company. Hawaii had been annexed in 1898 and become part of the United States. Under the Chinese Exclusion Act, Immigration Inspectors could bar Chinese from entering the United States even if they were US Citizens.

1 *Hawaiian Gazette*, June 25, 1897, p5.
2 *Utica Observer*, January 2, 1909, p6.

Kentwell often made trips abroad, travelling first class. He returned many times to mainland USA ports without trouble, most likely because he was travelling first class and because his skin colour was relatively fair. However, in 1904, after returning to Hawaii from a trip from the Philippines, an immigration officer singled him out for investigation under the Chinese Exclusion Act. Kentwell protested his treatment all the way up to President Theodore Roosevelt saying that he should not be treated as Chinese because he was English, having been born in Hong Kong to an English father. The Immigration Officials in Hawaii did not agree and in their correspondence simply referred to him as the "Chinaman."[3]

Once in 1905, returning to San Francisco on board the *China*, he actively sought to be excluded on arrival. The *San Francisco Chronicle* reported that as the ship docked:

"He walked the decks of the *China*, waiting anxiously for some Chinese Bureau official to treat him with discourtesy. He wanted to be insulted. He would have welcomed an assignment for the night to the meanest bunk in the detention shed, and would have greeted as brother the Government official who asked."[4]

He also gave speeches, in Cantonese, to the Chinese community encouraging them to fight discrimination.[5]

Kentwell did later become an American citizen. However, by 1911 he had moved to Oxford in England with his wife and four young children and in 1915 re-naturalised to become a British subject.[6] At Oxford, he also faced discrimination because of his race and was refused entry to the Officer Training

3 E. Lee, *At America's Gates: Chinese immigration during the exclusion era*, 1882-1943.

4 *San Francisco Chronicle*, August 24, 1905, p4.

5 *San Francisco Call*, August 28, 1905, p12.

6 *London Gazette*, April 6, 1915, p3366-67.

Corp because he was not of pure European descent.[7] The English Bar did not discriminate on the basis of race and he was admitted to practice as a barrister in England in 1916.

Soon after his admission in England, Kentwell moved to Shanghai. He left his wife and six children behind in Oxford. As we shall see, he was not lonely in Shanghai, having at least one French "lady friend" with a very sexy name.

Upon arrival in Shanghai, he was admitted before the Supreme Court for China by de Sausmarez, and quickly built up a substantial practice appearing in many cases in the British Supreme Court, the US Court for China, the Mixed Court and other consular courts. One of the first cases he appeared in was in the Mixed Court in 1917 with a watching brief for the Chinese authorities over a prosecution of a Mr Hung Chi-Tsu for his role in the conspiracy to murder Sung Chiao-Jen, the leader of the Nationalist Party in 1913. Sung had been shot at the Shanghai Railway Station, most likely on orders Yuan Shikai, after arriving from Peking. He was also in court when Fischer and Fleming made their nasty allegations against each other.[8]

During the course of his practice, Kentwell locked horns with the Assistant Judge, Peter Grain, on many occasions. It appears Grain did not like Kentwell, possibly because of his mixed race. Kentwell directly suggested this was the reason in one case. The Chief Judge, Skinner Turner, on the other hand, appears to have been more sympathetic.

Soon after Grain arrived in Shanghai, in 1922, Grain and Kentwell butted heads over Shanghai land law in a simple case where rent had not been paid and Kentwell was seeking possession of the premises. The Defendant admitted he had not paid. Grain asked Kentwell if he wanted ejectment. Kentwell said yes, he had claimed possession, which is ejectment.[9]

....

7   G Horne, *Race War: White Supremacy and the Japanese Attack on the British Empire*. See also file no. A63/IV/61/478-557 held at the Hertfordshire Records Office.

8   See Chapter 42

9   *Abdoolaly Ebrahim & Co v MS Mehta*, *North China Herald*, August 5, 1922, p410.

Grain asked Kentwell: Do you know that the land law is technical?

Kentwell: In Shanghai it is simple.

Grain: Not in a British Court. We have to go by British land laws. They are very technical.

Kentwell: It is the custom in Shanghai.

Grain: It is not a question of custom in Shanghai. It is a question of British law. Shanghai custom has nothing to do with me.

Grain then adjourned the hearing for two weeks for Kentwell to consider the law. What must have been galling to Kentwell is that he was right. As may be recalled, Frederick Bourne had decided some years before that Chinese law and custom should be applied to questions of land law in China.[10] There is no record of the hearing being restored and presumably the case was settled.

This was not the last time Kentwell was given a hard time by Grain over his knowledge of the law. In another case some time later, Kentwell appeared before Grain on behalf of an Indian moneylender, Pakai Singh, seeking payment from Mr H. Ossim who had guaranteed a debt owed by a Mr Pierce. Ossim said that Pierce could pay the debt so there was no need to sue him. Kentwell told Grain that there was authority for the proposition that the plaintiff could claim from either the guarantor or the debtor, regardless of the debtor's ability to pay. Grain adjourned the case for two weeks, commenting sarcastically, "it will give you time to read some law, Mr Kentwell."[11]

Kentwell defamed

Kentwell did not just get himself into trouble with judges.

10 See Chapter 37.

11 *Pakai Singh v H. Ossim*, *North China Herald*, July 3, 1926, p30.

278   GUNBOAT JUSTICE

Kentwell's practice of law, or probably more correctly the supervision of his practice, got him into trouble with clients on
a number of occasions.

In one case, newspapers reported he was a co-defendant
with his interpreter, Mr G.R. Grove, in a lawsuit relating to the
sale of some properties by a client, Mr H.B. Clough, to Grove.
The writ said that Clough "was induced to sign the deed by the
false and fraudulent misrepresentation of the defendant and
Lawrence K. Kentwell, counsel for both parties to the deed."
This resulted in Kentwell being subpoenaed as a witness in the
British Supreme Court and in Kentwell bringing an action for
defamation in the United States Court for China.

Kentwell had represented Clough in the Mixed Court in
a claim against a Mr Sia and obtained judgment for $5,944.
Sia owned 17 houses on Avenue Road (now Beijing West
Road). They were sealed by the Mixed Court to satisfy the
judgment. Some mortgagees had come forward, reducing
the value of the properties. Kentwell told Clough that his
interpreter, Grove, was interested in purchasing the properties. Clough agreed to this and signed a deed, drafted by
Kentwell, giving up his right to claim the $5,944 in return
for a payment of $3,000. Clough later found out that Grove
had then quickly on-sold the properties for $3,300 making a
tidy profit of $300. He brought action in the British Supreme
Court to rescind the deed on the basis of misrepresentation
by Grove and Kentwell. Clough, however, only sued Grove
and not Kentwell.[12]

When the action was commenced in 1923, it first came
before Gilbert King, the Registrar. Kentwell had protested
against the publication of the writ mentioning him and asked
that the press be directed not to print his name. King left this
to the discretion of the reporters. The British-run *North China
Herald* and *North China Daily News* did not mention Kentwell's

12 *Clough v Grove*, North China Herald, March 3, 1923, p614; *Kentwell v The China Press Inc*,
North China Herald, March 24, 1923, 831 and March 31, 1923, p906.

name, but two America-run newspapers, the *China Press* and *Evening Star* did. The *Evening Star's* headline was:

"Fraud Charge made against Atty.
Kentwell: British Lawyer is co-defendant in action by
Mr Clough"

The *China Press'* headline was:

"Charge of Fraud is brought against Local Attorney:
Mr. L. K. Kentwell is made defendant in British Court
Suit"

Both headlines were inaccurate and clearly defamatory. Kentwell had not been made a Defendant to the action. Kentwell filed a suit in the US Court for China seeking damages.

Clough's action against Kentwell's interpreter, Mr Grove, was heard first before Judge Skinner Turner without a jury. Kentwell was subpoenaed to give evidence for Clough. Kentwell said that he had told Clough that Grove was interested in buying the properties, Clough and Grove had agreed terms and Kentwell had drafted the agreement. There was nothing untoward in the transaction. Clough had known that Grove was his interpreter because Grove had interpreted the proceedings in the Mixed Court.

Clough said that it was Kentwell who had dealt with the matter, not Grove. Kentwell had told him he had an offer of $2,500 and was trying to get a better offer. Eventually, Kentwell had told him $3,000 was the best he could get and he had better accept it. Clough said he had signed the agreement with Grove not realizing that he was giving up his rights under the judgment.

Turner stopped Clough there. He had had enough:
"The difficulty about this case is, that it is a fierce attack on Mr. Kentwell who is not a party to the proceedings. It

is nothing but an attack on Mr. Kentwell. Nothing whatever is said about Mr. Grove, the actual defendant."

Turner pushed Clough who eventually admitted he had no complaint against Grove but that he thought Kentwell and Grove had colluded together to cheat him. His lawyer, Mr P.W. Goldring, called this an "accumulation of suspicions."

Grove's lawyer, Ranald McDonald, argued there was no case to answer. Turner agreed and dismissed the action with costs. He added that:

> "It seems to me hard, that, under the guise of an action of fraud against one man, and this charge being withdrawn early in the case, opportunity should be taken to hurl charges of fraud against another man who is not a party to the suit; and, as far as I am at present advised, I doubt if he could have been made one."

Kentwell proceeded with his action for defamation in the US Court against the *China Press* and the *Evening Star*. Charles Lobingier heard the case just a few weeks before the end of his term in office. Kentwell instructed Chinese American attorney, Dr Hua-chuen Mei (who had represented Gilbert Reid when he was charged with sedition). The newspapers got in big guns, instructing Stirling Fessenden, soon to be elected Chairman of the Shanghai Municipal Council, and Ferno Schul, the Commissioner of the United States Court. The actual reporting of the writ against Grove was privileged under American (and British) law, so could not be the subject of a defamation suit. The only defamatory part of the article was the heading that described Kentwell as a co-defendant. One witness called by Kentwell, Mr R.C. Faithfull, said that after seeing the report he had contacted Allan Mossop, the Acting Crown Advocate to make enquiries about Kentwell. He also said he had been told by one member of the press that "something ugly was coming against Kentwell in the near future." Mr J.E. Doyle the city editor of the *China Press* and managing editor of the *Evening News* said that in writing the headline he had merely tried to summarise the writ. He had "no animus against Mr Kentwell."

Dr Mei argued that such a scandalous report could only damage Kentwell's reputation in a small community like Shanghai. There was nothing in Clough's writ to justify such glaring headlines. Fessenden, kept is simple. He pointed out that Kentwell had been vindicated in the British court and it was for Lobingier to decide if Kentwell had been so injured as to deserve damages.

In his decision, Lobingier clearly had some sympathy for Kentwell, but said that if any damage had been done to Kentwell it was from the report of the writ, not the use of the words co-defendant. He therefore decided not to award him any damages but did award him his costs on the basis that Kentwell was "not unjustified in bringing the action."

Kentwell the criminal mastermind?

Kentwell did not stay out of trouble for long. As Mr Faithfull had been told, there was indeed "something ugly coming against Mr Kentwell." He was charged by the British Crown Advocate, Harrie Wilkinson, as a criminal mastermind. On March 21, 1925, Detective Sergeant Maurice Tinkler of the Shanghai Municipal Police arrested Kentwell on charges of possession of and uttering (that is, making use of) counterfeit banknotes.[13]

Wilkinson, in prosecuting the case, made it clear that although the charges were only for possession and uttering of counterfeit bank notes, his case was that Kentwell was most likely the mastermind of the operation. Or, as Wilkinson put it: "he must have known of the forgeries and he might or might not have been the intellectual head in the matter."

---

13 *R v Kentwell*, *North China Herald*, May 2, 1925, p200.

These were very serious allegations to make of a member of the British Bar. However, the reasons to suspect Kentwell were damning. Kentwell, who obviously was doing well, had three premises in Shanghai. He owned or rented a house at 1 Soochow Road (Suzhou Road) along Soochow Creek, a house "in the country" at 200 Warren Road (now Gubei Road in Hongqiao) which he leased and had another house in Nanziang (Nanxiang), in Putong far out of town. At the Warren Road house, Chinese men had been arrested photographing genuine banknotes. At the house in Nanziang, printing presses were found which were being used to print counterfeit banknotes.

Kentwell's Chinese assistant, Johnson Dzung, had at one time owned the property in Nanziang. But by either a lease or mortgage Kentwell had claimed the house was his. Kentwell had applied to the British Consulate-General for an official notice declaring that a British subject who was protected by extraterritorial rights occupied the house. This would ensure that the house would not be interfered with by Chinese soldiers or others. The notice had been given to Kentwell and it was placed outside the house.

Kentwell had not been arrested in possession of any counterfeit banknotes. The evidence against him came from two Chinese men who had been caught by the French police with fake currency. The French police investigations had led to the searches of Kentwell's houses and the discovery of the counterfeiting operation. The French police had then requested the SMP to arrest Kentwell and search his Soochow Road premises, which were in the International Settlement. The case was passed to Detective Sergeant Tinkler who arrested Kentwell. Nothing was found at the Soochow Road premises. Kentwell told Tinkler "Well, I think you will find all this is false." He soon after added that he thought the case might have a connexion with him having unsuccessfully defended some Chinese in counterfeiting cases.

Kentwell was released on bail. At his committal hearing before Registrar Gilbert King, Kentwell reserved his defence and he was committed to trial in the Supreme Court.

Between the committal and the trial, the case had an extraordinary twist. Kentwell had employed another British lawyer, Mr M.L. Heen, to assist to run his practice while he was being prosecuted. Heen had come into Kentwell's office on Szechuan Road (Sichuan Road) to find a Chinese assistant in conversation with some Chinese men. Heen asked what the men wanted. He was told that they were Chinese police from Nanziang who had in their possession a document that Mr Kentwell may wish to buy from them. The document was a letter signed by Kentwell addressed to the Chief of Police in Nanziang confirming the house in Nanziang was his and asking the police to leave the house alone because it belonged to a British national who was protected by extraterritorial rights. The letter read:

"Sir,—Upon the report by my servants that you have sent a police sergeant accompanied by two constables to my house demanding the use of the same as the commander's headquarters, I beg to say that this house was mortgaged to me on loan of Tls. 100,000. Prior to the outbreak of the war, registration of same was made in Our Consulate and protection asked for through the Envoy. As I am going to remove to this house, such an action on your part will cause my application to our Consul to file a strong protest with your honourable government. For the sake of national friendship, I hope nothing of such nature shall occur again."

The Chinese police thought they were sitting on a gold mine. And, in Chinese courts, where documentary evidence is king, they would have been. They however, did not appreciate that in British courts where oral evidence can be decisive, Kentwell may be able to explain the letter. The Chinese police put a very high price on the letter: $25,000.

Heen told Kentwell of the Chinese police's offer. Kentwell's response could have come out of a bad American detective novel.

"Collar them."

The SMP were called and a sting operation was set up. Because of the pending prosecution against Kentwell, this required permission from the Commissioner of Police who himself confirmed with the Crown Advocate that arrests could be made. Two foreign detectives and two Chinese detectives hid behind a partition in Kentwell's office while Kentwell met with his visitors. The Chinese said the French police had offered $50,000 for the letter but they were willing to offer it to Kentwell for $25,000 because they wanted to help him out.

The SMP detectives pounced and arrested the Chinese men who turned out to be the Chief of Police at Nanziang, Po Sa-tien, his secretary and a man who was said to be the teacher of Kentwell's interpreter, Johnson Dzung. Kentwell had them prosecuted them in the Mixed Court before Magistrate Zau and the British Assessor, Mr A.J. Martin, on blackmail charges. The case was adjourned until after the case in the British court against Kentwell was finished. William Fleming represented the Chinese. Fleming was still his feisty self, pushing hard for bail despite opposition from Kentwell's lawyer. Fleming said that it was with "ill grace indeed" that Kentwell objected to bail "when he himself was out on bail at that moment." Very high bail of $30,000 was set on the grounds that it was likely it would be difficult to get the Chinese police back to the International Settlement if they refused to return.[14]

Kentwell's counterfeiting trial started before Skinner Turner and a jury on March 23, 1925. Harrie Wilkinson prosecuted together with R. N. Macleod. Kentwell had three de-

---

14 Blackmail Case. *North China Herald*, April 4, 1925, P24

fence Counsel, Mr K E Newman, Mr Heen and a French lawyer, Mr R Cremieux.

Wilkinson called numerous witnesses including Tinkler
and Detective J. C. Giuuhs of the French police who had raided the house in Nanziang where two printing presses and numerous other printing equipment had been found. Kentwell
and Dzung's professional letter paper had also been found
there. The French police had also obtained a warrant from
the Chilean Consul to arrest Dzung but could not locate him.
He eventually surrendered himself when the police found he
was no longer Chilean and then obtained a warrant from the
Mixed Court. Other detectives from the French Police also
gave evidence.

The questioning of Detective Giuuhs, a French policeman
in a British Court, produced one very (for a lawyer at least)
funny moment when Newman cross-examined him about the
blackmail attempt by the Chinese policemen:

Newman: What was it the French police said at Nan-
ziang, which led to these two men calling upon Mr.
Kentwell?
Witness: The French police said nothing at all to them.
The chief of police at Nanziang himself told the French
police that he had received a letter from Kentwell
informing him that the property was his. Upon this, we
applied for a subpoena to bring the chief of police to
Shanghai, but he deceived us in the matter of getting
the Chinese magistrate's permission. On returning to
Shanghai, we found he was here, trying to blackmail Mr.
Kentwell.
Newman: All that is irrelevant.
The Crown Advocate: Then why did you ask the ques-
tion?

The key witnesses for the prosecution, Kentwell's alleged

accomplices in counterfeiting, were then called. The first was Tsu Sing Tseng who said he was an insurance broker. He said he had overheard Kentwell and Dzung talking about getting a proclamation for the Nanziang house and hoisting the British flag to keep Chinese soldiers away. He said he had met Kentwell at Kentwell's office where Kentwell had told him that banknotes were nearly ready. He and Kentwell had negotiated a price for the counterfeits.

Wilkinson's next witness was Tsang Zien-sung who had given information to the French police about the operation. Tsang had been employed by Tsu as a cook at the house. Tsang said that he had seen Kentwell at the Warren Road house and that Kentwell had been on a launch near the Nanziang house when counterfeiting equipment was loaded. Notably, he did not say he had seen Kentwell in possession of counterfeit bank notes. He said that there were seven forgers at work at the house. Turner asked Tsang if he had been paid his wages. Tsang responded: "Tsu is my relative." Turner could not resist. Showing that he had come to understand the Chinese he said, amidst laughter: "That means you didn't get them." Tsu confirmed this, saying, "I didn't get cash. Arrangements were made."

Wilkinson's final witness was Kentwell's interpreter, Johnson Dzung, who said that he had arranged with Kentwell to get the proclamation for the Nanziang house and that he had been to the Warren Road house and seen men working there. He did not know anything about counterfeiting activities.

In defence, Kentwell gave evidence on his own behalf and put the blame firmly on Dzung. He said that Dzung had been his interpreter but that he had realized later that "he was a bad lot." He recalled one case in particular when Kentwell had been handling a case in the Mixed Court involving a nun. Dzung had been given a title deed to a property to hold and had promptly mortgaged it. Asked why he had not dismissed Dzung immediately, Kentwell responded that "he had to act carefully, that he could not dismiss the man at a day's or a month's notice, and that unless he acted diplomatically in the matter it was possible that Dzung, who knew a great deal about his practice, might do damage to it if he thought he had ground for complaint." He added in response to a further question that "the greater part of my business was Chinese business, and if I had dismissed him instantly he might have done me an injury."

Carmen Roderique, who was described as Kentwell's "lady friend", told the court she lived at 1 Soochow Road and had been to the Nanziang house but had never seen any counterfeiting paraphernalia. She said the Warren Road house was used for riding and tennis. A number of office staff were called to say they had seen Tsu who had spoken to Dzung but never spoken to Kentwell. Finally, Mr Heen was called to recount the blackmailing incident.

Turner summed up to the jury with a very clear direction to acquit. He said the real evidence against Kentwell came from Tsu and Tsang. A jury could rely on the evidence of accomplices, however they should be very careful if they wished to do so. Kentwell was a very well known legal practitioner and that there was no evidence that he had actually ever slept at either of the houses where the counterfeiting was occurring.

Not surprisingly the jury returned in 35 minutes with a verdict of Not Guilty. Turner agreed, saying: "I think, gentlemen, it would have been dangerous to have convicted on the evidence brought before you."

Kentwell was in the clear and ready to fight another day.

Not so farewell to my concubine
Kentwell continued with his practice and in one case later in 1925 was clearly right on the law, much to the distaste of both Turner and Grain. Kentwell was defending a Mr Browne in a claim brought by his former Japanese common law wife, Sono Fujiyama.[15] Browne had been a solider then a policeman

---

15 *Fujiyama v Browne*, *North China Herald*, November 28, 1925, p 398; *NCH* December 5, 1925, p446 and *NCH* January 30, 1926, p201.

in Burma. Browne and Fujiyama had moved to Shanghai and it appeared Browne fell down on his luck, ending up at one point in prison. Despite this, Fujiyama stayed with him and supported him, even taking him food in jail. Browne then left her for a younger British woman.

Fujiyama brought an action for payment of $250 due under an agreement Browne had signed with Fujiyama after he had broken up with her. The agreement had been drawn up by her Japanese lawyer and stated that it was "signed, sealed and delivered" but it had not been formally sealed. Fujiyama applied for summary judgment for the payment of $250. Kentwell appeared on behalf of Browne to oppose the judgment on the grounds that the agreement was invalid. English law did not allow for cohabitation to be the foundation of a contract. Skinner Turner asked Kentwell what cases he relied upon. This led to the following amusing exchange, which shows again Turner's kinder side, admonishing Kentwell in much the same way as Grain had previously but much more gently.

Kentwell: I thought the point was so very well known that illicit cohabitation does not constitute a consideration for payment that it would not be necessary to cite cases.

Turner: You must never assume that a judge knows anything (laughter). Please bear that in mind.

Turner then asked Kentwell to get authorities while he dealt with other cases. Kentwell returned and argued that the document needed to be properly sealed. Tyco Wing, for Ms Fujiyama, then suggested the case be adjourned for argument on the validity of the seal. Turner agreed, saying that the agreement was virtually an annuity and that a lot of money may be hanging on it. Kentwell consented to this, adding that the Fujiyama might live for 125 years. Turner with his customary joke responded: "Quite so. I think it is very likely she will. Annuitants have a habit of living a long time."

At the next hearing Turner refused to grant summary judgment and allowed Browne to defend the action on the basis that there was an argument the agreement was not properly sealed. He, however, allowed Fujiyama to amend her case and apply for a court order ordering Browne to put a seal on the contract.

Peter Grain then had the unpleasant duty of hearing the trial. Kentwell, without looking up the cases, had been right about the law from the start. Grain found the agreement should be under seal and it was not appropriate to order Browne to seal the document. The agreement was therefore invalid. The payment of the money was only a moral obligation and not a legal obligation. Grain concluded his judgment:

> "I say I have come to the conclusion with some regret because I cannot forbear saying that I consider the defendant has treated this woman harshly. She helped him when he was in trouble, worked for him and gave him the best years of her life and then he callously casts her off because he wants to marry some one else, presumably a younger woman. I must in this case find for the defendant, but I shall make no order as to costs."

In making no order as to costs, Grain was making clear his distaste for Browne's position. As the winning party, Browne should have been entitled to the costs.

Grain, actually went further and at the end of the hearing asked Kentwell: "I don't know whether you can persuade your client to do anything for this woman."

"I understand that whilst the case was on he was prepared to give her $200 so that she could go back to Japan, which was what she wished to do," Kentwell replied.

"Then let us hope that he has not changed his mind. It is the least he can do."

Kentwell defends himself

Very soon after this, Kentwell was again fighting for his professional life in the British Supreme Court. By this time, reflecting the current mood of Chinese generally, he had become a shrill Chinese nationalist.

In July 1926, Grain heard a case against Kentwell brought by one of his former clients for professional misconduct. In 1921, Kentwell had assisted a Chinese businessman, Chow Kwei-Ching, to register a Spanish company at the Spanish Consulate under the name of "Chinese Coal Produce and Stock Exchange Co." In order to do so, Kentwell had registered Chow as a Spanish subject, born in the Philippines. Chow said that he took no part in the registration, save giving Mr. Kentwell his photograph and paying to Mr. Kentwell's office $380 as the registration fee.[16]

Chow said at the trial that he never went to the Spanish Consulate, that he was a Chinese subject, born in China, and had never been to the Philippines. He said he had never claimed to be Spanish. Kentwell knew he was a Chinese subject. Kentwell did not deny that he carried out the registration, stating, "I effected the registration of Chow Kwei-ching;" and that he had "probably attended at the Spanish Consulate to do so."

Chow paid in total $46,650 to establish the company. The company was soon after put into liquidation with Kentwell as the liquidator. Mr Chow only received back $26,000 of the money he put in. Of this, he paid more than $10,000 to Kentwell in fees. Chow sued Kentwell to provide a proper account of what had happened to his money. The trial lasted for 13 days. Kentwell made the foolish decision to defend himself.

Kentwell's primary defences as summarized by Grain in his judgment were that it was a Mr Gonzales of the Spanish Consulate, the Official Trustee, who received all the money;

---

16 *Chow Kwei Ching v Kentwell*, Trial: *North China Herald*, July 31, 1926, p222; August 14, 1926, p416; Judgment: *North China Herald*, September 4, 1926, p462.

many things had been done by Kentwell's interpreter without his knowledge; and, that he had been compelled to carry on the liquidation by the Spanish Consulate under the orders of the Official Trustee and without any powers as liquidator; and, that all his duties were superseded by the appointment of the Official Trustee almost directly after his own appointment as liquidator.

Finally, Kentwell said that the matter had taken place so long ago that he had forgotten many things that happened and many of the details. "I forget" is usually the defence of scoundrels. However, any practicing lawyer will have some sympathy for Kentwell. He was running a busy practice in many courts and consulates. It is very difficult to remember what has happened five years before.

The initial registration at the Spanish Consulate was not a direct issue in the case. Chow had not claimed that this was improper. Grain, however, thought it was grossly improper and said so in his judgment:

> "It is most distressing and regrettable that a man who has been called to the English Bar for about 10 years and has practised as an admitted legal practitioner before this Court for about the same time, should have lent himself to obtaining a false and fraudulent registration. This registration is only a side issue, but it is part of the history in the case and also, as it concerns a legal practitioner in my Court, I felt bound not to pass it by without some comment."

Grain then said that Kentwell's various defences were not believable, but more importantly:

> "There is a rule among members of the English Bar which is highly prized. Namely, that one's first duty is to consider and protect the interests of one's client. I

regret to say that in this case that rule does not seem to have been adhered to."

He concluded by ordering Kentwell to give the account requested by Chow showing the money he had received from Chow and how he had spent it. To punish Kentwell further, he ordered that Kentwell pay Chow's costs on the highest scale.

Kentwell was not going to take this lying down. After the judgment was delivered, Kentwell stood up and accused Grain of being "hostile to him throughout the proceedings." Then he accused him directly of racism:

"the whole atmosphere was so hostile that at I considered it was bordering on racial prejudice."

Grain tried to call Kentwell to order but Kentwell refused to stop. The *North China Herald* reporter noted that, "it was difficult to follow his remarks, but he was heard to say: 'This country is my motherland.'"

When Kentwell finally stopped, Grain reprimanded him: "I cannot have platform speeches. I am under the impression that you are a countryman of mine. You are a member of my own profession and a British subject, aren't you?"

"Yes, I am," replied Kentwell.

Grain had had enough and lectured Kentwell:

"I am satisfied that anybody who listened to the proceedings during the many days that the hearing of this case occupied will agree that I exercised the most extraordinary patience. I don't mind saying on my own behalf that if you had not been the defendant there were many things I should have objected to you saying, and the case, instead of lasting 13 days, would have lasted six. You have the right of appeal and you can state as the grounds of your appeal that the Judge was prejudiced."

He then asked if Kentwell wanted leave to appeal. Kentwell replied in the affirmative. Grain granted him leave.

Kentwell disbarred

Kentwell did not appeal. After the appeal period expired, Allan Mossop, now the Crown Advocate, applied for Kentwell's disbarment on the basis Grain had found that Kentwell had fraudulently assisted Chow to register as a Spanish national at the Spanish Consulate so he could register a Spanish company.[17]

Skinner Turner was out of Shanghai so the application came before Grain. Because the reasons for seeking disbarment were based on Grain's findings in the Chow case, Grain recognised in his judgment that he was not the most appropriate person to be dealing with the case. He said:

"I much regret that the present motion has come before myself and not before my brother Judge ... but unfortunately it was unavoidable owing to the absence of Judge Sir Skinner Turner."

This time, Kentwell was smart enough to get another lawyer to represent him. Tyco Wing, who Kentwell had been against in the Fujiyama case, appeared on his behalf. While Kentwell had admitted registering Chow as a Spanish national, all was not lost. The Privy Council had, many years before, overturned a decision to disbar an attorney who had put a false recital in a contract.[18] The effect of a false recital is that the other party would sign the contract believing something to be true when it was not. The Privy Council had found "the

17 "Mr L.K. Kentwell's Penalty", *North China Herald*, November 27, 1926, p414. It is not clear if Mossop personally made the application. The hearing was in chambers on November 8, 1926. Grain delivered judgment on November 24, 1926. At that hearing Mr Lipson-Ward as Acting Crown Advocate appeared.

18 Re Stewart (1868) L. R. 2 Privy Council Appeals, p.88

reason assigned for the false statement, though unsatisfactory, had any fraud whatever followed upon the transaction, was not inconsistent with the possibility of honest motives." More importantly, the document had not been used fraudulently. Wing argued that the facts were similar in Kentwell's case. The Spanish Consulate had not been deceived and, in fact, the "the Spanish Consulate was ready to accept registrations without inquiry."

Grain took a very dim view of the practice of obtaining false registrations. He emphasized the need for British lawyers to maintain the highest possible standards while practicing in an extraterritorial jurisdiction:

> "Even if this particular Consulate did at that time give great facilities for the registration of Chinese subjects, there was all the more reason for Mr. Kentwell as a member of the English Bar and a legal practitioner in this Court to do nothing that might in any way directly or indirectly encourage this irregularity.
>
> "Foreigners in China by Treaty are in possession of extraterritorial rights and it is most essential at all times, and more especially at the present period, that foreigners should not abuse those rights. It is still more essential that a trained lawyer, a member of the English Bar and a legal practitioner in H.B.M. Supreme Court for China, should do nothing in any way to abuse those Treaty rights which he in the course of his profession does so much to uphold, and administer."

Grain acknowledged that disbarment would be the end of Kentwell's career as a barrister. However, he said "it is the duty of the official presiding over these courts to do all in his power to maintain the high standard of integrity and honesty." He ordered that Kentwell be permanently disbarred.

When Grain had finished reading his judgment, Kentwell

leapt to his feet to protest. His lawyer, Wing, "made an ineffectual attempt" to restrain him. When this failed he walked out of the court leaving Kentwell arguing.

Kentwell complained that the decision was politically motivated because of his support for Chinese nationalism. Grain said that he had no knowledge of Kentwell's political views. But, that if Kentwell objected he could appeal to the Privy Council. Kentwell retorted that this would be futile.

Kentwell did not appeal. He did, however, write a stream of letters to the British judicial and political authorities in Shanghai and London denouncing the decision and British imperialism. He took particular pleasure in attacking Grain personally. The following year he wrote to Grain:

> "You know from the bottom of your stony heart that you have illegally and arbitrarily removed my name from the roll of legal practitioners .... Are you a product of Oxford or Cambridge? I suspect you belong to neither, hence refinement and nobility of character and good conscience are not in your reach ... the good name of the British nation has been polluted by you ... I will not resort to bombs, dynamites or revolvers, I would soil my hands if I did. I am content to leave the matter in the hands of the just Providence."[19]

He wrote later that:

> "the earthly dissolution of said Peter Grain will surely be a painful and agonizing one. Even hell fire is too mild and pure to roast the putrid carcass of the said Peter Grain."

Grain in his own defence, some years later, wrote to the

19 This and following quotes are all source from B. Wasserstein, *Secret War in Shanghai*, pp185 to 187

British Minister:

> "L. K. Kentwell usually states that he was disbarred
> merely because he caused a Chinese subject to be reg-
> istered as a Spanish subject. But the facts against him
> were far more serious than that. L. K. Kentwell con-
> stantly speaks of China as his 'Mother Land' or some
> title, but the grave charge against him when the court
> was moved to disbar him was that he had taken large
> sums of money from one of his Chinese brothers."

Kentwell returns

Kentwell was back in the Supreme Court two months after
his disbarment. He was now a journalist having founded the
China Courier, "an anti-British Journal" with another Eurasian, G.R. Grove, his former interpreter. Needless to say, the
Municipal Police were keeping a close eye on him.[20]

He had been summonsed for payment of the money he
had been ordered to pay Mr Chow in the case he had lost
the year before and for payment of back rates to the Shanghai Municipal Council. He had by this time become a fervent
Chinese nationalist and a strong supporter of the Nationalist
Government in Canton.

In the council rates case, Kentwell had written to the Municipal Council Inspector, Mr Inwood, stating:

> "I have to inform you that the undersigned will not pay
> the above taxes until Shanghai is handed back to the
> Chinese people, whose sovereignty the imperialistic
> countries of Europe have continually infringed. The
> Council collects taxes from the Chinese but allows them
> no voice in the deliberations of affairs of the Council.
> Fair play indeed."[21]

20 G. Horne, *Race War: white supremacy and the Japanese attack on the British Empire.*
21 *North China Herald*, November 20, 1926, p269

When summonsed to appear in the British Supreme Court, he responded in a letter to the court stating: "I have taken steps to become a citizen of the Republic of China, my motherland, and I throw myself heartily into the fight to recover her rights."

Kentwell did not appear in court. Judge Peter Grain, however, agreed that if Kentwell had taken Chinese nationality then his British nationality would go, leaving the British Supreme Court without jurisdiction. But, until satisfactory evidence could be produced to show that he had become Chinese, Kentwell would be considered British. Because Kentwell had not appeared, Grain issued a warrant for his arrest.[22]

Kentwell was arrested by Plain Clothes Constable Rhind on Sunday, January 31, 1927 outside his Chinese lawyer's house on Burkill Road (Fengyang Road), just behind Bubbling Well Road. Kentwell had been expecting to be arrested. He had in his pocket a letter he had pre-written addressed to the *North China Daily News*, which read:

"Sir, I shall thank you for the courtesy of publishing this brief communication in the valuable columns of your esteemed paper.

"I am aware that the local British Supreme Court has issued a warrant for my arrest. I am advised not to surrender myself, being a Chinese citizen. The local British court has no jurisdiction over me. I can only be brought before the British Court under duress, that is by being arrested wherever I happen to be."[23]

Kentwell was brought the next day before Registrar Gilbert King. Mr M.B. Brown and H.R. Snyder appeared for Chow and Mr E.T. Maitland, the prosecuting solicitor, appeared for the Council. Mr H. Lipson Ward, the Acting Crown Advo-

22 *SM Council v Kentwell; Chow Kuei-Ching v Kentwell*, North China Herald, January 29, 1927, p162.
23 "L.K. Kentwell arrested", *North China Herald*, February 5, 1927, p191.

E.T. Maitland prosecuted Kentwell on behalf of the SMC

cate, was also in court. Watching Kentwell in court must have been great entertainment. Many of the British lawyers in Shanghai had found that they had business in court that day and the legal benches were "closely packed."[24]

Kentwell said to King:

"I told the policeman that I would appear under duress and would only appear here by force. I am a Chinese citizen and do not recognise this court."

King said that there were judgments against him made when he was registered as British subject. He was asked how he was going to prove he was Chinese.

Kentwell responded:

"I have my Chinese legal adviser here who went with me to the City Court when I renounced my allegiance to Great Britain because of the snobs who have brought disgrace to Great Britain. I am ashamed of them as my nationals and I renounce my allegiance. This is the class of people who have brought on the disgrace. They are snobs and proud people who are looked upon with shame by the Chinese. I did not register this year at the British Consulate."

He and his Chinese lawyer gave evidence that he had

....
24 *SM Council v Kentwell; Chow Kuei-Ching v Kentwell, North China Herald*, February 5, 1927, p301.

applied to become a Chinese citizen but could not produce evidence that it had been granted. His lawyer said it was possible for foreigners to naturalize to become Chinese if they had lived in China for more than five years or if their father or mother were Chinese. Kentwell interjected: "And my mother was Chinese."

At one point Kentwell said in an outburst:

"I demand my immediate release as a Chinese citizen. This is the Gunboat Policy again."

A heated outburst followed and waving his hand over the legal benches he shouted: "These snobs also secured the rendition of the Mixed Court"

King, exasperated, retorted: "Oh Mr Kentwell, please!"

"That's right," continued Kentwell, "Snobs all of them! The Shanghai Club and Country Club! I am ashamed of their behaviour as Englishmen!"

King responded:

"I do not propose to act like a judicial gunboat, but I have to obey the law."

King required Kentwell to prove he was Chinese. Kentwell said that if he was not granted Chinese citizenship he would be stateless, to which King said, that no, he would be British. Kentwell said, "I don't recognize the Crown." King as a judge of the court could only reply, "But I have to."

Kentwell was cross-examined as to his assets. He said he had none. He had invested all his spare cash in the *China Courier* and had sent any other cash back to England to support his six children. King asked him if he had any money now.

"I have money which I put into a newspaper," replied Kentwell, "but that is just like throwing it into the Huangpu

River. I put in $50,000 to fight this arrogant British snobbery."

King's famous patience was wearing thin. "Perhaps that shows the futility of fighting the arrogant British snobs," he suggested facetiously.

Kentwell then gave evidence concerning his businesses. Then, as the *North China Herald* court reporter put it, he made "an uncomplimentary remark about Judge Grain which had been made several times previously."

This brought a quick and strong reproof from King: "I have great admiration for Judge Grain and I will not allow you to speak evil of him. What he did was not a personal matter but as Judge of the Court."

Kentwell said his wife had means and property in Honolulu and that he had wired her for some money, but added, "If I get the money from her, I am willing to put $50,000 more into the paper to exterminate this British snobbery."

The case was adjourned soon after this for two months with Kentwell being granted bail. The *North China Herald* has no record of the case being heard again. Presumably Kentwell, in a moment of rationality, paid his rates and reached a compromise with Chow.

Later that year, it was reported that Chinese President Chiang Kai-shek was considering Kentwell for the position of President of the Provisional Court that had replaced the Mixed Court in Shanghai, a suggestion surely opposed by the British. Kentwell's British nationality was, four years later, revoked for "disloyalty and disaffection."[25]

Kentwell wants to come back

Ten years later, Kentwell sought to be allowed to practice before the British Supreme Court. Kentwell had continued to practice law in Shanghai at some point qualifying as a Chinese lawyer, but, he could not appear in the British courts.

---

25 Provisional Court: *Bakersfield Californian* March 22, 1927, p2. Denaturalisation: *London Gazette*, October 6, 1931, p6392.

In 1935 he had been involved in a case where Percy Moe had contacted him to bring a case in the British Supreme Court. Kentwell instructed a British solicitor, Mr E.T. Maitland, to bring the case. Maitland, ironically, had prosecuted Kentwell on behalf of the Municipal Council eight years before. Moe later claimed that Kentwell and Maitland had agreed that if they won the case they would be paid a success fee. $353 was paid into court as a deposit. Moe then decided not to proceed with the case. Maitland took the money out of court to settle his fees which he claimed had been agreed at $1,000. Moe then sued Maitland to get back the $353 and Kentwell's involvement came to light. The then Assistant Judge Penrhyn Grant Jones heard the case and found that a success fee had been agreed and declared the agreement to be invalid on the basis it was champertous.[26] The *North China Daily News* wrote in an editorial:

"It is well that the Court thus should show itself vigilant in penalizing a practice which, although not illegitimate under the laws of other countries is rigidly condemned by English law in order to discourage the evil of litigiousness."

Then in a clear dig at Kentwell, it added:

"Inevitably in an international community, the conflict of codes exposes some practitioners to the danger of laxity in observing the principles under which they have been enrolled. Strict correction from the bench is therefore to be welcomed as a guarantee that the high standards of the British bar will not be lightly allowed to fall into neglect."

26 "Client is Given Judgment against Mr Maitland", *Shanghai Times*, June 19, 1935; "Champerty", *North China Daily News*, June 19, 1935. (Both Mossop Law Reports)

The year after the Moe case, Kentwell wrote a very polite letter to Penrhyn Grant Jones who at the time was Acting Judge, requesting the right to appear before the British courts. He based his application on the fact that he was a practicing member of the Chinese bar as well as still being admitted as a barrister in England. He noted that:

> "Your Honour are no doubt aware that the Chinese Government extends to all British legal practitioners the courtesy to practice in all Chinese Courts where British interests are involved and in return it seems only fair that the British Government extends the same courtesy to qualified Chinese legal practitioners to appear in H.B.M. Courts in China."[27]

Grant Jones, passed the letter on to the Registrar who responded in a terse letter on his behalf that "as you were struck of the Roll of this Court on the 24th November, 1926, he is precluded from hearing you."

Kentwell replied in a less polite letter complaining his disbarment was a "travesty of justice and a terrible reflection on the integrity of H.B.M. Supreme Court." He said that Judge Grain had been motivated by political considerations related to Kentwell's "extreme political views on Anglo-Chinese relations." Many American lawyers and a British law firm had all obtained similar registrations at the Spanish Consulate. Kentwell asked for reconsideration of the Grain's decision on the basis that "assuming that I did advise the Chinese to obtain registrations," the penalty of permanent disbarment did not fit the crime:

> "It is too drastic and too severe. It is like cutting off both my hands and my feet with the removal of my

---

27 All correspondence is in FO656/221 items 70 onwards.

eyesight. I cannot endure it any longer."

A dramatic plea that may have had a chance, but, Kentwell surely did not help his cause when he wrote: "I did intend to shoot Judge Grain and his co-conspirator" - presumably referring to Allan Mossop who as Crown Advocate had applied for his disbarment - "but the thought of my six young children and wife restrained me from transplanting my wish into action. As each year rolls by, my desire for revenge the injustices and wrongs done me by Judge Grain grows stronger and stronger."

He called Grant Jones' attention to the famous case of Captain Dreyfus who had had wrongful convictions annulled against him. He then begged: "I implore your Honour to assist me to redress the wrongs and injustice done to me by reviewing my case. Please do so for you have the power." Kentwell asked for vindication of his name and compared himself to Germany who had suffered injustice under the Versailles Treaty:

> "I have suffered so much more than Germany in my permanent disbarment, after having spent so many years and money in acquiring a profession and to be deprived of earning an honest living by the vindictive pen of a vindictive judge, you can well imagine my feelings."

The Registrar closed the correspondence with a short letter that followed instructions written by Grant Jones on the top margin of Kentwell's letter. The reply to Kentwell stated, simply, "the Acting Judge has no power to review the decision of Sir Peter Grain in this matter."

What drove Lawrence Kentwell?

Kentwell had faced institutionalized racism all his life: in America as a Chinese; in England when he was refused a military commission because of his mixed blood; and, most certainly for the whole time he was in Shanghai. He was refused admission to the Shanghai Club despite being a barrister and an Oxford graduate - as he was to repeat on many occasions in his own form of snobbery. It is impossible now to say whether Grain disbarred him because of racism as Kentwell alleged. Nevertheless, there can be no doubt he genuinely felt that many of his problems were caused by his mixed heritage.

Kentwell wrote plaintively to the British Ambassador to China in 1940:

"There is no doubt that I was regarded as a despised Eurasian, a half-caste outcast with all sorts of hidden indignities heaped upon me like Hitler by the people of my fatherland as unworthy of their association in spite of the fact that I was British born, a gentleman, an Oxford graduate and a member of the English bar and father of six wonderful children, two of whom are Oxford graduates. The golden portals of the Shanghai Club dubbed the 'home' of British snobs and racial prejudice may not be soiled by my unworthy feet because I am not a person of 'pure' European descent. Do you think any human being with any spark of self respect and pride in him will take such outrageous treatment lying down? Never!"[28]

Reading these words almost three-quaters of a century later, it is impossible not to have complete sympathy for Kentwell. He was, of course, right. But, he was also a man before his time.

As we will see in the next chapter, the British system (as well as those of other countries) was not quite ready to treat other races as equals.

....

28 Letter to the British Ambassador in 1940 reproduced in B. Wasserstein, *Secret War in Shanghai*, p191-192.

CHAPTER 46

The Rise of Nationalism

LAWRENCE KENTWELL WAS NOT the only nationalist to appear before the British Courts in the 1920s. The world was changing quickly. The new socialist Soviet Union offered hope of change to the down-trodden around the world. Nationalist movements were established around the world. In 1920, Gandhi had taken over the leadership of the Congress Party in India and was agitating strongly for independence - agitation that spilled over to Indians in China. A decade after the Qing Dynasty had fallen, Chinese were becoming more and more conscious of their rights and willing to take steps to protect them.

This rise of nationalism brought a number of cases before the British courts, a riot in Shanghai and, at last, to the formation of the long promised Extraterritoriality Commission.

The Indians revolt
Throughout the 1920s British authorities were very concerned about sedition being spread amongst Indians in China. In late 1920 an Order in Council was enacted specifically prohibiting the publication of seditious materials in China.[1]

Disaffection amongst Sikhs led, in June 1923, to a case which the *North China Herald* headlined as a "Curious Case of Alleged Slander." Har Charan Singh brought a defamation action against the one of the senior Sikh Policeman in Shanghai, Budda Singh, at the time, the Jemadar (or Lieutenant) of

---

1 China Amendment Order In Council, No. 3 of 1920, printed in the North China Herald, April 31, 1921, p340.

the Police. Har Charan, who had at one time been in the Arm-
ritsar Police, alleged that Budda Singh had told others that he
had been passing information on disaffected Sikhs in Shanghai to Captain Barrett head of the Sikh Branch of the Municipal Police. The case was tried before the newly-knighted Sir
Skinner Turner and a jury of five. Har Charan said that Budda
Singh's statements had meant "he was acting as a traitor to
his fellow Indians. The words complained of brought [him]
into contempt among his compatriots and especially in the
Sikh Gurdwara." Har Charan said that he lived in fear of his
life because he had been identified as an informer. Turner was
having none of this. He said that it was "a very worthy object
to give information against disloyal Sikhs." This could hardly
be defamatory. Turner had some sympathy for the position
Har Charan was in and made a point of stating in court that
Har Charan had denied on oath being an informer. Nevertheless, Turner all but directed the jury to find for Budda Singh.
The jury, without leaving the jury box, did so.[2]

In the spring of the following year, Sikh disaffection, led
to one of the most extraordinary scenes ever to occur in any
British court in China.

At 10am on Tuesday, April 22, 1924, the trial of Harbak
Singh on charges of sedition was due to resume in the Police Court which was located on the ground floor with a door
opening directly to the consulate gardens. The case had started the previous Saturday morning before Registrar Gilbert
King. The public gallery of the court was packed with Sikhs,
all wearing black turbans. Another hundred or so black-tur-
baned Sikhs, who could not fit into the court, were in the garden of the Consulate, surrounding the court on two sides.[3]

Singh had been charged with sedition for publishing sev-

---

2   *Har Charan Singh v Budda Singh, North China Herald,* June 16, 1923, p767. The jury
members were F. Milner, A.J. Stokes, C. Holdsworth, H.E. Middleton and I.A. Levis. For
Turner's knighthood see *London Gazette,* 10 April 1923, p2640.

3   *R v Harbak Singh, North China Herald,* April 26, 1924, p146.

eral pamphlets, including "British Barbarism in India" and "British Justice gone Bankrupt." A few months before, King had convicted Singh after a trial on a similar charge and released on giving two recognisances in the amount of $250. After publication of the new pamphlets, a warrant was issued for his arrest. This was passed to Detective Sergeant Tinkler of Central Police Station to execute. While Tinkler was looking for his man, Singh went to Central Police Station on Foochow Road (Fuzhou Road) to ask if there was a warrant out for his arrest. He waited for Tinkler to return. Tinkler searched Singh's shop, Rose & Co at 478 Chapoo Road (Zhapu Road) and found nothing. But pamphlets ready to be printed were found at a printing company, E. Shing & Co. on Szechuan Road (Sichuan North Road).

It appears that Singh wanted to be prosecuted. Captain Barrett, Superintendent of Police, testified that he had received a copy of the pamphlet through the post addressed to him in Singh's handwriting.

When first brought into the court on the Saturday, Singh had adopted a policy of strict non-cooperation with the court. He refused to plead or to recognise the court. When asked by King if he objected to Tinkler's evidence concerning his arrest he merely said: "I don't object to anything. You can do as you like." He similarly refused to question witnesses from the printing company. When the prosecutor, Mr Maitland, asked for an adjournment until Tuesday, Singh said: "I am a strict non-cooperator. I do not recognize your court. You can do what you like." King told Singh that he wished to see the case against him proved to the hilt and ordered that the case continue on Tuesday. Singh was ordered to be held in custody.

The adjournment gave Singh's supporters the opportunity to attend the trial and, although they were there in large numbers, they were relatively well behaved. The *North China Herald* reported:

"Remarkable scenes were witnessed in the grounds of
H.B.M. Consulate and in H.M. Police Court on Tuesday morning at the termination of the trial of Harbak
Singh. The court room was filled with Indians and the
grounds outside harboured some fifty to a hundred
others."

On the Tuesday, one more witness for the prosecution was
called who confirmed receiving the pamphlet in Nanking
Road.

Singh then asked if he could make a statement. King said
that he could. Singh produced a number of pages of closely
written words, which he read out in "quite good English."
Singh started by saying that Shanghai was part of China. He
had done nothing seditious against the Government of China. The International Settlement was not a British colony so
he could not therefore be charged with sedition against the
British Government.

He went through Indian history, covering various injustices and broken pledges by the British government. He complained about the treatment of Sikhs in Shanghai; how there
were special registration rules for them, and, that many had
been deported by Captain Barrett during World War I. Captain Barrett and the Jemadar of the Sikh Police Sirdar Sahib
Budda Singh were singled out for their abusive treatment of
Sikhs and personal persecution of Harbak Singh.

He said that in India sedition was not a crime. He knew
he was about to be deported to India but did not care. "He
would only be one of many innocent Sikhs sent out from
Shanghai." Then in a flourish of rhetoric he added:

"What did it matter? By sending me to gaol you do but
send me from a large prison to a smaller one. You can

imprison my body, but not my soul."[4]

He emphasized that he did not hate the English.

"I love all men as my brothers. All men are my brethren. I hate the system of Government by the British in India."

But, he said, he would fight for the freedom of India, even if it "led him to the gallows." King, who it should be remembered was born in India and spent his early years there, went through the statement with Singh to try to convince him of the errors of his ways. Singh asked King why he was being prosecuted for sedition when most of what he printed had passed the censor in India. Some of the papers in India had even described "the British Government as the Government, not of His Britannic Majesty, but as the Government of His Satanic Majesty."

At this point King broke protocol and asked Captain Barrett directly if that was true. Barrett responded: "I believe that is so, Sir. Some of them I know are very hot stuff." Singh then tried to produce the papers, but King said he would take his word for it.

Mr Maitland prosecuting then said there was nothing really to say. Singh had admitted everything and "was so bigoted in his ideas he could hardly be considered a reasonable being."

King, was not having this and dressed down Maitland telling him:

"Every British subject had a right to hold any opinions he wishes, no matter how much anyone else differs from him. He can only be stopped when the expression of those opinions is likely to cause trouble."[5]

King clearly did not want to convict Singh, at least not without hearing a defence. He made one last exhortation to Singh to "make some plea on his own behalf." Singh refused.

King said he had no choice but to convict Singh and sentence him to the maximum sentence of two months imprisonment. At the end of his term of imprisonment he would be bound over to keep the peace on his own surety and that of three others for $250.

At the end of the hearing and before King could leave the bench, "the crowd broke into loud cheers for the prisoner, which were taken up by their fellows outside — cheers which could not be suppressed by the police." A rush was made for the doors, which King ordered to be closed but the mob was too strong for the police. Some of the crowd was arrested and the rest of the crowd then "cheered more and threw flowers and confetti over them." King ordered that they be released and the crowd moved towards the Bund Gardens before being headed off by the police. They then marched to the Sikh Gurdwara on North Szechuen Road.

The *North China Herald* published a hand-wringing editorial, headed the "Sikhs and Sedition", about the case. And they were right to wring their hands. The Sikhs had always supported the British. They had put down the Indian mutiny; they had formed the backbone of the British army in the Opium Wars; and, they served as the muscle of British power in the treaty ports. Without the Sikhs, Britain would not have been where it was in China.

The editorial acknowledged that "in the history of India, we find much to feed our pride, great deeds of endurance and feats of courage and in nearly all we find the Sikhs fighting side by side with our soldiers, sharing in our victories, bear-

---

5   This quote has been changed from past tense to present tense.

ing with us the burden of our defeats... In the Indian Mutiny the Sikhs stood by us to a man, and it was largely due to their aid we soon turned the dreadful tide which threatened to engulf us." The article boldly stated that "there are even less essential differences between the Englishman and the Sikh that might appear at first sight." They acknowledged a similarity of features; that ideals were the same; and, that "even the God we worship is the same." The editorial firmly put the blame for the disturbance on the lower levels of the Sikh community and expressed the "hope that the saner and more educated Sikhs will have done something to calm their brethren and show them the foolishness of their ways."[6]

After Singh completed his sentence, having failed to find sureties, he was brought to court for deportation. Normally, a judge would hear such an application, but both Turner and Grain were absent from Shanghai and Singh came before King as Acting Assistant Judge. King ordered Singh be deported.[7]

The Chinese fight back

Chinese were not subject to British jurisdiction, so normally protests by Chinese would not find their way in front of the British courts. However in 1923, in a very high profile case, Chinese in Shanghai decided to use the British justice system to fight back against a gross injustice.

That year, a Ningpo native, Loh Tse Wah, 43, had found himself in serious trouble with the Shanghai Municipal Police.[8] He had joined Hongkew Police Station on February 2, 1923 as the "boy" of Inspector Prosser. He resigned three days later on February 5, 1923, very soon after $400 had been stolen from a new recruit to the force, John Gavan. Detective Superintendent J.F. Gabbutt was determined to get the money back;

6   *North China Herald*, April 26, 1924, p125.

7   *North China Herald* September 27, 1924, p516.

8   Details of case from R. Bickers, *Empire Made Me*, p123 to 126; *R v Gabbutt, North China Herald*, March 31,1924, p904 and April 7, 1923 p57 (Committal); *North China Herald*, April 21, 1923 p194 and April 28, 1923, p255 (trial); and, *Straits Times*, May 3, 1923, p12.

it was too much loss of face for money to be stolen from a police station. He was certain he had his man; the only problem was how to get him to confess.

Loh was subjected to "intensive questioning" by Gabbutt, Sergeant Alfred Balchin, a Japanese detective Sergeant Okajima and two Chinese detective constables Woo Zer-yung and Yang Tse-shang. Plain and simple, he was tortured. He confessed at least twice but the confessions were not considered satisfactory because he could not produce the money. Okajima had been brought in at midnight after two other interrogation sessions to see if he could extract the location of the money from Loh. Loh was finally brought before the Mixed Court, which acquitted him despite his confessions.

Loh's injuries were horrific. He had been hung by his thumbs, garroted, hung from a ladder with his hands behind his back, had lit opium pipes put up his nostrils and been stripped and beaten on his genitals. Loh said Gabbutt had personally beaten him with a leather belt and had told him in Chinese that he would hang him from a ladder until he died.

Following his acquittal by the Mixed Court, his former employer, Mr Chang took him to a doctor, Dr Stafford Cox, for treatment. Chang was a leading member of the Chinese community, fluent in English and a director of the Commercial Press. Dr Cox said Loh was extremely exhausted when he came to him. He had a black eye, wounds on his ears, hands and elbows. His right side had significant swelling from the kidneys to the hip caused by deep injuries. He had blood in his urine. His feet were badly injured and the right foot looked like gangrene was starting. Dr Cox immediately sent Loh to hospital for treatment.

The injuries to Loh caused outrage in the Chinese community. Circulars were issued denouncing the torture of Loh and demanding an end to extraterritoriality. The Ningbo Guild went one step further. They determined to use the extraterritorial system against the foreigners. The Guild decided to bring a private criminal prosecution against Gabbutt and Balchin in the British Supreme Court. Okajima was also prosecuted in the Japanese Consular Court and Woo and Yang in the Mixed Court.

The Ningpo Guild instructed a senior British barrister R.N. MacLeod to bring committal proceedings in the Police Court. The hearings were held before Peter Grain sitting as magistrate. MacLeod appeared with a Chinese barrister, Y.S. Ziar, who had stud-

Mr MacLeod prosecuting on behalf of the Chinese

ied in England. MacLeod asked for leave for Ziar to appear because there was considerable Chinese evidence. This was granted. R.F.C. Master represented Gabbutt and Balchin. After the evidence was heard, Master suggested that there were political motives for the prosecution and argued that there was no direct evidence against either Gabbutt or Balchin. Grain disagreed saying: "It would be proper for me not to make any comment now, and I shall say I consider this is a case which should go before a jury."

The jury trial started two weeks later before Skinner Turner. The prosecution was taken over by the Crown Advocate, Harrie Wilkinson. Reader Harris defended. The jury was an all-white panel of Britons made up of Messrs A.T. Pike, P.C. Inglis, W.S. Read, A.T. Lavington and S.E. Hill.

The court was packed the entire time, mainly with Chinese who had come to see if the British courts would deliver justice. Turner found the entire case extremely distasteful. When Harris tried to suggest that there was some political motive for the prosecution because the Guild had paid for the committal proceedings, Turner made it clear he saw nothing improper with this and pointed out that for the trial, the case was now in the hands of the Crown Advocate, Harrie Wilkinson.

It appears, however, that Wilkinson did not prosecute the case with any "perceptible zeal." On a visit to the Hongkew Police Station, he was recorded as telling the police: "you had better keep the ladder out of the way." There could be a number of reasons for this. Wilkinson was a believer in extraterritoriality. It was 33 years since he had arrived in Shanghai and 26 years since he had been made Crown Advocate. He had usually prosecuted on behalf of the police, and he may have found prosecuting British policemen distasteful.

Wilkinson also appears to have been going through a bad time. He was now almost 57, the age his father had been when he had become a judge. His younger brother, Thomas, had died three months earlier in December 1922 of injuries sustained trying to stop the robbery of an excise office by members of Sinn Fein. His father was now all alone in Ireland. Reflecting

Major Hilton-Johnson seeks to justify "intensive questioning"

his personal mood, the week before Gabbutt's trial started, in a speech moving the admission of a former chief clerk of the Supreme Court, he made a speech of "an unusual character" criticizing harshly the pay and conditions of court staff.[9]

Perhaps because of Wilkinson's lack of zeal, Turner on many occasions took over the questioning of witnesses himself. He wanted to know if they approved of "intensive

9 TG Wilkinson wounding and death, *North China Herald*, February 24, 1923, p522; "H.M. Court Officials Poor Rewards", *North China Herald*, April 21, 1923, p193.

questioning" and why Okajima had been brought in at midnight. When the Deputy Commissioner of Police, Major Hilton-Johnson, tried to justify "intensive questioning" as being an acceptable investigation method, Turner almost exploded saying in open court, "Well, I don't think you will find many people will agree with you."

Gabbutt and Balchin both gave evidence in their defence denying being involved in any assault on Loh. Turner summed up as fairly as he could. He made it clear he considered the Ningbo Guild had been acting entirely properly in assisting Loh. The one weakness in the case against Gabbutt was that Loh had not picked him out in an identity parade.

The jury retired for 50 minutes and returned with a verdict of not guilty on all charges. They did, however, add an important rider:

> "We are convinced that Loh received his injuries while in the hands of the Police."

The two or three hundred Chinese watching the proceedings retired quietly but certainly not happy. Gabbutt and Balchin did not get off scot-free; they were both dismissed from the SMP.[10]

Following the acquittal in the British court, the charges against Okajima in the Japanese Consular Court and against Woo and Yang in the Mixed Court were withdrawn. In withdrawing the cases in the Mixed Court, Mr MacLeod on behalf of Loh said that he had been "instructed to withdraw the charge on the ground that the evidence must be the same as that in the British Court. The most serious charges were against Det-Insp. Gabbutt who had been acquitted." He did not wish to see subordinates convicted when Gabbutt had been acquitted. William Fleming who was appearing for Woo

10 Minutes of the Shanghai Municipal Council, 1922-1924, p341.

and Yang consented to this. The British assessor, Mr Mead, with perhaps deference to Chinese sentiments, said that the Mixed Court "knew nothing about the British Court or any other court, and was not bound by decisions of such courts. If counsel did not wish to put in evidence and wished to withdraw the charge, the case would therefore have to be dismissed."[11]

All police in Shanghai knew that the result of the case had deeply upset the Chinese. Detective Sergeant Maurice Tinkler, a good friend of both Gabbutt and Balchin, wrote that as a result of the case, "the feeling amongst the Chinese was at fever heat."[12]

More trouble in Canton

The situation in Shanghai was nevertheless better than that in Canton. The British and other foreign powers still controlled Shanghai and the area around it. This was not the case in Canton. The Nationalist Government there had grown militarily very strong. They did not have the power to throw foreigners out. They did, however, have the power to make life for them very difficult.

The British and French concessions in Canton were located on Shameen Island, a Manhattan shaped island separated from the Chinese city of Canton by a narrow river about 10 metres wide. Aerial photos of the time show it as an oasis of green with grand European style buildings protuding through the tree cover surrounded by the large grey city of Canton.

Numerous anti-foreign protests were held in Canton in the 1920s. In 1923 the British and French authorities had tried to limit Chinese access to Shameen Island leading to an anti-foreign strike.

That year the Bank of East Asia (BEA), a bank incorpo-

11 "Charge Against Police Withdrawn", *North China Herald*, May 12, 1923, p413.
12 R. Bickers, *Empire Made Me*, p126.

rated in Hong Kong, bought some land on Shameen Island in the British Concession. BEA was one of the first banks established in Hong Kong by ethnic Chinese soon after the end of the Qing Dynasty. It was established as a bank for Chinese. Originally, its Articles of Association stated that shareholders in the bank could only be ethnic Chinese but this was later amended to allow non-Chinese to invest as well.

BEA applied to register the transfer of land at the British Consulate in Canton. The registration was refused on the basis that the Land Regulations for Shameen forbade the sale of land on the island to Chinese. BEA brought an action in the Supreme Court seeking an order that Sir John Jamieson, the Consul-General, and the Mr Frank Wallis, the Vice-Consul, register the transfer.[13]

The case brought before the court vexed question of the status of Hong Kong Chinese. Normally, the British considered them to be British, and the Chinese considered them to be Chinese. In this case, the roles were reversed, the British (or at least the Consul-General in Canton) wanted to treat them as Chinese. The Hong Kong Chinese wanted to be treated as British. Such dual nationals had been a problem since the British first entered China. Some Hong Kong Chinese would claim to be Chinese when it suited them, for example to live in cities not opened to foreigners and buy land; and, to be British when it suited them, mainly to avoid the jurisdiction of the Chinese courts. This had been such a problem in the 19th century that Sir Rutherford Alcock, the British Minister, in 1866 issued a notification first that any Chinese British subjects found living in breach of the treaties would be arrested by the Chinese authorities and handed over to the British consul for punishment. When this had only a limited effect, in 1868 a further circular was published that any Chinese British

13 *Bank of East Asia & Anor v Jamieson & Anor*, *North China Herald*, November 1, 1924, p127; November 8, 1924 p243; December 13, 1924, p429 (judgment); *Straits Times*, May 14, 1925, p9 (withdrawal of appeal).

living in China who concealed their British nationality could not claim extraterritorial protection. In order to do so, they must dress in a way to distinguish themselves from local Chinese, that is, to dress as a foreigner.[14]

The BEA case was heard by Skinner Turner in late October 1924 in Shanghai rather than in Canton. That may have been because only two months before Canton have been blockaded by Chinese protesters for five weeks and the presence of HMS Tarantula had been necessary to "dissuade Sun Yat-Sen from bombarding Shameen, which is protected at all times by American, French, Portuguese, and Japanese gunboats."[15] Both sides instructed high-powered lawyers. The Bank brought up Eldon Potter KC from Hong Kong. Harrie Wilkinson, the Crown Advocate, and his assistant, Victor Priestwood, represented Jamieson and Wallis.

In evidence, Consul-General Jamieson said that even though BEA was incorporated in Hong Kong, the owners were Hong Kong Chinese. The Chinese government and, particularly the Nationalist government in Canton did not recognize the British nationality of Hong Kong Chinese and he was obliged to refuse registration. He described the very difficult situation that the British faced at the time in Canton. Because the local authorities did not consider Hong Kong Chinese to be British, he had had to deal with a case in 1921 where a Hong Kong Chinese was due to be executed. Jamieson had contacted the Chinese authorities to demand the man's release on the basis he was a British national. This was refused. After considerable correspondence, the man had been dropped at the bridge near the British Concession. Jamieson was told by the Nationalists that he had better get him far away from Canton as soon as possible.

Jamieson said the partial closing of the Shameen in 1923

14 G. Keeton, *The Development of Extraterritoriality in China*, Vol 1, p246.

15 Letter from John Maitland Philips to PS Jones 29 August 1924; Imperial War Museum JMP/1/No. 6.

had been necessary due to the "overwhelming numbers" of Chinese who had been coming on to island. Jamieson said that the presence of Chinese on Shameen could lead to great difficulties:

"No purely Chinese institution, no association of Chinese, can at the present day dissociate itself from politics and in the course of the various political disturbances that arise, one can never be sure which particular party may want to persecute another particular party, and at no time can one be certain what steps a man's enemies may take to arrest him or assassinate him."

He came to the real objection in the case. He wanted to keep things quiet on Shameen:

"Were Chinese or British subjects of Chinese descent, to reside on the island, there would be danger of attempts being made against them on political grounds, and thus the government would be hampered and the inhabitants involved in trouble."

He said the nature of BEA's business was different to other British banks such as the Hongkong & Shanghai Bank or the Chartered Bank. BEA dealt solely with Chinese, implying that BEA did not need to be on the island. Then, in a bombshell that would be widely reported in the newspapers, Jamieson said: "If I am correctly informed they are associated with the opium trade."

Turner, the following day, said that he "regretted the statement had been reported in the newspapers. There was no suggestion in the pleadings or elsewhere that the Bank was not conducted in all respects as a perfectly proper banking business."

Potter, on behalf of BEA, made a simple argument. The

Mr. E. P. Eldon Potter, K.C., eloquently demonstrates that a Hongkong Company cannot conceivably be "a native of China."

Eldon Potter KC from Hong Kong argues for BEA that it is British

bank was incorporated in Hong Kong and was a British subject. It should be entitled to have the transfer of title registered. Wilkinson, on the other hand, argued BEA was "an artificial person of double nationality," and it should not be the responsibility of the British authorities to protect "the bank from Chinese authorities across the creek."

Turner, in a long judgment, found in favour of the bank. He ruled that a corporation's nationality is derived from where it is incorporated and not from the nationality of the shareholders. The bank was therefore British and was entitled to register the land. As to the policy that the British Government was trying to enforce, Turner said:

> "I am only concerned with the law. If the law has not provided for that policy, it is the fault of the legislature. I can only administer the law as I understand it, irrespective of the views of the Executive as to what the law ought to be."

Jamieson and Wallis filed an appeal but this was later withdrawn. They had decided to deal with the case another way. Rather than fighting in the courts, they amended the Shameen Land Regulations to provide that "British Companies" did not include companies controlled by persons of Chinese race. They also told BEA they would refuse to renew their lease. BEA never built its new premises, but did keep the land.[16]

The May 30 Movement

Turner handed down his decision in the Shameen case at the end of December 1924. This was probably the high water mark for foreign judicial power in China. Foreign courts could deal with issues involving foreign and Chinese nationals with limited concern for Chinese interests. But within one month this was to change.

May 30, 1925 marked what Professor Robert Bickers has called "Britain's single biggest disaster in China."[17] On this day, Shanghai Municipal Police officers at Louza Police Station on Nanking Road shot and killed Chinese protesters outside the station. The day had been marked by protests around Shanghai against the killing of a Chinese worker at a Japanese mill. Inspector Everson in charge of the station had arrested 15 protestors. A large crowd of protesters gathered outside the station seeking their release. Everson, fearing the station would be overrun, ordered Sikh and Chinese police to fire into the crowd. After the shooting subsided, 12 Chinese lay dead in Nanking Road for all of China and the rest of the world to see. Numerous others were injured.

The shootings sparked furious protests. They were a propaganda godsend to the Chinese authorities. The Ministry of Foreign Affairs published photos of the dead and injured, as well as photos of clothing they were wearing at the time. Two days later, on June 2, some of the survivors were tried in the Mixed Court and given very light sentences. The fact that protesters were prosecuted further enraged Chinese sentiment. Attacks on foreigners continued for days after the hearings.[18]

16 *Growing With Hong Kong, The Bank of East Asia 1919-1934*, p38. Chapter 2 of this book tells the story of the case from the bank's perspective.

17 R. Bickers, *Empire Made Me* p166. See generally, p163 to 172 for more on the May 30 Movement.

18 Verbatim reports of the trials were published with the *North China Herald* in early

Kitaro Suga   *Finley Johnson*   *Henry Gollan*

In part, to try to quell the Chinese rage, the foreign powers set up an International Commission to investigate the
killings.[19] The Chinese were invited to participate but refused
to. The foreign Commissioners were: from Britain, Sir Henry
Gollan, the new Chief Justice of Hong Kong; from the United
States, Judge Finley Johnson, Chief Justice of the Philippines;
and, from Japan Judge Kitaro Suga, Chief Justice of the Hiro-
shima Court of Appeal. The Commission sat in October 1925,
with Judge Johnson presiding, at the Shanghai Town Hall. It
heard evidence from the police officers involved and other
foreigners. Chinese had been encouraged to boycott the Commission and no Chinese gave evidence.

The three commissioners could not agree on a joint report
so all three issued their own findings in January 1926. They es-
sentially cleared the Municipal Police of misconduct. Johnson
was the most critical in his report. He set out his views of what
caused the disturbances. These included the Municipal Council
control of the Mixed Court and the inherent unfairness of extraterritoriality. Perhaps most importantly, he listed as a cause:

....
June. Mr Maitland prosecuted. Dr Fischer appeared for the Ministry of Foreign Affairs.
Mr Ho Fei and Dr H.C. Mei appeared for the accused. For reports on further attacks, see
North China Herald June 6, 1925, p417.

19 On the establishment of the commission see, *North China Herald*, October 10, 1925,
p55. For a summary of the Commission Report, see, *North China Herald* January 9, 1926,
p59.

"The failure on the part of the foreigners in China to
realize that the Chinese people have made greater
advancement during the past 10 years in civics, in the
fundamental principles of government and in the better
understanding of individual rights under the law than
they have made in any 100 years during their entire
history."

China was to keep on advancing and the killings put
much more pressure on the Municipal Council to return the
Mixed Court to Chinese control; something that Chinese lawyers had already been pushing for a number of years. By the
end of 1926, the Mixed Court was abolished, to be replaced by
a Provisional Court.[20]

Extraterritoriality Commission

For Chinese, there was further hope for change. The Extra-
territoriality Commission, promised since the end of World
War I, had finally been formed in late 1925. It was made up
of representatives from each of the treaty powers and a Chinese representative. Turner, as Judge of the British Supreme
Court for China, was appointed the British representative.
The United States Representative was Silas H. Strawn of
Chicago, an "eminent attorney" and personal friend of President Coolidge and the Secretary of State, Frank B Kellog. The
Commission was due to commence work in late 1925. The
on-going civil war in China meant that battles between warlords made it difficult to travel to Peking in 1925. The Com-
mission, therefore, did not hold its first session until January
1926. Strawn was elected Chairman of the Commission and
Dr Wang Ch'ung-hui, the Chinese Minister of Justice and
Chinese Commissioner, Honorary President. This position of
Honorary President had no powers but was created to save

20 See Chapter 50

face. The Chinese had previously insisted that a Chinese be Chairman.[21]

The members of the commission first reviewed the development of the new Chinese legal system. Then, from May 1926, a travelling committee went around China for more than 4,200 miles (6,700 kilometres) to study the implementation of new codes and to inspect the new courts and Chinese prisons. As can be expected, on many occasions, the courts and prisons had received special treatment to improve facilities before the arrival of the Commission. The travelling committee returned in June 1926 and the drafting of a final report commenced. This was finalized in September 1926 and, not surprisingly, did not recommend an end to extraterritoriality.

The report effectively put off any promise of an end to extraterritoriality until China had developed a fully functioning Western legal system. The key recommendations were that China must develop an independent judiciary and that there should be further reforms of the judicial, police and prison systems. Numerous laws were required to be completed or put into force, including civil and commercial codes; a revised Criminal Code; Banking and Bankruptcy laws; a patent law; and a land expropriation law. In addition, the report required that a uniform system for enacting and publishing laws should be enacted and that the modern system of courts, prisons and detention houses should replace all Magistrate's courts and old style prisons and detention houses.

If, and only if, these reforms were carried out, then the extraterritorial powers said they may consider the abolition of extraterritoriality on a progressive basis.

"May consider" on a "progressive basis." This was a procrastinator's charter and fell far short of what the Chinese people and government expected. Dr Wang, the Chinese representative of the Commission, added a disclaimer to his

---

21 See W. Fishel, *The End of Extraterritoriality in China,* Chapter VI for full details of the workings of the Extraterritoriality Commission.

signature that "by signing this report my approval of all the statements is not implied."

As the cases in the next chapter show, in an ever connected and internationalizing world, things would have been easier for everyone if one court system could have had jurisdiction over all people and companies in China rather than the hodgepodge of jurisdictions under extraterritoriality.

CHAPTER 47

Intermingled Jurisdictions

IN SHANGHAI, THE INTERMINGLING of numerous legal systems required by extraterritoriality in a more and more sophisticated and internationally connected economy, meant parties could find themselves caught up in mind-numbingly complex disputes. Two cases handled by Skinner Turner in 1925 in the British Supreme Court brought these issues to the forefront.

In the first case, Dent & Co a large British trading firm filed for bankruptcy. Dent & Co had borrowed money from a French bank, Banque de l'Indochine, for onward payment to a silk mill. After the bankruptcy, the silk mill repaid the money to Dent & Co's Chinese compradore, who then paid the money to the International Mixed Court. The compradore then brought an action in the International Mixed Court to have rival claims to the money resolved. The bank brought an action against the compradore in the French Mixed Court to seek recovery of the money. The International Mixed Court transferred the money to the French Mixed Court. The French Mixed Court ruled that it did not have jurisdiction and transferred the money to the British Supreme Court. For technical reasons, the Banque de l'Indochine became a defendant in the British court, meaning that the court did not have jurisdiction over it. The only way the case could proceed in the British Supreme Court against the bank was if the French Consul agreed for it to be a defendant in the British Court. Otherwise the case would have to be transferred to the French Consular

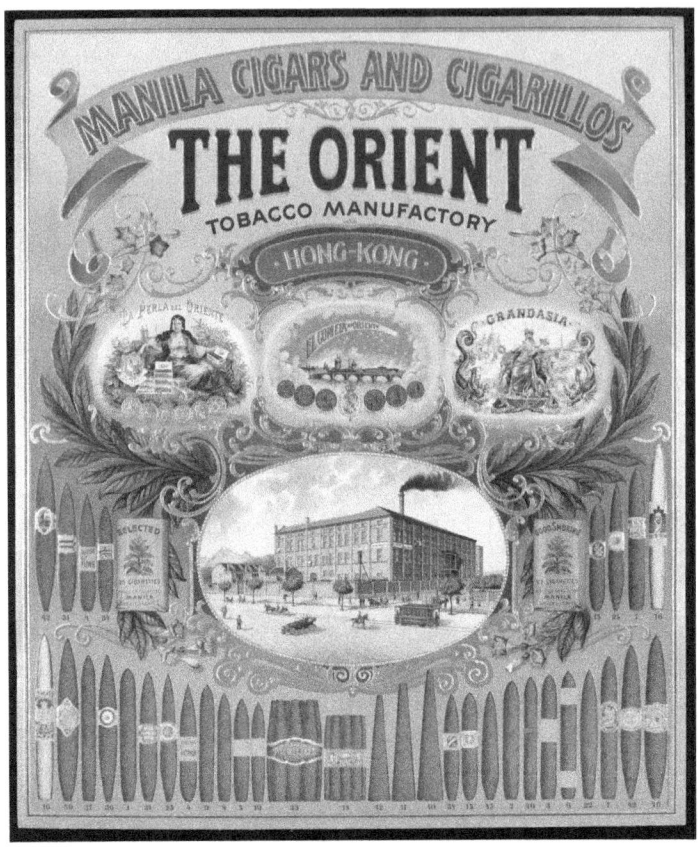

A poster advertising Ingenohl's cigars. Courtesy of Edward Schneider.

Court. The French Consul gave his consent.[1]

The second and far more interesting case originated from a World War I seizure of assets from Mr Carl Ingenohl in the Philippines under the American equivalent of the Trading With the Enemy Act. The case ended up with numerous decisions being made by British courts in Shanghai, Hong Kong and London and American courts in Manila and Washington DC.

---

1   *Trustee of Dent & Co v Banque de l'Indochine, North China Herald,* January 19, 1925, p61.

Ingenohl had been born in Germany and in 1886, he was naturalized as a Belgium citizen by an act of the Belgium parliament. In 1882 he established a cigar factory in Manila with his own headquarters being in Belgium. In 1910, he started a cigar factory in Hong Kong. Both factories sold cigars under the name "El Oriente Fabrica Tobacos. C. Ingenohl, Manila." They both also used the trademarks "Perla", "Cometa" and "Mundo."

During World War I, Ingenohl came under suspicion because of his German origin and the fact that his family was still German. A flavour of what was thought of Ingenohl can be found from a leading article published in the *Straits Times* in Singapore in August 1915 about Ingenohl and his family connections:

"The proprietor of the 'Perla del Oriente' brand of cigars is C. Ingenohl. He lives in Antwerp and is a naturalized Belgian citizen, but he is German by birth and his brother is Admiral Ingenohl, lately Chief Admiral of the German Grand Fleet. The manager and European staff of at the La Perla factory are all Germans. Ingenohl also owns 'The Orient Tobacco Manufactory.' All the profits of the Ingenohl businesses are sent to Germany via Antwerp."[2]

For loyal British readers of the paper, this was a damning indictment.

Ingenohl responded in a letter to the Editor seeking to allay these concerns. First, he confirmed that he had been German but was now Belgian having been granted citizenship by a vote of the Belgian parliament. Second, only 1/7th of his profits went to Germany, some went to Switzerland and England and the balance remained in Belgium. However at the

---

2 *Straits Times*, October 27, 1915, p 11.

The box cover of Ingenohl's cigars: "Removed to Hong Kong"

moment, due to the war, there were no profits. His brother, Admiral Ingenohl, was now retired. He explained that he employed only Germans in the Philippines because he could find no Belgians willing to go. The manager of his Hong Kong factory was a Dane.

Ingenohl was being a little clever with this. His brother, Frederich von Ingehnohl, had been the Admiral commanding the German Baltic Fleet and had been responsible for an aggressive policy of attacking the English coasts during World War I. He had only recently been relieved of his command. Still, Ingenohl's letter was quite convincing up until he wrote:

> "I do not deny that I was born in Germany and have sympathies for the land where my parents lived and died. Where it not so, I would be a man without character or moral principles and ought to feel ashamed for

myself before my Belgian fellow-citizens. I fully agree with the German people in defending themselves in this terrible war with all fair means although unfortunately they are the enemy of my adopted country."

Not surprisingly given these sentiments and who his brother was, his Hong Kong factory was put under supervision by the British authorities during the war. It was released back to him at the end of hostilities.

Ingenohl was not so lucky in the Philippines. When the United States entered the war in 1917, Ingenohl's Manila factory was seized as enemy property and sold to Messrs Olsen & Co Inc, an American company. Following the war, Ingenohl complained through the Belgian authorities about the seizure. After an investigation, it was conceded by the Government of the Philippines that the seizure had been improper. However, under the legislation under which the seizure was made Ingenohl could not get his factory back. He was paid, instead, the purchase price paid by Olsen & Co.

Not surprisingly, Ingenohl was not happy about the loss of his factory and he brought court actions against Olsen & Co around Asia. In 1922, Ingenohl sued Olsen & Co in the Supreme Court of Hong Kong for trademark infringement and passing off. Olsen & Co defended on the basis that they had acquired all the assets of the Manila factory, including the goodwill in Hong Kong and thus they had the right to sell their products in Hong Kong. The case was heard by Chief Justice William Rees-Davies who held that the assignment in the Philippines could have no extraterritorial effect in Hong Kong. In making his decision, Rees-Davies relied on the English case of *Rey v Lecouturier* involving the forced seizure by the French authorities of the Chartreuse liquor business in France belonging to Carthusian monks. One of the key reasons for the decision in the *Rey v Lecouturier* case was that the monks' process for making Chartreuse was a secret. Olsen &

MANILA CIGARS

NOTICE

The Trade Mark above depicted is the property of Mr. C. Ingenohl, Manufacturer of the well-known brand of LA PERLA DEL ORIENTE Cigars. Until the year 1919 these cigars were made both in Manila and Hongkong and were well-known and extensively consumed in the Straits Settlements. At the end of 1918 Mr. Ingenohl's Manila Factory and the right to use his trade mark in the Philippine Islands were sold by order of the United States Government. Mr. Ingenohl, since the sale of his Manila factory, has continued to manufacture his LA PERLA DEL ORIENTE cigars at the Orient Tobacco Manufactory in Hongkong. They are made of MANILA tobacco and are in every respect identical in quality with those formerly made by him in Manila. They are still sold in this Colony under the above Trade Mark. The label, however, as will be noticed, now bears the word "HONGKONG" instead of the word "MANILA."

Co did not appeal from Rees-Davies' decision.[3]

Ingenohl then tried to enforce the award for costs he had obtained in Hong Kong in the Philippines. At first instance he was successful, but the Appeal Court in Manila ruled that the Hong Kong decision was wrong and therefore should not be enforced. Ingenohl appealed to the US Supreme Court who, some time later, ruled in his favour holding that whether to enforce a judgment of a foreign court involved "delicate considerations of international relations." Ingenohl had obtained his award for costs "after a fair trial" by a court having jurisdiction and this was sufficient to allow enforcement of the award. The US Supreme Court added that the transfer of assets by the Custodian of Enemy Property could only be good outside US jurisdiction if there "was no opposing interest or right."[4]

Having won in Hong Kong, Ingenohl decided to bring an action in Shanghai to seek to recover some of his very substantial market in China. In 1919, just after the war ended, Olsen & Co had had a contract to supply over 24 million cigars to China. Ingenohl did not, however, sue in the US Court for

3   *Ingenohl v Olsen* 1922 HKLR 4.
4   *Ingenohl v Olsen & Co*, 273, US 541, (1927).

China, presumably because he had been advised that the US Court would find that the assignment of the goodwill in the Philippines was valid in China.

Rather, already having a favourable decision in Hong Kong, Ingenohl decided to sue a British defendant, the Wing On Department Store, in the British Supreme Court for China. The Hong Kong court had applied English case law in deciding in Ingenohl's favour and Ingenohl must have been advised he had a good claim in China.

Both Ingenohl and Olsen & Co instructed leading lawyers in Shanghai. Duncan McNeill and J.E. Badeley represented Ingenohl. Olsen & Co instructed Mr R. Macleod and Mr E. Platt. McNeill and Macleod had both been practicing in Shanghai for more than 20 years and had both acted as Crown Advocate in the past.

Judgment was delivered on May 922, in an action brought by Mr. Ingenoh n the Supreme Court of Hongkong agains Messrs. Walter E. Olsen & Co., Inc., o Manila, the present owners of the El Orient actory at Manila formerly owned by Mr ngenohl, under which Mr. Ingenohl is en itled in Hongkong to the exclusive use o he Trade Marks "LA PERLA DE RIENTE," "EL COMETA DEL ORIENTE nd "IMPERIO DEL MUNDO" used i onnection with the sale of his cigars. Mr ngenohl is also the sole owner of thes rade Marks in the Straits Settlements igars now sold in the Straits Settlement nder the Trade name "LA LINDA FILI INA, MANILA," are NOT the manufactur f Mr. Ingenohl and are not the same bran f cigars which Mr. Ingenohl now sells an as always sold under the trade name "LA ERLA DEL ORIENTE."

WARNING.

The application of the above Trade Mar o boxes containing cigars, which are no he manufacture of Mr. Ingenohl constitutes breach of Mr. Ingenohl's rights. Actio as recently been successfully taken unde rdinance No. 161, (Merchandise Marks gainst certain persons selling cigars not o r. Ingenohl's manufacture in boxes bear ng Mr. Ingenohl's labels, and all vendor f cigars are hereby warned that proceed ngs will be taken against any person selling r offering for sale cigars not being th anufacture of Mr. Ingenohl's factory i oxes which bear the labels of Mr. Ingenohl actory or any colourable imitation thereof

RODYK AND DAVIDSON,
Solicitors for the
Orient Tobacco Manufactory C. Ingenohl,
Hongkong.
O. STUTZ,
Hotel van Wijk,
Sole Agent for the S.S. and F.M.S.

A warning notice published by Ingenohl in Singapore after winning in Hong Kong.

The Ingenohl trial lasted, for then, a very long time of seven days.[5] Macleod knew he had a hard case to argue. The decision in Hong Kong would be very persuasive in a British court in China. He took the brave decision to attack it head

5   Judgment: *Ingenohl v Wing On, North China Herald*, April 25, 1925, p154; Argument: *North China Herald*, February 28, 1925, p309.

on. He focused almost his entire case on proving that there was no secret process to making the cigars and therefore the Carthusian monk case should not apply. He called a number of witnesses to show that there was nothing secret about the process. Macleod even went so far in his argument as to concede that the decision in Hong Kong was correct in Hong Kong, where the Hong Kong factory had registered trademarks, but not applicable in China where no trademarks were registered.

In his judgment, Turner disposed of both the Hong Kong and Manila decisions quickly by saying they were not binding on him. He added that, "both are to be treated with that respect and courtesy which is always shown to the judgments of a foreign Court of competent jurisdiction."

Turner immediately noted that the case was anomalous because:

"In the case before me the position is peculiar: this Court sitting under a Treaty with China exercises jurisdiction at the suit of nationals of all countries over British subjects; and we find here a British Company (Wing On Co., Ld.) as the (nominal) defendants. But the real party to the action is Messrs Walter Olsen & Co., Inc.: an American Company: therefore the plaintiff being a Belgian citizen, this Court is in effect being asked to decide a dispute between a Belgian and an American - neither subject, save by consent and submission, to the jurisdiction of this Court."

So, what he really had was the case of a Belgian citizen who was once German suing an American in a British Court in China for the British common law tort of passing off.

The first hurdle that Ingenohl needed to overcome in order to be able to sue for passing off in the Supreme Court for China was that he needed to prove that Belgian courts in China would give British subjects protection in the Belgian courts if their trademarks were infringed. The Judge of the Belgian Consular Court signed such a certificate, which Turner accepted.

Turner then turned to whether the assignment of the assets of the Manila factory included the goodwill in China. Turner noted that more than 90% of the factory's business at the time of the assignment had been export business and that the intention of the Custodian of Enemy Property must have been to assign the goodwill in China. With regard to the Carthusian monks case, Macleod's arguments succeeded. Turner said he disagreed with the analysis of Rees-Davies CJ and held that it did not apply to the case. The principal reason for this was that the Carthusian monks had had a secret process for making their Chartreuse. The secret process could not be assigned. There was no secret process for making the cigars and the assignment of the goodwill was effective. Turner then had to consider whether the Hong Kong factory had any goodwill in China. He held that it did not as it was really the Manila factory which had the goodwill in China. He in fact went so far as to suggest that the Hong Kong factory could be sued by Olsen & Co for passing off in China. He therefore dismissed the claim with costs. Given the complexity of the case, he awarded costs on a special scale and allowed for the costs of two counsel to be claimed rather than the normal practice of allowing for only one counsel's costs.

Ingenohl appealed to the Privy Council in London. The Privy Council described Turner's judgment as "able and exhaustive." They disagreed that the assignment in the Philippines had assigned the goodwill in China. The Privy Council found instead that the assignment allowed Olsen to say that they were not passing off their cigars as those of Ingenohl's provided they did not claim they were cigars produced by

Ingenohl himself. They dismissed the appeal but did require Olsen & Co to undertake to remove words from the cigar box labels that the products were guaranteed by C. Ingenohl.[6] This was not the end of the dispute. Ingenohl and Olsen & Co continued litigating around the world in to the 1930s. Ingenohl himself died in 1934, but his company continued to sell his cigars in Hong Kong and Shanghai through luxury boutiques right up to WWII.

Turner later used the case and the conflicting decisions of the Shanghai and Hong Kong courts to illustrate the "peculiar and somewhat unsatisfactory positions" that could arise under extraterritoriality. The decision of Rees-Davies CJ and that of Turner and the Privy Council, however, were not necessarily contradictory. As Macleod had argued, Rees-Davies was dealing with trademarks that had been registered in Hong Kong. They were a property right actually registered in Hong Kong. Turner was dealing with the tort of passing off which requires a party to prove they have goodwill.

The Ingenohl case was to be one of the last major cases tried by Skinner Turner. It was also one of the last cases to be appealed directly from the Supreme Court for China to the Privy Council before a local appeal court was established. A number of changes were coming to the court.

---

6 *Ingenohl v Wing On* (1927) 44 RPC 343 (Appeal No. 81 of 1925).

CHAPTER 48

Recognition, Retirements and Advances

THE PRAISE BY THE PRIVY Council of Turner's "able and exhaustive" judgment in the Ingenohl case was not the only recognition given to the Supreme Court in Shanghai from London. In 1925, Gilbert King, the Registrar of the Supreme Court, was awarded the Order or the British Empire for his services. Some time after, special arrangements were made for Judge Skinner Turner to present the OBE to King. Peter Grain, the Assistant Judge, Mr Barton, the Consul General and members of the bar all attended.[1] Sir Skinner praised King's devotion to duty:

"It is a matter of great satisfaction to me to be able
to be here today. We all like to see some recognition
very paid to long and faithful service and we have an
instance of that in Mr. King, whose record it would be
hard to beat. ...
"Mr. King has been ever ready to give such assistance
as he properly may to all who applied for it and I
should like publicly to thank him for all the help he
has given to me since I came here first as Assistant
Judge, ten years ago, and after I became Judge. He has
shown a constant and steady devotion to all his duties,

1 *London Gazette*, 3 June 1925, p3777 for award of OBE; "The Fine Record of Mr G.W. King", *North China Herald*, June 5, 1926, p446.

notwithstanding some discouragements and at times
ill-health. ...
"May you live long to wear the insignia."

King replied, first by thanking Sir Skinner and then adding his gratitude that the work of the court had received some
recognition from Home:

> "We of the judicial branch of the Foreign Office service
> may be forgiven if sometimes we get the impression
> that we do not bulk too largely in the eyes of the Home
> authorities. Numerically, we are a very small service
> vis-à-vis the executive branch, but it may be that our
> impression is a mistaken one. For all that, my personal
> gratification today is the greater in that, in my person
> as a judicial officer of this Court, some recognition of
> the work of the Court has been shown."

The end of a dynasty: Harrie Wilkinson retires

King was awarded his OBE just before the longest legal dynasty of extraterritorial courts in China came to an end. In October 1925, Hiram Parkes Wilkinson, at the age of 59, retired
after 28 years service as Crown Advocate. On his retirement,
together with his father Hiram Shaw Wilkinson, a "Hiram
Wilkinson" had been Crown Advocate in Shanghai for a total
of almost 44 years.

Wilkinson had had a very successful career: He had been
Crown Advocate, Judge for Weihaiwei, Acting Assistant Judge
in Shanghai, Acting Judge in Siam as well as Acting Chief Justice and member of the Full Court in Shanghai. But he had
missed out on the main prize: following in his father's footsteps as Chief Judge of the Supreme Court. Timing had not
been favourable to him. Ernest Satow did not want to appoint
him straight after his father retired and de Sausmarez had
served for a long time. Skinner Turner had replaced Frederick

Bourne as Assistant Judge and then become the Chief Judge.

At his last hearing, Judge Skinner Turner wished Wilkinson a "long life and happiness on his retirement." Wilkinson thanked Turner in return as well for what he had said as a farewell in 1921. A few days later, the *North China Herald* reported that Wilkinson had left Shanghai for home "for good."[2]

One of the reasons for Wilkinson's retirement at the still relatively young age of 59 must have been to spend some time with his father, who had just turned 85. His father had kept himself busy in retirement, serving as the Pro-Chancellor of Queen's University, and as a justice of the Peace. In 1917, he was also appointed a member of the Irish Convention. Harrie, however, must have felt that his father would not live for much longer.[3]

Harrie moved with his family to join his father in the townland of Moneyshanere, just outside Tobermore in Northern Ireland. His father died the following year and was buried in a family plot next to Harrie's brother, Thomas, in Kilcronaghan Churchyard in Tobermore. The grave has a beautiful view over the lush green valley outside Tobermore.

Harrie also kept himself active in retirement. He served as a Justice of the Peace and founded the Tobermore Unionist Club. He was admitted as a barrister in Northern Ireland in 1926 and was appointed a King's Counsel in 1928. In 1930, he was appointed as Sherriff of Londonderry County. He did not, however, stay Home "for good" and, as we shall see, returned to China in the early 1930s.

Peter Grain was appointed as the new Judge of the High Court of Weihaiwei to replace Wilkinson.

Wilkinson was not the only long serving lawyer to retire. Duncan McNeill, who had acted as Crown Advocate in Har-

---

2 *North China Herald*, October 31, 1925, p200. HP Wilkinson's reminiscences are also published in this article. For the rumour that he might be retiring in 1921, see *North China Herald*, April 30, 1921, p318.

3 H.S. Wilkinson obituary, *Times*, September 29, 1926, p14.

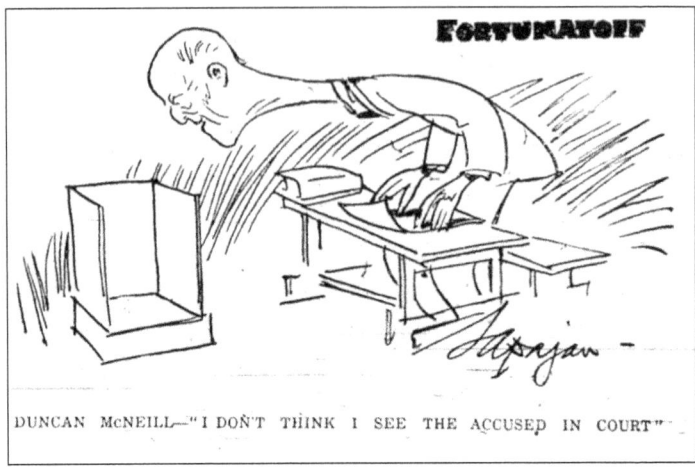

DUNCAN McNEILL—"I DON'T THINK I SEE THE ACCUSED IN COURT"

Just before retirement Duncan McNeill appeared prosecute a Russian Dr Eugene Fortunatoff for bribery. Fortunatoff jumped bail.

rie's place between 1901 and 1903 (and who had accused H.S. Wilkinson of being unjust in 1905) also retired in late February 1926. His son John, had just arrived in Shanghai and been admitted a few weeks earlier before Peter Grain. Grain had wished him well and said: "I hope you have as successful career as your father." At a farewell speech for Duncan McNeill at a meeting of the St Andrews Society, the President, Colonel Gordon, said:

"Our President in 1902-03 has always take a keen interest in things Scottish and he has left us means by which we can still tak' a cup o' kindness for auld lang syne, and he is doing yet a nobler deed, he is leaving us a hostage in his son John so that the human touch with him is not lost. We look forward to the anxious father visiting again to see how John is following in the paternal footsteps."

As we shall see, John did very well in career and was even more successful than his father.[4]

New Crown Advocate

Allan Mossop, who since 1915 had acted as Crown Advocate on many occasions in Harrie Wilkinson's place, was appointed the new Crown Advocate for China.

Mossop appears to have been a very private person and little was written about his personal life. His nephews and nieces recall him as having a love of children and being a great storyteller. He also had a life-long love of animals and served as president of the Shanghai Society for Prevention of Cruelty to Animals (SPCA) for many years. Once when making a presentation of prizes for the SPCA essay competition, he told the children how he had kept a pet snake as a boy in South Africa: "Most of the boys at school kept pets of some sort, and I kept a little snake. It lived up my sleeve and during lessons it was secreted in my desk. It used to follow me, answer to its name, drink milk etc." His love of animals extended to his Alsatian dogs which had their own special amah to feed them and walk them. The dogs had their own sets of leather booties that they wore to keep their feet clean when they went out on Shanghai's filthy streets.[5] He also later adopted and kept a pet goose.

As a young man he also served in the Shanghai volunteer fire brigade and recalled to his nieces and nephews in South Africa how they had a small two man tender to get into the Shanghai slums. Perhaps because of his South African heritage, Mossop was keen on watersports. He was described as one of the "pillars of the Shanghai Rowing Club" and as a "yachtsman of no mean pretensions."

....

4   John McNeill Admission: *North China Herald*, February 6, 1926, p252; Farewell to Duncan McNeill: *North China Herald*, February 20, 1926.

5   *North China Herald,* April 21, 1937, p108; Conversation during 2013 with Judy Bekker, niece of Sir Allan; Email from Marian Naude, niece of Sir Allan, dated July 20, 2013.

The Shanghai volunteer fire brigade of which Mossop was a member.

Shanghai becomes more appealing

Mossop was the Crown Advocate when the first major change in many years to the structure of the British courts in China was made: the establishment of a proper appellate court in Shanghai. Up until this time, as we have seen, a party who wanted to appeal had two choices, either bring the case to a two-judge panel in Shanghai or appeal to the Privy Council. In the first case, if the judges disagreed, the decision of the Chief Judge prevailed. Both methods of appeal were considered unsatisfactory. The first because the Full Court not a truly independent tribunal, particularly if the appeal was from a decision of the Chief Judge; the second, because of the expense and trouble of taking an appeal to London.

A new Order in Council changed this by creating a Full Court in China. The first appeal was heard on October 8, 1926. The *North China Herald* headlined this as an "Important Innovation" and reported:

"Yesterday witnessed a new departure in the procedure of HM Supreme Court and one of very great importance. It is that three judges for the first time in the

history of the Court sat to hear appeals, and the fact
they do so constitutes a very important advance in the
procedure of the Court. Several important cases are on
hearing list, and it will be appreciated how the authorities at Home has given due regard to the subject of
appeals here."[6]

Under the new Order in Council, appeals from the Su-
preme Court were to be heard by the Judge and Assistant
Judge together with the Chief Justice of Hong Kong, or if the
Chief Justice was not available, another judge of the Hong
Kong Supreme Court.[7] The President of the Court was the
most senior of the Judge or Chief Justice. Appeals from the
Registrar of the Supreme Court and the Provincial Courts in
China remained to be decided by the Judge and the Assistant
Judge or the Judge sitting alone.

The first full appeal was heard by Sir Skinner Turner,
Judge; Sir Henry Gollan, Chief Justice of Hong Kong; and,
Peter Grain, Assistant Judge. Allan Mossop appeared as the
Crown Advocate.

Sir Skinner, at the beginning of the hearing, first said a few
words noting the recent deaths of Robert Mowat and H.S.
Wilkinson. After briefly recounting their careers he said:

"Though to most of us here today they are only names,
it seemed to me fitting to record our sympathy with
their relatives and to show they are not forgotten in the
history of H.B.M. Supreme Court for China."

6   *North China Herald*, October 9, 1926, p67. The China Order in Council 1925, Article
22(2)

7   Until the Supreme Court ceased to exist judges from Hong Kong came to sit on
Shanghai Full Court, including Chief Justices Joseph Kemp and Atholl MacGregor as
well as Acting Chief Justices John Wood and Roger Lindsell. See the *Luna Park* and
MacKellar cases in following chapters for cases heard by Kemp and MacGregor. See also:
Chun Nich Realty Investment v Clark, North China Daily News, 8 December 1933 (Wood)
and *China Realty v Kew & Anderson*, North China Daily News, 1 December 1937 (Lindsell)
(Both from Mossop Law Reports).

He then welcomed the introduction of an appeal court:

"This is the first sitting of the Full Court as constituted
under the Order-in-Council of 1925. The old Full Court
consisted of the Judge and Assistant Judge of the Court,
with a casting vote, in the case a difference of opinion,
in the hands of the Judge: not a very satisfactory arrangement, and hence litigants were apt to take their
appeals directly to the Privy Council in London without any first appeal in China. In 1925, I was enabled
to get this altered and, thanks to the co-operation of
the Colony of Hongkong, we have now a Full Court of
three Judges and appeals only lie to the Privy Council
from decisions of that Court, thus ensuring to litigants
one appeal in China and that to a Court in which the
majority of the Judges sitting can have had nothing to
do-with the case in the Court of First Instance.
"I doubt not that this change will be welcomed, and,
though this is not the first time he has sat with me in
Shanghai, I should like, on behalf of the Judges of this

THE APPEAL COURT SITS IN SHANGHAI
For the first time in the history of the Supreme Court for China, a full Court of Appeal sat last Friday. The Judges, from left to
right are Sir Henry Gollan, Sir Skinner Turner and Judge Peter Grain.

The First Appeal Court Henry Gollan, Skinner Turner, Peter Grain

Court, to add a word of welcome to Hongkong's Chief Justice on this, the first sitting of the newly-constituted Full Court."[8]

While much better than the previous system, the new system of appeal still had the flaw that the original trial judge would still sit on the panel that heard the appeal. It was also not, as Skinner Turner had alluded to, the first time Sir Henry Gollan had sat on the Shanghai Full Court. Since 1917, if a judge was not available, the Judge (or Acting Judge) had the power to appoint "any fit person approved by the Minister" to sit with him on the appeal. Gollan had sat with Skinner Turner in an appeal in 1924 under this provision.[9]

The first appeal was in a civil case from a decision made by Grain where he had found in favour of the Defendants in a case for breach of contract involving the sale of lumber from Russia. The Full Court upheld Grain's decision. Interestingly, Grain admitted that he had been mistaken in one point in his original decision but said this did not affect the ultimate result. The second appeal was by Hasura Singh against a conviction for grievous bodily harm. The appeal was dismissed on the spot.[10]

Skinner Turner retires
Soon after the first appeal hearings (and issue of the report of the Extraterritoriality Commission), Turner took home leave. While there, he retired due to ill health, probably partly brought on by the pressures of being a member of the Extraterritoriality Commission and, perhaps, some personal distaste at its recommendations. Turner died eight years after his

8   *North China Herald*, October 16, 1926, p126.

9   China (Amendment) Order in Council 1917, s.3; *Siberian Agricultural Corporation Ltd v R Fermus, North China Herald*, December 13, 1924, p460.

10   *R v Husara Singh, North China Herald*, October 16, 1926, p126 Decision in the civil case: *Shanghai Import & Export Lumber Co v Mackenzie & Co Ltd, North China Herald*, November 20, 1926, p367.

Gilbert King promoted to Assistant Judge

retirement, in 1935, at a nursing home in Winchester at the age of 67.

On Turner's retirement, Peter Grain was promoted to Judge of the Supreme Court while also remaining the Judge of the High Court of Weihaiwei. Gilbert King, the Registrar or the Court, was appointed Assistant Judge. By the time King was appointed a judge, he had served as Registrar of the Supreme Court for 19 years. A replacement for King as Registrar was not appointed for three years which perhaps explains why Grain remained as Judge for Weihaiwei. King would have continued to supervise the Registry until a new Registrar was appointed.

Two years after his retirement, Turner gave a talk on extraterritoriality where he made it clear that he thought extraterritoriality should end soon. He said that the system had "difficulties and inconveniences arising from it," and concluded with a suggestion that as an interim step, extraterritorial courts could apply Chinese statute law before the eventual abolition of extraterritoriality.[11]

In his talk, Skinner Turner also said that:

"By a gradual process of evolution the British machin-

---

11 S Turner, "Extraterritoriality in China", 10 Brit. Y.B. Int'l L. 56 1929.

ery for the exercise of jurisdiction has become complete."

He was in many ways correct. After more than 60 years, almost every legal issue that needed to be considered had been considered and the Orders in Council or decisions of the court provided for a complete system. Even the US Court, despite the scandals covered in the next chapter, had by this time created an almost complete system of rules and jurisprudence.

It is one of those ironies of life that just when a system is finally complete, it is also about time to have it dismantled. But for the intervention of Japan, this is what would have happened to British and American extraterritoriality in China.

The cases in the next chapter certainly provided fodder for those who considered extraterritoriality to be a corrupt system.

CHAPTER 49

The Dirty DA

MILTON PURDY ON HIS arrival as the US Judge in Shanghai at the hearing to welcome him commented on "how fortunate had been the U.S. Government in getting men of such excellent quality and ability as the officials of this court."

At the very end of 1926, he learnt how wrong he had been. The US Court for China saw the trial of two of its officials for engaging in serious criminal misconduct.

First, Purdy had the sad duty to pass sentence on the former Clerk of the US Court, William Chapman, who had pleaded guilty to embezzling G$15,000 from the court. He had originally fled to Seattle, but was caught on arrival in the US and was brought back to Shanghai for trial. During his days on the run, he had found God. In a personal statement to the court he cited the scriptures and promised that whatever the sentence he would do his best in prison to improve himself. Purdy called it a "most distressing case" and said when he heard of the offence he was "literally astounded and crushed." He said if he could dismiss the case with the words, "go and sin no more," he would. But, as a judge he had a duty to uphold the law. He sentenced Chapman to three years and five months imprisonment. Having arrived in Shanghai to be sentenced, Chapman was then put back on the same boat, the *President Roosevelt*, heading back to Seattle.[1] Long-term US prisoners from China were no longer sent to the Philippines. Instead, they were now im-

---

1 *United States v Chapman*, *North China Herald*, December 31, 1926, p63.

HON. JUDGE MILTON PURDY.

DR. GEORGE SELLETT, U.S. DISTRICT ATTORNEY.

LEONARD G. HUSAR, THE ACCUSED.

MRS. PORTER, COURT STENOGRAPHER

U. S. v. HUSAR: THE CHIEF PERSONALITIES

prisoned at the federal penitentiary on McNeil Island in Puget Sound just near Seattle. This was to be Chapman's new home.

At that very same time that Chapman arrived in Shanghai to be sentenced, a scandal of far greater proportions, in fact the largest scandal to occur in the 37-year history of the US Court for China, was unfolding. Leonard Husar, the United States District Attorney, was arrested for corruption. The allegation was that he had solicited and taken a G$25,000 bribe to hand over to Tracy Woodward, an opium smuggler, a file detailing Woodward's dealings in opium. Woodward's file had been sent to Shanghai from the US Consular Court in Persia.

A few month's earlier, Husar's wife, Mary Jo Grubb Husar, had filed for divorce in California. As part of her divorce petition she alleged that Husar had taken the bribe. She said Husar was so worried afterwards that he had slept with a gun under the pillow. She claimed that he had finally told her of the problem after the US Consul had started investigating and he had suggested she return to America.

As soon as the allegations were made, Husar resigned as District Attorney. He also decided to hit back, filing his own divorce proceedings in Shanghai, accusing Mary Jo of drunkeness and infidelity. He said in court that her drinking had "caused him severe embarrassment and had greatly interfered with his social standing in the community, so much so that certain families had intimated that they could not receive him and his wife in their homes." He had also kept watch on a hotel once and had seen a man leave. He had found her in bed so drunk that to remove her would have required an ambulance. He later filed a cross-complaint in the US proceedings where he "named 10 men with whom she openly consorted" and called her a "vulgar-minded woman without any sense of decency, pride or shame." He added she habitually drank to excess and danced nude at a party.[2] All

2   *Oakland Tribune* November 13, 1926, p1; *North China Herald*, December 31, 1926, p63; *Oakland Tribune*, January 28,1927, p8.

terribly scandalous, but the best was yet to come.

The new, very young, District Attorney, Thomas Sellett, prosecuted Husar. Sellett, who held a PhD, had been appointed to replace Husar. Sellett had been born in November 1898 making him 28 at the time of his appointment. He had graduated from the University of Michigan in 1923 and come to Shanghai where he commenced practice as an attorney. He also taught at the Comparative Law School of China for a year before becoming Dean of the school.[3]

The allegations against Husar were that he had arranged for another American lawyer, Neil Heath, to approach Woodward who was at this time running a successful business. Heath blackmailed Woodward by telling him that Husar intended to prosecute him for his dealings in opium unless Woodward paid a bribe of G$75,000 to get the file back. This was bargained down to $25,000. Woodward then said that he had arranged to meet Husar and Heath at the Shanghai American Club on Foochow Road (Fuzhou Road) where Husar handed over the file. He had arranged to pay $25,000 Mexican, but Heath told him it was Gold Dollars, take it or leave it. Woodward paid and then took the file home and with the assistance of his chauffer burnt it.

Sellett decided that he would only be able to get a conviction against Husar and Heath if he offered Woodward immunity from prosecution. Woodward then became the star witness in two trials: *United States v Heath* and *United States v Husar*. In both cases, Sellett faced a major problem that his star witness was a convicted opium smuggler and generally regarded as being of low moral character.

The US Marshal arrested Husar as he left the US Court following a hearing where he had been defending an action brought against him personally for the price of 12 dresses his wife had bought. He was released on bail of G$15,000 set by

3 *North China Herald*, May 30, 1934, p 306.

Judge Purdy.[4]

Heath's trial started first before Purdy with Sellett prosecuting. Heath was represented by a phalanx of Shanghai's leading American lawyers, including William Fleming, Cornell Franklin, P. Faison and Norwood Allman. Heath also represented himself. Surprisingly, given the allegations that were to be made in both trials, Husar also appeared to defend Heath. Heath was charged with two counts of receiving and taking government property and one count of larceny of US property.

Woodward was the main witness and gave evidence of how Heath had contacted him to shake him down and how over a course of four meetings he had negotiated a price of G$25,000 plus a 2,000 taels commission for Heath. He said that he had not met Husar when he came to club to hand over the file, but had instead stood with his face to the window so he did not see him. However, as he left the club he had seen Husar standing outside of the bathroom.

A letter Heath had sent to Woodward when the case was being investigated was the most damning evidence. The letter read:

> "The situation is serious for both you and I, it is
> dangerous.... Husar's wife has made a full report to
> Washington and filed a divorce suit against Husar, us-
> ing our names... I tried to keep her from filing it, but
> could not... I did persuade her from using our names
> and substituting John Doe ... I got a lawyer for her who
> I know that I can control, Mr J. G. Moser ... The Secret
> Service in Washington obtained our names some way
> ... they are looking for me now, I feel that they will get
> me ... there is no question but that I will be carried back
> (removed under the Removal Act) ... I am using a false

---

4 *North China Herald*, January 22, 1927, p114. The original complaint against him is set out in the article.

name … You know that the U.S. Government will not let drop a case as this … Husar thinks that I had relations with his wife, this is not true, although he alleges it … I would spend a year in prison to see him get the limit ... he will be begging me on bended knees to save him. I am going to write to Dr Sellett … I'm busted, this worry is driving me crazy, I wish I could get to South America and outlive the statute of limitations … trusting that we will be out of this jam soon. I am etc., Neil McKay Heath."

A number of other witnesses were called from the banks confirming that Woodward had drawn a large sum of money on the day he paid Heath. His chauffeur also gave evidence that he taken his master to the club and helped him destroy a file.

Detective Inspector Tinkler of the SMP who had been sent by his superiors to inspect the file was called to give evidence what he had seen on the file. He said the SMP had decided to take no action against Woodward because they believed the US authorities would prosecute him. Tinkler said the documents were black bound with two binders. He remembered certain telegrams and letters and that most of the material was typewritten. He said that about eight charges had been brought against Woodward in Persia and he had pleaded guilty to about half of them. Tinkler added, mysteriously, that, "certain foreigners were mentioned, including Father Costello, Mr Kentwell and Lissie Bell."

Even in such an important case as this, the mention of Kentwell's name was too good an opportunity even for the erudite and serious Dr Sellett to resist. He asked Tinkler, who of course knew Kentwell well having arrested and given evidence against him two years before in the British Supreme Court:

"Do you know Mr Kentwell's nationality?"

"No", deadpanned Tinkler to laughter in the court.

One suspects that even Purdy was forced to have a chuckle at this entirely irrelevant question and answer.

After the prosecution closed its case Franklin and Fleming argued that Purdy should dismiss the charges on the basis that Woodward was a co-conspirator and that the law required that his evidence be corroborated by other evidence. Purdy

Detective Inspector Maurice Tinkler tells the court L. K. Kentwell was mentioned in the opium files

agreed that much of the evidence was not corroborated. But Purdy considered the Heath's letter to Woodward to be totally damning. He said: "I cannot imagine a letter being written more clearly linking the author with a crime. You would have a hard time convincing any jury in Christendom that this letter did not refer to this case." He dismissed the application.

Heath chose not to give evidence. His only defence was to attack Woodward's credibility by calling a number of witnesses to testify as to his bad character. This included Major Holcomb who gave evidence that, in 1918, when he was District Attorney he had prosecuted Woodward in Shanghai for opium smuggling.

At the close of the case, Franklin applied for a dismissal of the charges on the basis that there was no evidence the file was US Government property and that Woodward's evidence was not corroborated. Purdy held that two of the counts had not been properly proved and acquitted Heath. However, he found Heath guilty on one count, larceny of government property. He then, over the objections of Heath's lawyers, put off sentencing of Heath until after Husar's trial.[5]

Husar's trial commenced on April 20, 1927. He was also represented by Fleming, Franklin, Allman and Faison. He pleaded not guilty. Much of the same evidence that was called in the Heath trial was given again. There was also evidence from the Consul-General and other consular and court officials and staff as to how the Woodward file had gone missing. The jailer at the Consular Jail, which was located in the consular building, said he saw Heath visit Husar on a number of occasions during the period in question. It was also formally admitted that Husar had been District Attorney at the time.

Woodward gave additional evidence of how he had met with Husar a few times after the bribe had been paid and that Husar had told him that he believed Heath had had an affair with his wife. Woodward said Husar told him of Heath that, "after giving him $17,000 in the book deal the sneak and dog had the impudence to eat at my table and conduct himself in a shameful way with my wife." Woodward also said Husar told him Heath was blackmailing him over the payment of the bribe. This time, Woodward said that, in fact, he had seen Husar when Husar came to the American Club in a ricshaw on the day the file was handed over.

The most damning evidence against Husar, however, was that on the day after the alleged bribe had been paid, December 16, 1925, Husar had opened a safety deposit box at the Hong Kong & Shanghai Bank. He had visited the box eight times until it was closed a little over a year later in mid-January 1927. There was also evidence that Husar had made other transactions at other banks.

Husar had two defences. The first was an alibi. He called witnesses and gave evidence himself that he could not have been at the American Club at the time in question. The first witness Cornell Franklin tried to call on behalf of Husar was

---

5 Sellett also preferred new charges against Heath. These were ordered to be tried after Husar's trial. See *North China Daily News*, April 21, 1927.

Heath. Heath had been subpoenaed. Heath had not yet been sentenced so the case against him was still pending. He had a right not to answer questions that might incriminate himself. He answered a few questions before Purdy warned him of his right against self-incrimination. He was then withdrawn as a witness.

Husar's second defence was absolutely startling.

He claimed he had made the money in his safe deposit box from dealing in guns!

He said that in 1924 he had befriended Colonel Hsu, the intelligence chief of a Chang Tsung-Chang who was then in charge of the defence of Shanghai. He said he had received $6,000 a year paid in cash. This had been increased to $750 per month (or $9,000 per year). From December 1925 he had acted as a go-between in an arms deal between an Italian named Parlani and Colonel Hsu. A total of 6,000 rifles with bayonets and ammunition had been sold and Parlani had offered him a 5% commission on the deal. He had introduced Parlani and Chang and then told them he would look to Chang for the commission because he was not familiar with Parlani. The sale price had been agreed at 500,0000 taels giving Husar a $37,000 commission. Colonel Chang paid the commission, he said, on December 15, 1925.[6]

Husar had asked for cash payment because he did not want to be identified with the deal "as anything that has arms connected with it in China carries a stigma." He, of course, knew this because two years before this purported deal he had prosecuted Kearny and his "gigantic organization" for gun running. Despite this he said, "at the same time, however, I did not feel I was doing any wrong. General Chang was the accredited militarist of this area at the time. I was simply offered a commission by his agent and took it."

Husar then said he took the bulk of the money and put it

6 *New York Times*, May 5, 1927 and June 13, 1928.

in the safety deposit box at the Hong Kong & Shanghai Bank. He also gave evidence by reference to his bank accounts to show the deposits he had received from Colonel Soo as well as to explain the payments out.

The day ended early before Husar could be cross-examined because all the members of the press present needed to attend the horse races, an obviously much more important matter than the trial of a former District Attorney for corruption.

The next day, Sellett cross-examined Husar. He first asked about Husar's domestic difficulties and Heath's relationship with his wife. Husar said that he had beaten Heath once - Heath had denied any relationship with his wife, but Husar said he was convinced they had committed adultery. He also admitted that having prosecuted Captain Kearny for arms smuggling he had, only two years later, turned around and made money the same way. He had interviewed Woodward when he had come to Shanghai and obtained a lot of useful evidence from him about opium smuggling. He had decided, however, not to prosecute him. Husar also admitted that he had paid Captain Kearny $20 for a photograph of Woodward. He said that he had given the photograph to a newspaper because he wanted the paper to publish it to embarrass Woodward. Husar said that Parlani was in Europe and he could not get Colonel Hsu to give evidence due to the political situation in Shanghai. This was, in relation to Hsu at least, probably true. Shanghai was at the time surrounded by Nationalist troops and the newspapers daily carried pictures of foreign troops preparing to battle the Chinese. Hsu had most likely long since vanished.

Sellett then changed tack completely to attack Husar's credibility. He suggested that the amounts of $500 and $750 that Husar had been paying into his bank account were, in fact, protection money he had extorted from two American prostitutes, Virginia Nelson and Blanche Bennett. Husar responded sarcastically: "That's the best insinuation I have heard you make today." Sellett pushed Husar to answer as to whether he had met Blanche Bennett.

Husar's response was telling in terms of showing the divisions in the American community in China and, given Husar's own admissions in the trial, how the old District Attorney and new one were like chalk and cheese. He said:

> "The only business I ever had with these unfortunate women was when some of your people – missionaries – came to me with an affidavit that they had gone into some of the houses and spent money and asked me to help get them out of town."

Even from the written page, you can almost hear Husar spitting the word "missionaries" out.

This closed the case. Both prosecution and defence agreed to make limited arguments in closing. Sellett said the case was clear and Husar's own admissions about the money in the safety deposit box made his defence impossible. Cornell Franklin, for Husar, asked simply, who would you believe, "a useful citizen, a man honoured with a responsible position of high trust and a man with an unblemished record" or a convicted opium smuggler of low character.

Purdy gave a very short judgment saying that after hearing all the evidence he believed the convicted opium smuggler, Woodward, and that Husar was guilty.

The next day, saying "it pained and grieved him" to be in the position of sentencing a government official he had been associated with since he occupied the bench, he sentenced Husar to two years in McNeil Island in Washington State. He granted Husar bail of G$20,000 pending appeal saying that bail had to be sufficiently high that if he absconded he would not benefit from his crime. He also sentenced Heath to 18 months in McNeil Island.

Husar appealed to the Ninth Circuit in San Francisco and the case was heard a year later in June 1928.[7] Husar had three grounds of appeal. The first was that the United States Court for China did not have jurisdiction over him. The second that Purdy had improperly not allowed Heath to give testimony and the third that the letter from Heath to Woodward sent in 1926 should not have been admitted in evidence.

The first ground, lack of jurisdiction, was the only one of real interest and was not raised by Husar until the oral argument before the appeal court. The charge against Husar had not stated that he was a United States citizen. The US Court for China only had jurisdiction over United States citizens. This needed to be stated in the charge.[8] Husar "freely admitted" that he was a US citizen but argued that the charge was technically defective. The Ninth Circuit dealt with this neatly by relying on the Supreme Court decision in the Ross case that gave the court jurisdiction over any seaman on a United States vessel. Husar had been prosecuted as the United States District Attorney for China, had been appointed as such by the US President and had taken an oath of office. This was more than enough to give the US Court jurisdiction. If the Consular Court in Yokohama had had jurisdiction over Ross as a British seaman on a US vessel, it surely had jurisdiction over Husar as a US District Attorney in a US court. The other points were rejected on the basis that Purdy had been right to caution Heath and that Husar had only objected to the evidence later. The Ninth Circuit therefore upheld the conviction. Husar was paroled in December 1929 after serving a year and a half in McNeil Island.[9]

....

7   *United States v Husar*, 26 F.2d 847 (1928) before Reidkin, Dietrich and Hunt, Circuit Judges.

8   The charge must have been amended at some time. The original charge published in the *North China Herald* of 22 January 1927 (at p114), alleged he was a United States Citizen.

9   Records of Prisoners Received at the United States Penitentiary, McNeil Island,

After Husar's appeal had failed, Heath also filed an application for *habeas corpus* against the warden of McNeil Island on the ground that the charge had not stated that he was a United States citizen and the court therefore did not have jurisdiction. This was successful and Heath was released. The government appealed. The Ninth Circuit allowed the appeal on the grounds that in a *habeas corpus* applications are treated differently to appeals. On appeals the record must show there is jurisdiction. In *habeas corpus* applications it must appear affirmatively on the record that the court did not have jurisdiction. Heath's conviction was restored and he was ordered to be returned to prison.[10] Heath did not immediately return, but gave himself up in San Francisco ten months later telling the police he had been "making good" in real estate.[11]

Everything about the Husar case was very strange. But the plot thickens even further. Douglas Valentine in his book, *Strength of the Wolf: The Secret History of America's War on Drugs*, suggests that Husar had been involved in a US Government investigation of opium smuggling and that only because of his wife's allegations was the government was forced to prosecute him.[12] This sounds like your typical American conspiracy theory, but there are a number of things that suggest it might be true. First, when Husar first married his wife in 1923, she bought an airplane to Shanghai. Aircraft were then (and are now) very expensive. Was it really hers or was it for some other purpose? Second, Husar's crime should have resulted in his disbarment anywhere in the world. There could be no greater breach of trust. But Husar was not disbarred. Instead, astonishingly, the Governor of California restored his civil rights upon release and he resumed practice

Washington record for Husar (No. 7184).

10 *Archer v Heath*, 30 F.2d 932 (1929).

11 *Huntsville Daily Times*, January 1, 1930.

12 Douglas Valentine, *Strength of the Wolf: The Secret History of America's War on Drugs*, p 13.

as a lawyer in California. Third, and perhaps most amazingly, only seven years after his conviction, Husar was appointed as a city attorney in Los Angeles.[13] While not conclusive, all this suggests that there was more to this case than meets the eye. No matter what, there was something funny in the state of United States justice in China. Perhaps Husar really did have a second job as secret agent. His position as District Attorney would have given him the perfect cover for snooping around in China. On the other hand, the fact he appears to have served substantial time in prison suggests he did not have complete protection.

The prosecution and convictions of Chapman, Husar and Heath were a very bad start to 1927 for the United States Court for China. For China, on the other hand, 1927 started with the hope for the first united government of China in more than a decade.

---

13 Plane: *The Morning Post*, February 12, 1923, p11; Civil Rights and City Attorney: *Nevada State Times*, July 9, 1935 p1.

CONCLUSION TO VOLUME II

THE FIRST QUARTER of the 20th Century saw many changes in East Asia. The legitimacy of the Qing Dynasty and the city of Peking had been all but destroyed by the failed Boxer uprising and war with the eight foreign powers. Japan had now joined the ranks of the world powers; eating up Korea as part of its continued imperial ambitions. This brought British journalist Ernest Bethell before the British courts on a number of occasions as he opposed Japan's occupation of Korea. Ultimately, British and American extraterritoriality ended in Korea with Japan's annexation of the country.

The United States, emulating Great Britain, established a United States Court for China. The court went through a baptism of fire with its first two judges retiring under a cloud. In the British Court, both HS Wilkinson and Frederick Bourne retired to well-deserved accolades after 40 years of service. Sir Frederick Bourne became the only Assistant Judge to be honoured with a knighthood.

The Republican Revolution in China in 1911 brought hope to the Chinese people for change but Yuan Shikai's greed for power soon brought this to an end with the country sliding into civil war and disorder and the Nationalist Party retreating to Canton. World War I brought new challenges for China and the British and American courts, including cases of sedition and how to deal with enemy aliens. China gained some judicial power over foreigners with Germans losing their extraterritorial rights in 1917 and the Soviet Union giving up its rights in 1922. They were, however, in Shanghai International Settlement subject to the jurisdiction of the International Mixed Court which had been taken over by the Municipal Council.

Havilland de Sausmarez also retired at the end of World War I. Skinner Turner, to the disappointment of Harrie Wilkinson, replaced him, serving for 7 years as Chief Judge before retiring. Harrie Wilkinson after 28 years as Crown Advocate had himself retired bringing an end to a 44 year dynasty with his father in that position. Charles Lobingier, despite William Fleming's vicious attack on him, had succeeded in building a strong and respected United States Court for China. Milton Purdy, in a lower-key way, continued this before having to face the disappointment of convicting two officials of the court for corruption.

The first seven years of the 1920s were a time of flux and change worldwide, but particularly in China. Rapid economic growth following World War I saw Shanghai expand further to the north and to the west as well as bringing many more complex cases before the court as multiple jurisdictions intermingled.

The weakness of the Chinese Central Government allowed foreigners to maintain their extraterritorial rights and privileges through the early nineteen twenties. Times were, however, changing fast. Chinese (and in the British courts, Indians) were more willing to defy foreign power. The prosecution by the Ningpo Guild of Inspector Gabbutt for torturing Loh Tse Wah and the Bank of East Asia's challenge to the decision of the Consul General in Canton to refuse to register a land transfer showed that Chinese were become more willing to assert their rights. The May 30 Movement marked the beginning of increased Chinese nationalism, which could be seen most overtly by Lawrence Kentwell's outbursts in the Supreme Court.

The American Commissioner on the International Commission investigating the causes and aftermath of the May 30 Movement, Finley Johnson, had correctly identified that the major problem was that foreigners did not appreciate just how far China and its people had developed in the previous

10 years. Despite this, the long awaited Extraterritoriality Commission recommended only very slow change. The foreign powers, failing to understand of the sea-change in thinking that had occurred amongst the Chinese people, still felt they could hold off Chinese aspirations to be masters in their own country.

As we shall see in the next volume, this would soon change. A newly strong China was about to stand up, altering the very nature of the foreign presence in the country and making the exercise of extraterritorial rights all the more difficult.

Introduction to Vol I

Extraterritoriality – an Extraordinary System

IN 1874, SIR EDMUND HORNBY, Chief Judge of the British Supreme Court for China and Japan, entered a court room in the northern Chinese seaport of Chefoo in the full red robes of a British criminal judge. All those in court rose and bowed to him. As he took his seat, behind him was the British coat of arms bearing the words "Dieu et Mon Droit" ("God and my Right"). Before him in the dock was Thomas Fawcett, a British foreman accused of killing a Chinese man. After a trial in which Chinese witnesses were brought to court in chains to give evidence, Fawcett was acquitted by the British jury. For the next three days and two nights, the local Chinese population besieged Hornby's house demanding proper justice. He wrote later: "Of course, I never tried another British subject accused of killing a Chinaman at an outlying port, unless there was a gun-boat at hand."

What was a British judge, bewigged and fully robed in red, doing trying a criminal case against a British subject in northern China? Why was there a British jury? Why the gunboat? The simple answer is: extraterritoriality.

In China, for almost a century, Britain, America and other foreign countries ran their own civil and criminal justice systems. These legal systems were, as far as possible, entirely separate from the Chinese system. They had their own courts, judges, lawyers and, even, prisons. In Japan, almost identical foreign legal systems to those in China also existed for just over forty years.

These justice systems were created as part of the forced opening of China and Japan in the 1840s and 1850s. Until then, for more than 200 years, both China and Japan had been closed to Westerners and in both countries, only limited foreign trade had been allowed at a single port far away from the capital.

Britain and America changed this. In 1842, following the two-year Opium War, a British Navy flotilla led by Captain Henry Pottinger forced China to sign - at the point of their gunboat barrels - the Treaty of Nanking which opened five ports to Western trade. In 1854, an American naval squadron, led by Commodore Matthew Perry, forced Japan – also at the point of their gunboat barrels – to open to Western trade and sign a Treaty of Amity and Commerce. Other Western countries were quick to follow Britain and America's lead and signed similar treaties with both countries.

The Chinese and Japanese, not surprisingly, hated the "unequal treaties" that had brought foreigners to their shores. They, however, had no choice but to accept them. The treaties allowed the treaty powers to base army and naval forces in China and Japan, and on numerous occasions, British, American and other treaty powers' gunboats and armies were brought in to enforce "treaty rights." Peking was attacked and the Summer Palace burnt to the ground by the British and French in 1860. Kagoshima in southern Japan was shelled and all but destroyed by the British in 1863. Shimonoseki was held to ransom by the British, American, French and Dutch navies in 1864. China fought and lost numerous wars with foreign powers in the late 19th century. Right up to the 1940s, foreign navy boats, exercising treaty rights, patrolled the coast of China and the Yangtze River to protect foreign interests. Foreign troops were stationed in Peking and all along the railway line between Peking and Tientsin.

China and Japan's reaction to their forced opening to the

West continues to this day to have a strong impact on how they both view and treat each other and the rest of the world. Each country faced an almost identical challenge, but the results were diametrically opposite. Japan was the big winner from the unequal treaties while China was the big loser. Neither country has forgotten this – and neither country will. Ever.

This history explains the deep enmity that exists to this day between the two countries and why the 21st century tensions between the newly-strong China and still-strong Japan are so dangerous. If pushed, neither side will back down to the other.

For Japan, its forced opening is, now, a matter for celebration. All over Japan can be found memorials to the arrival of the foreigners and their contribution to the development of Japan. Museums commemorating the foreign settlements and the foreigners who helped build them can be found in all treaty ports. In a country where land is scarce, and despite having fought the British and Americans in World War II, foreign cemeteries from the 19th century have been preserved and are well maintained. On the 150th anniversary of the British and Japanese Treaty of Amity and Commerce, the Japanese Foreign Minster, at the Foreign Office in London, launched a "Japan-UK 150" celebration.[1] In Yokohama, you can enjoy lunch at "Le Jardin de Perry" near where Matthew Perry landed.

For China, its forced opening and the 100 years that followed are now described as "the Century of Humiliation." Anti-foreign sentiment is taught in schools, fills China's history books and is on display in all its museums. Foreign cemeteries have all been destroyed. You could never imagine any Chinese Foreign Minister celebrating an anniversary of the

....

1   Speech by Mr Shintaro Ito, State Secretary for Foreign Affairs, at a Reception to celebrate 150 Years of Diplomatic Relations between the United Kingdom and Japan at the Foreign & Commonwealth Office, London, September 16, 2008.

Treaty of Nanking anywhere, let alone at the Foreign Office in London. There is no "Le Jardin de Pottinger" in modern-day Nanjing.[2]

How can two countries which faced almost identical challenges have travelled such different roads?

In Japan, the opening of the country led to a civil war between reformers and those who wanted to retain the old feudal government under the Shogunate. The reformers won. From the late 1860s, the basic policy of the Japanese government was "reform or die."

Japan launched headlong into a program of rapid and large scale Westernisation. The Shogunate and old feudal system was abolished; foreign laws were studied and adopted; and, democracy was steadily introduced. The results were amazing. Japan went through a period of massive industrialization and economic growth and year after year became, politically, economically and militarily stronger. In less than 40 years, by 1894, Japan was strong enough to be able to reach agreements with all foreign countries to abolish all the unequal treaties. The following year, it defeated China in war and imposed its own unequal treaty on China. It continued to go from strength to strength, defeating Russia, annexing Korea and, over time, taking over large parts of China. Ultimately, during World War II, Japan occupied almost half of Asia.

China, on the other hand, was at the time of its forced opening already ruled by foreigners, the Manchus from Manchuria in what is now northeast China. The basic policy of the Manchu-run Qing Dynasty can be summarized as "if we reform we will die." Any change in China's system of governance, they believed, would weaken Manchu rule. One large-scale revolt in the 1850s and 1860s, the Taiping Rebellion, did threaten the government (and the Foreign Settle-

---

2   There is a Pottinger Street in Hong Kong, but that is another story.

ment in Shanghai), but was put down. The Qing Dynasty futilely resisted reform, relying instead on "self-strengthening," modernization in certain limited areas. This response, which led to further wars with foreign powers which China almost invariably lost, allowed China's sovereignty to be chipped away by more and more unequal treaties.

The Republican Revolution in 1911 offered hope, but collapsed into civil war. Germany's defeat in World War I and the Russian Revolution brought the end of extraterritorial rights for Germans and Russians, but saw Japan take over most of Germany's interests in China. Unification under the militarily powerful Nationalists in 1927 offered even more hope; the European powers and America were willing to give up some rights. But by this time Japan was too strong for China to resist alone. By the time World War II started, Japan occupied more than half of China.

To this day, anti-foreign and particularly anti-Japanese propaganda is a fundamental part of the Chinese Communist Party's hold on power. Regular anti-Japanese protests are encouraged (and then, when they get too big, discouraged) by the government. In the 2010s, Sino-Japanese tensions have been upped by the Chinese by the use of military threats to assert China's claims over the Diaoyutai/Senkaku Islands. In March 2014, almost eighty years after World War II finished, the Secretary General of the Chinese Communist Party and President of China Xi Jinping said on a visit to Europe that the "war of aggression committed by Japanese militarism alone inflicted 35 million Chinese military and civilian casualties. These atrocities are still fresh in our memory."[3]

How Japan which until the mid-1840s had co-existed relatively peacefully with China has became China's sworn enemy is a story that for most Westerners has long been forgotten. But given modern-day tensions between the two countries,

3 "Japan's wartime atrocities 'still fresh in memory'", *South China Morning Post* March 30, 2014, p3.

it is well worth remembering. The story is not just Chinese Communist Party propaganda: China was treated appallingly by foreign powers, including Britain and to a lesser extent, the United States, for over 100 years. Japan's treatment of China, after it threw off the unequal treaties that had been imposed on it, was even worse.

Extraterritoriality - foreign justice in foreign lands - was a fundamental part of this humiliation. Extraterritoriality underpinned the foreign presence in China. It served day to day to remind Chinese they were not sovereign in their own land and the assertion of "treaty rights" often resulted in military force being used against China.

Extraterritoriality meant that the governments of China and, while the treaties were in force there, Japan had almost no power to control foreigners enjoying treaty rights. Foreigners were allowed to freely enter the treaty ports, they were not subject to local laws and, could not be punished by local authorities. The most local officials could do was to arrest foreigners and hand them over to their own consular authorities for trial. They could not even deport them. Any threat by the Chinese or Japanese to breach these rights resulted in the dispatch of gunboats to enforce them.

Extraterritoriality created a remarkable system. Each treaty power established courts staffed by consular officers to try cases against their nationals. At its peak, in Shanghai, there were at least 23 different courts operating in the city: 19 foreign courts, three Chinese courts, and a Court of Consuls for bringing cases against the foreign-run Municipal Council. Close to twenty courts operated in the main Japanese treaty port, Yokohama. The consular courts were an alphabet soup of jurisdictions including German, Italian, Austro-Hungarian, Russian, Belgian, Danish, Dutch, French, Hungarian, Spanish, Mexican, Chilean, Norwegian, Swedish, Russian and Spanish courts.

While they hated the unequal treaties that allowed for-

A scene from the Italian consular court in Shanghai in 1920s. Italian and British witness give evidence before an Italian judge and assessors.

eigners freely to enter and trade with their countries, Chinese and Japanese attitudes towards extraterritoriality, at least at the beginning, were equivocal. Despite later protestations and propaganda, neither China nor Japan were against extraterritoriality in the early years. Extraterritoriality had been demanded to protect treaty foreigners from the "barbaric" Chinese and Japanese legal systems which, to be fair to the foreign powers, did regularly torture parties before the courts. For both the Chinese and the Japanese, foreigners handling disputes between other foreigners seemed like a good idea.

Indeed, perhaps most telling of their early attitudes to extraterritoriality is that in the 1870s, China and Japan agreed to provide for mutual extraterritoriality for their citizens in each other's countries. In the 1880s, when foreign countries entered into unequal treaties with Korea, both China and Japan also imposed extraterritoriality on Korea.

The real problems with extraterritoriality came as more and more foreigners arrived in China and Japan and interacted with the locals. Particularly in China, foreigners in the form of missionaries, traders and officers of the foreign-run Imperial Maritime Customs spread across the country. Everywhere they went they mixed with local Chinese, creating friction that lead to disputes and, in the worst cases, to a number of killings. The Japanese managed, for the most part, to restrict foreigners to treaty ports but even in these ports, just as in China, disputes would arise with and crimes be committed against Japanese. Local Chinese and Japanese could only seek justice – in their own country - by going to a foreign court using a foreign language and applying foreign law. They often felt that justice was not done when foreigner judged foreigner. This could lead to violence. The first British Chief Judge, Sir Edmund Hornby, quoted above, had had to call in the gunboat in Chefoo because a mob had besieged his bungalow for three days, angry at the acquittal of the British foreman.

The problems were exacerbated by the fact that most

countries did not appoint trained lawyers to handle legal cases. Cases were instead handled by consuls, often with no legal training. For many countries, consuls were not even professional consular officers, but merely local merchants appointed to handle their country's interests. Cases could be, and often were, very poorly handled and decided.

In order to deal with some of the problems with consular courts, the British, by far the largest Western power in East Asia, were the first to establish a formal court system in China and Japan staffed by professional judges. In 1865, the British Supreme Court for China and Japan was established in Shanghai. It was run from the British Foreign Office in London. The British Court for Japan, under the Shanghai Supreme Court, was established in Yokohama 14 years later. America, as its economic and political interests grew in China, established the United States Court for China in 1906 in Shanghai. This was for most of its life run by the Department of State from Washington DC.

These three courts tried in China, Japan, and, for a period, Korea (or Corea as it was then known), cases of every type imaginable: murder, sedition, rape, contract disputes, divorces, mass fights on board merchant ships, assault, battery, theft, fraud, ship collisions, and even, patent, copyright and trade mark infringement cases.

The courts were in almost all respects fully functioning British and American courts. They were staffed by professional judges. Qualified lawyers appeared before the courts. British or American law was applied and British and American rules of evidence and procedure were used. In the case of the British courts, juries were empaneled for all major civil and criminal cases. British judges and barristers all wore the traditional wigs and gowns, even in the oppressive heat of summer. Case reports were published and full records kept. Every quote from a judge, lawyer or witness in this book is from a contemporaneous report or record.

The only major anomaly was that there were no juries in the American courts. The United States Supreme Court had, in 1891, ruled that the constitutional right to a jury did not apply in extraterritorial courts. This was challenged on a number of occasions with Americans making comparisons to the much-preferred practice in the British courts of trial by jury. Even American judges would from time to time lament not having a jury to assist them in trying cases.

The following chapters tell the story of these British and American judges, their courts, and the lawyers and the parties that appeared before them. The story is told in 13 parts in chronological order beginning from the treaties that established extraterritoriality and continuing through to the end of extraterritoriality in, first, Japan and then China.

At a much higher level, this book also tells the story of China and Japan's forced opening to the world and how extraterritoriality influenced and guided the development legal and political systems of both countries, so much so that the history of extraterritoriality still has a strong impact on how both countries view the world today.

The men who came to the Far East as judges and lawyers of these court were all adventurers; being willing to travel far away from home to be a judge or practice law in what in the early days were primitive conditions. For the British all, perhaps bar one or two lawyers, were men of Empire. They all believed in extraterritoriality and the benefits it brought to British interests.

The British judges of the 19th century were truly remarkable. The founder of the court, Hornby, was a force of nature who by his own personal will established a fully functioning legal system. His assistant, Charles Goodwin, was a genius, a world famous Egyptologist and Bible scholar. Many other judges had come to China and Japan as British consular officers, committing themselves to spend their entire career in the Far East. They all learnt Chinese or Japanese and could read, write and speak their chosen language fluently. As consular officers they were required to conduct official business with the Chinese or Japanese in the local language. Others were barristers from England who had come to China at a young age seeking their fortunes; one, Nicholas Hannen, achieving the rare honour of becoming both Chief Justice and Consul-General in Shanghai.

The 20th century brought many more changes. Extraterritoriality had been abolished in Japan. The United States Court for China was established to oversee the US consular courts. China was starting to reform its government and legal system, spurring further changes. Shanghai had also grown to be a cosmopolitan city and was no longer the hardship posting it had once been considered to be. These developments brought a new type of judge and lawyer to the courts. For the most part, in both the British and American courts judges were brought in from outside China, not always successfully - the first two American judges were forced to resign. The American legal profession also improved, helped in no small part by the overzealous efforts of the first judge of the US Court to clean up the quality and standards of the bar.

Change also brought new challenges to the courts. They had to deal with two Chinese revolutions, civil war, warlords and rising Chinese (and, in the British courts, Indian) nationalism. World War I brought cases of sedition to both courts as well as tricky questions of how to deal with enemy nationals who lived side by side with Americans and British in China. The entire existence of the US Court was challenged by one American lawyer who launched a large-scale attack on the court in Washington DC. One half-Chinese British barrister denounced the British court for practicing "gunboat diplomacy."

The Japanese incursions into and ultimate occupation of most of China in the 1930s and World War II brought its own difficulties. There were numerous cases before the courts involving spies; murders of, and by, Japanese soldiers; *habeas corpus* applications for the release of Chinese prisoners wanted by the Japanese; and, even whether it was necessary to pay rent when Chinese and Japanese troops were fighting pitched battles outside your front door.

Milton Helmick the last judge of the United States Court for China, who served right up to the commencement of the Pacific War, described the job of an extraterritorial judge:

"For ordinary every day judging he ought to have known ... all about extraterritoriality, a little international law, a smattering of the laws of other countries, something of Chinese law, a great deal about China, a lot about international politics, considerable about diplomatic usages, a bit of anthropology and a modicum about bomb dodging."[4]

So, where did extraterritoriality come from?

4 M. Helmick, "United States Court for China", Far Eastern Survey, Vol. 14, No. 18 (Sep. 12, 1945), p252.

INDEX

Name

A

Admiralty, jurisdiction in (British) Vol 1: 138, 279, 282, 322-4

Alaska, law of, application in US Courts Vol 2: 85, 184, 192, 252

Alcock, Rutherford Vol 1: 39, 42, 46, 123, 125 Vol 2: 317

Allman, Norwood

    Attorney Vol 1: 102 Vol 2 : 56n, 247n

    Cases Vol 2: 353, 356 Vol 3: 19-20, 90, 92

    Internment and repatriation Vol 3: 172, 175, 180n, 199, 204

    Judges, comments on Vol 2: 117 (Thayer), 266-7 (Purdy), Vol 3: 80-81 (Helmick)

    Shunpao (Shenbao), owner of Vol 3: 138-9

    Student Interpreters, on Vol 1: 88

Amalgamation of British Judicial and Consular positions Vol 1: 189-91, 304-6, 379-81

American Oriental Banking Corporation Vol 3: 90-99, 97i

American-Chinese See: Nationals, dual

Anderson, Charles Graham Overbeck Vol 3: 36

Andrews, Lorrin Vol 2: 81, 86, 97-99, 104, 110-1

Aoki (Viscount) Vol 1: 287-9, 328, 392, 396, 398

Arthur, Chester Vol 1: 219

Appeals

    British Consular/Provincial Courts, from Vol 1: 46, 135-8, 207, 258, 274, 278

    British Court for Japan, from and to Vol 1: 138-9, 207, 322

    British Supreme Court for China, from:

        • Jurisdiction Vol 1: 61, 111, 135-8, 141, 205-6 Vol 2: 59-60, 342-5

        • Full Court (Civil) Vol 2: 345 Vol 3: 21-24

F

W

Z

www.ingramcontent.com/pod-product-compliance
Lightning Source LLC
Chambersburg PA
CBHW061547120626
46550CB00004B/1397